THE POLITICS OF GENDER AFTER SOCIALISM

THE POLITICS OF
GENDER AFTER SOCIALISM

A COMPARATIVE-HISTORICAL ESSAY

Susan Gal and Gail Kligman

PRINCETON UNIVERSITY PRESS   PRINCETON, NEW JERSEY

Library of Congress Cataloging-in-Publication Data

Gal, Susan, 1949–
The politics of gender after socialism : a comparative-historical essay /
Susan Gal and Gail Kligman
p.   cm.
Includes bibliographical references and index.
ISBN 0-691-04893-2 (cloth : alk. paper)
ISBN 0-691-04894-0 (pbk. : alk. paper)
1. Sex role—Europe, Eastern. 2. Post-communism—Europe, Eastern.
3. Europe, Eastern—Social conditions—1989– I. Kligman, Gail.
II. Title.
HQ1075.5.E852 G35   2000
305.3′0947—dc21   00-021231   CIP

This book has been composed in Galliard

The paper used in this publication meets the minimum requirements of
ANSI/NISO Z39.48-1992 (R 1997) (*Permanence of Paper*)

www.pup.princeton.edu

Printed in the United States of America

10 9 8 7 6 5 4 3 2 1

10 9 8 7 6 5 4 3 2 1
(Pbk.)

For Anna and Hannah

Contents

Acknowledgments

THIS VOLUME was born of the comparative research project that we codirected, *Reproducing Gender: Politics, Publics, and Everyday Life after Socialism*, published by Princeton University Press. We wish to thank again all those who participated in that collaborative effort. We are indebted as well to the two readers for Princeton University Press who urged us to expand and publish as a separate shorter book what had been our lengthy introductory essay to the project's coedited volume. A grant from the MacArthur Foundation's Program on Peace and International Cooperation gave us much appreciated resources to pursue our research and writing. We are also grateful to our universities for additional support as well as funds from UCLA's Academic Senate and the Lichtstern Fund of the Department of Anthropology, University of Chicago. The Collegium Budapest provided an elegant and congenial environment in which to work; Albert and Lori Kligman's generosity and hospitality provided us with another.

The administrative staffs of the Department of Sociology at UCLA and the Department of Anthropology at the University of Chicago extended indispensable support. Thanks are also due to Mary Murrell, our editor at Princeton University Press, for her enthusiasm and encouragement, and to Cindy Crumrine and Paula Durbin-Westby for fine editorial work.

We are grateful to Eva Fodor for her research assistance and conceptual contributions. For their ongoing intellectual stimulation and goodwill we thank Andrew Abbott, Leora Auslander, Susan Crane, Norma Field, Christy Glass, Sam Hamburg, Robert Levy, Sasha Milićević, Ruth Milkman, Carole Pateman, Leslie Salzinger, Dawn Waring, and Viviana Zelizer. Last but not least, we thank each other for being steadfast colleagues and friends.

THE POLITICS OF GENDER AFTER SOCIALISM

1

After Socialism

THE UNEXPECTED collapse of communism a decade ago changed the world. For the men and women of the former socialist states, Western freedoms and consumer goods seemed closer than ever before, but so did daunting financial uncertainty. For them, as for all of us, the familiar Cold War dualisms that divided Europe into West and East formally disappeared; the countries of East Central Europe and the former Soviet Union became members of a reconfigured global economy. As East Central Europe looked with hope to the West, Western politicians, bureaucrats, scholars, experts, and volunteers of all sorts headed east to help establish democratic practices in East Central Europe. In the years that followed, increasing class and ethnic differentiation, a rise in unemployment, and a decline in state subsidies were among the costs considered necessary to transform moribund socialist economies into thriving markets. These costs however, have been experienced differently by women and men.

It is our goal in this essay to explore how discourses and practices of gender play a major role in shaping the post-1989 reconstitution of states and social relations in East Central Europe. Since the end of state socialism, most studies have focused directly on the economic processes of marketization and privatization or on the political processes of democratization, constitutionalism, and the emergence of civil society. We propose, instead, to consider the processes of the postsocialist transformations from a gendered perspective. We contend that democratization comes more clearly into view if one asks how men and women are differently imagined as citizens, or how "politics" itself is being redefined as a distinctively masculine endeavor. Similarly, by examining how women and men are differently located in the emerging economies, one foregrounds the usually unremarked yet pervasive and often feminized phenomenon of small-scale, service-sector marketization. Attending to gender is analytically productive, leading not only to an understanding of relations between men and women, but to a deeper analysis of how social and institutional transformations occur. To this end we raise two crucial questions: How are gender relations and ideas about gender shaping political and economic change in the region? And what forms of gender inequality are being shaped as a result? By making central what has been marginalized, this essay seeks to outline an alternative analytical agenda for research.[1]

Recognizing that these processes are intertwined with events happening simultaneously in Western Europe, the United States, and elsewhere, we do not consider East Central Europe in isolation, but within a broader political geography. In discussing postsocialism, we will note parallels, interactions, and contrasts with other regions in policies and social trends, as well as in discourses. Of particular interest is the way that the public arguments about gender in one part of the globe influence those occurring in another; the way politicians can score points by aligning with or contrasting themselves to images and policies in other regions. The historical context of postsocialism is equally important in our analysis. As other scholars have noted, the sometimes subtle and hidden continuities with socialism are as powerful as the dramatic ruptures. Social actors all over the region have been reaching into the presocialist past, claiming historical models, inspiration, and justification of current political policies and gender arrangements. Nostalgia for earlier historical periods—different ones for different constituencies—is a pervasive aspect of making the postsocialist future. By attending throughout to historical comparisons as well as cross-regional interactions and contrasts, this work engages both the literature on East Central Europe, and also the broader feminist literature that has persistently asked: How are states and political-economic processes gendered? How do states and markets regulate gender relations?

Gender is defined here as the socially and culturally produced ideas about male-female difference, power, and inequality that structure the reproduction of these differences in the institutionalized practices of society. What it means to be a "man" or a "woman," to be "masculine" or "feminine," varies historically. Such cultural categories are formed through everyday interactions that are framed within larger discourses and within specific institutions. We argue that there are reciprocal effects here: Not only do state policies constrain gender relations, but ideas about the differences between men and women shape the ways in which states are imagined, constituted, and legitimated. Thus, states themselves can be imagined as male, even though both men and women are involved in their operation; social categories such as "worker" can be identified with a single gender as well, even if both men and women work. Such socially constructed ideas linking femininity and masculinity to other social categories are often embedded in state policies. Ideas about gender difference also contribute to the forms of market expansion. In shaping institutional change, ideas about gender difference interact with other central cultural constructions such as the nation, the family, the public good. At the same time, the ideologies and policies that states promote, as well as the constraints and incentives of economies, circumscribe the range of possible relations between men and women. We therefore focus here on how gender relations both form and are formed by different kinds of states, different kinds of economies, and different types of political action.[2]

While the category of gender is central to social life, gender arrangements are diverse. One of the important lessons of empirical studies about the socialist past is that if there ever was a single gender regime of state socialism, it has long been replaced by many different ways of understanding the relations between men and women. Scholars agree, nevertheless, on some of the broad features of socialist gender orders. There was an attempt to erase gender difference (along with ethnic and class differences), to create socially atomized persons directly dependent on a paternalist state. Yet, women in socialism were also sometimes constituted as a corporate category, becoming a special object of state policy, with ministries or state offices dedicated to what were defined as their concerns. Women's full-time participation in the labor force was dictated by the state, on which women were more directly dependent than they were on individual men. In short, the ideological and social structural arrangements of state socialism produced a markedly different relation between the state, men, and women than commonly found, for instance, in classic liberal parliamentary systems or in various kinds of welfare states. Gender as an organizing principle, male dominance, and gendered inequality can be found in all these systems, but with profoundly different configurations.

Socialist gender arrangements themselves varied significantly over time and space. Indeed, socialist regimes were often characterized by contradictory goals in their policies toward women: they wanted workers as well as mothers, token leaders as well as obedient cadres. While officially supporting equality between men and women, the regimes countenanced and even produced heated mass media debates about issues such as women's ideal and proper roles, the deleterious effects of divorce, the effects of labor-force segregation—such as the feminization of schoolteaching and agriculture—and the fundamental importance of "natural difference." These debates revealed the paradoxes and contradictions in official discourses, as well as more general tensions in both policy goals and the system of political-economic control.

Such diverse relations between official discourses and the everyday practices of men and women are a central focus of this book. People in the region reacted as much to the representations of themselves in official communications as to the often unforeseen and unintended consequences of state policies about reproduction, sexuality, and family life.

Observers—from both East and West—have made infamous the gap
between image and practice in state socialism, between what was said,
what was done, and what was experienced. Our reflections take this as a
point of departure. The development of public spheres and capitalist
mass media have swept away censorship and "official" discourse in this
classic sense. There are now numerous alternative narratives—ways of
looking at the world—that vie for popular attention, attempting to
achieve persuasiveness and thus domination. Yet the apparent plurality
and openness of mass media obscure the fact that certain issues remain
undiscussed, some perspectives on gender relations and possible futures
are suppressed. We argue that the disjuncture between public discourses
and ordinary practices in a multitude of contexts has not disappeared.
Rather, it now takes different forms and continues to be crucial for the
maintenance of power differences and for understanding changing social relations in the region.

We intend this gendered perspective to be a part of the more general
scholarly debates on what is happening after socialism. Therefore, we
situate this work with reference to current frameworks for the study of
East Central Europe. These frameworks differ in the way they analyze
change in two key dimensions: space and time. With respect to space,
the definition of the region itself is controversial. During the communist
period, debates about the regional divisions of Europe, and the justifications for them, were coded ways for critical elites to publicly discuss different political alignments from those of the Cold War. They provided
a means to express subversive visions of the future. But the idea of European regions has deep historical precedents. The countries to which we
primarily refer in this essay—Poland, Hungary, Romania, Yugoslavia,
Bulgaria, Croatia, the Czech and Slovak Republics, and (East) Germany—undoubtedly have much in common, not least their geographi-
cal contiguities; some very general patterns of economic and political
relations to earlier empires that were based to the east, west, and south;
and forty years of communism. But we understand that definitions of
regions and their boundaries are not self-evident categorizations arising
out of uniform historical experience. Still less do they reflect cultural
similarity. On the contrary, the image of unity is in part an effect of politically charged cultural constructions both in the West and the East.
Indeed, the centuries-old European discourse of East/West oppositions—in which the East is the less civilized, less economically advanced
pole—remains pervasive across the continent. The apparent separation
of regions was and is a consequence of political economic relations and
discursive interactions among them. The peace treaties following World
War II put hard and definite borders around what had been the more
shifting boundaries of "Eastern Europe," "Central Europe," "South-

eastern Europe," "the Balkans," without eliminating the differentials of wealth and power that the East/West discourse both marked and helped to create.[3]

The geopolitical borders and definitions of the region have, of course, shifted again. The events of 1989 along with the impetus of the Maastricht Treaty have brought the "hardness" of boundaries dramatically into question. Acceptance into Western political, economic, and military clubs has been a goal of many of the region's countries. Some have been welcomed into NATO, others have been kept at bay. In keeping with these changes, scholarship itself has been deeply affected. The notable differences in access to money and influence between those studying East Central Europe from the "inside" and those coming from the "outside" to do so have increased since the end of communism, and interactions among scholars have sometimes been fraught. Some social scientists from the region have noted that, as in orientalist and colonial relations all over the globe, those native to the region and living there have often been assumed to be able to theorize only about the region itself; "Western" scholars, in contrast, seem to be empowered to make theoretical statements about social process "in general." Without denying these very real tensions and inequalities, we suggest that in this case neither "side" is so simple to characterize. For instance, there are many historical models for the ways in which intellectuals from what is now called East Central Europe have contributed to the Western canon. And in the current scholarly context, it is indisputable that many groundbreaking conceptualizations now widely used in all of social science— soft-budget constraints, second societies—originated in the social science scholarship of East Central Europeans.[4]

Our own approach to these familiar dilemmas of scholarly interaction, and the relations between power and knowledge that they index, has been twofold. First, on a practical level, this essay emerged out of a collaborative and multidisciplinary research project on gender that we co-directed. We consider this book a companion volume to the original collaborative work. The project included scholars from East Central Europe as well as Western Europe and the United States; it attempted to bring these scholars together to create a broad framework within which we could raise questions about gender, conduct research, and then compare our results. But it did not try to apply uniform methods or analyses. In making our own points in the present essay, we highlight the evidence and theoretical insights of our colleagues who contributed to that project. In the spirit of intellectual and political debate—which was as present among the East Central Europeans in the collaborative project as between "East" and "West"—we sometimes argue with their positions.[5]

Second, on a more conceptual level, it is necessary to think analytically about Cold War discourse itself and scholarly participation in it. Predicated on underscoring difference, American social science during the Cold War implicitly limited the sorts of questions considered appropriate in discussions of communist countries. It kept discussion of communism in the East of Europe institutionally separate from the study of the capitalist West. This remained true despite the efforts of some scholars to make political and intellectual alliances across the divide. As a result of this separation, important parallels and their impacts were often obscured.[6] For example, all over the former communist world, public discussions assume or assert that women were in an unholy alliance with the communist state, that women were specially favored before 1989. Certainly, state socialism claimed to "emancipate" women by ensuring their participation in the labor force. It frequently instituted liberal divorce laws and sometimes attempted to socialize some household tasks. Nevertheless, much empirical evidence suggests that far from enjoying an advantageous alliance with the state, women were in fact more at the mercy of state policies than men were. Communist states manipulated both men's and women's participation in wage work. But in the case of women, states also intruded significantly on reproductive lives, in a directly embodied manner. Yet the assertion of women's advantageous position in communism continues as an aspect of public discourse, one that—we argue—serves to delegitimate women's political activity in postcommunism. This makes it difficult to publicly formulate criticisms of neoliberal state policies adopted across the region since 1989 that have often resulted in higher rates of women's unemployment and the dismantling of public services such as childcare and food kitchens that were of particular help to women.[7]

Interestingly, women's relation to the state has become an equally controversial topic in the rest of Europe and the United States over the last two decades. As in East Central Europe, public discourses about this subject have palpable political consequences. Long-standing American representations of the dubious morality of "welfare mothers" played an important role in preparing public opinion for recent decreases in state support. Similarly, in the European Union, public discussions about single mothers, abortion, and social citizenship are highly contested. They raise the issue of women's relation to the state in the face of EU pressures to streamline public spending. These pressures threaten the high levels of state provisioning that, in different ways in different countries, have been characteristic of Western Europe since World War II.

Until recently, such parallels between "East" and "West" were rarely analyzed. By assuming a categorical difference between them, Cold War discourse—in general public forums as well as in social science—took largely for granted, and therefore left unexamined, the fact that "East" and "West" constituted politically important audiences for each other; as such, "East" and "West" reacted to each other's actions. This was not limited to the arms race. Vivid and often questionable images of the other were used by both sides for internal and international political purposes. Frequently, the rivalry between East and West was veiled and indirect, each side assuming instead of mentioning the other's existence as a competitive or negative model. Official discourses juxtaposed idealized images of self to more empirically real pictures of the other—to the other's disadvantage. For Eastern leaders, the West was a foe whose defeat in economic and political terms would produce the ultimate legitimation of state socialist regimes. But the West also appeared in the East as a source of positive identity, at first for the disaffected, later for anyone importing blue jeans and rock and roll. Meanwhile, politicians in the West scored points by emphasizing the "totalitarian" aspects of "communism," as an "evil empire" in implicit contrast with a democratic West. As a result, what could have been appreciated as the achievements of socialism, such as mass educational efforts, were ignored. In the Eastern version of Cold War discourse, communist leaders harped on imperialism, or on the drug abuse and violence that they identified as the deleterious consequences of too much "individualism." They could thereby discount the significance of individual rights. Gender arrangements were part of this Cold War shadow boxing. Communist theories and policies about families were framed in part as critiques and responses to the West. Emblematic of the role of gender in this competition was the famous kitchen debate of 1959 when Khrushchev and Nixon met at a Moscow exhibit of American goods. Significantly, the two leaders argued about which system would produce the most and best labor-saving devices for women's household work.[8]

One way of taking into account the effects of these Cold War assumptions on our own thinking is to include such mirroring and self-differentiating interactions in our analyses. We examine the former communist states not only in regional terms, but from a gendered perspective that deliberately attends to the construction of regional images in such interactions. The features that socialist states share with a variety of welfare states then become more evident. One advantage is that such comparisons raise questions not only about socialism and the trajectory of change in postsocialism. They also open the possibility that a view from East Central Europe can change our understanding of the West and of the gendered intellectual framework itself. For instance, we can analyze more precisely how, in the East, as in the West, discourses about women, family, and reproduction were and continue to be crucial in the legitimation of politics. As another instance, current patterns of political

activism among women in East Central Europe become more comprehensible if we see that women's politics are not immune to East/West
competition and mutual stereotyping. In this way, the examples of East
Central Europe can contribute to a renewed examination of the category of "feminism" itself as a social-political movement. Or, as yet another example, analysis of the postsocialist contraction of the state in
East Central Europe, juxtaposed to simultaneous changes in European
and American social provisioning, points to general questions about the
nature and effects of state support in different contexts, and about the
way states of different kinds structure the relations between men and
women. The comparison also casts a new light on the dilemma of
women's "autonomy" versus their "dependence" on men, states, and
markets, which has been such a salient feature of recent feminist theorizing in the United States and Western Europe.

The issues we have just discussed revolve around the implications of
spatial definitions and imagined boundaries. Another set of questions
preoccupying studies of the region, and to which we wish to orient our
own investigation, is the nature of social change after socialism. These
questions involve analytical and popular notions of time and history.
The massive dislocations provoked by the collapse of communism immediately gave birth to what English-language observers have called
"the transition," in concert with common usage in the countries involved: *átmenet* or *rendszerváltás*, *Wende*, *tranziţie*, *tranzicija*, or
schimbare. Thus "transition," like many social scientific terms, has been
not only an analytical tool, but a part of everyday politics and common
sense.[9]

But increasingly, scholars have been noting the disadvantages of
using the metaphor of "transition." As many critics have remarked,
"transition" is as consonant with Marxism-Leninism as with American
modernization theory because it assumes evolutionary progress from
one well-known "stage" of history to another. It thereby inadvertently
continues the Cold War morality tale we have already discussed, one
that pitted two "sides" against each other in an implicit contest for who
was "ahead." The competition occurred even within the countries of the
former Soviet bloc themselves, as each compared itself to the others, and
was so compared by outside observers. It used to be a matter of who had
the highest standard of living. But the competition continues today.
Now it is often a question of whose economy is more privatized, which
country most "Western," which the most "democratic," which is accepted into NATO or the European Union. Feminist analyses of
women's situation in East Central Europe have not escaped this pitfall.
Early studies bemoaned the lack of feminist activity in the region without reflecting on the relative lack of a strong feminist movement, let

alone a mass movement, anywhere else in the world during the late-twentieth century. The question too often has been: Which is better for women, communism or capitalism? And some feminist analyses simply reversed the valences of the discussion, asking: What have women lost in the transition?

Furthermore, the "transition" metaphor too readily invites one kind of comparison at the expense of another. Because "transitions" to democracy have arguably happened in the last twenty years in numerous parts of the globe, the term implies the primacy of typological comparisons among "transitions" as such, regardless of the contemporaneous historical circumstances in which they occur. In contrast, we are interested in "transitions" as parts of simultaneous conditions and transformations occurring in the world political economy and in widespread discourses that go well beyond the region's shifting boundaries. Rather than comparing Latin American, for instance, with East European "transitions" as different examples of a single process, we sketch how East Central Europe's interactions with other polities and economies, along with continuities and paradoxes from the past, produce patterned, if historically particular, results. We want to know how the pressures exerted at a particular historical moment by capitalist investors or the Catholic Church or the policy recommendations of the World Bank intersect with local debates about the proper roles of men and women and local forms of political action to produce present-day policies and patterns of action. By the same token, in the realm of discourse, we are observing a region in which the recent valorizations of the "individual," "private enterprise," and even "family values" echo similar emphases of neoconservatism farther to the west. This is not to say that "privatizations" of public services in the United States and Western Europe are the same as the contraction of the state in East Central Europe. They are quite different in process and effect. Yet we think it worth attending to their contemporeneity: they are justified by parallel arguments and ideologies and pursued by interrelated, overlapping groups of elites, who are often personally and corporately linked to each other in an increasingly globalized world.

Finally, another important criticism of the metaphor of transition from socialism—or for that matter transition to socialism—is that "transition" assumes a theory of history in which all aspects of society change in concert and in the same direction. This homogenizes state socialism, which, despite its distinctive ideological and systemic structure, nevertheless took many forms and had many phases in the different countries of the region. The approach also homogenizes capitalism, glossing over its varying and uneven forms, and the partially contingent, open-endedness of social change. Stage-thinking and the concomitant expectation of predictable change make it as hard to notice genuine innovations as to take account of continuities with the past.

Thus, we join recent critics of "transition" studies in rejecting teleological assumptions and in giving causal weight to "pathways" from the past. With them, we recognize the significance of the dramatic political ruptures that captured the world's imagination, but nevertheless insist that there are less salient but no less important continuities in many areas of social life. Some of the most interesting questions about social process are lost if we fail to note continuities between pre- and post-1989 East Central Europe, and between capitalist and socialist societies before 1989. Such continuities are repeatedly highlighted by a study of gender, and attending to them is indispensable for understanding the relations between men and women. For instance, gender segregation in the occupational structure is often longer lasting than political regimes; the division of household labor has changed at yet another pace. In this way, a gendered perspective reveals not only continuities, but quite different temporalities in the various processes occurring in the region and across the different versions of "transition" in different countries.

We depart from most critics of "transition" studies, however, in focusing on gender as an analytic category and on the dynamic discrepancies between discourses, institutional practices, and subjectivities. This allows us to note contradictory and paradoxical aspects of current processes that require novel conceptualizations. They are not easily categorized as either continuity, rupture, or path. We ask how social actors—institutions as much as individuals—working with the cultural and communicational materials at hand, and in the face of the open-ended contingencies of social life, create a sense of themselves and of social continuity. We examine how ideas about gender difference and sexuality are often recruited to construct continuities with the past, with nature, with the general good. They can thus be used to gain authority for postsocialist political institutions, practices, and political actors when there are not yet well established rules of the game for political activity.

Yet, some practices and institutions that seem continuous with those common under socialism are nevertheless experienced quite differently by social actors since 1989. They are reinterpreted and often revalued. Meanwhile, what seem to outside observers as novel activities and self-understandings, even new subjectivities, go unremarked because they are cloaked in the guise of continuity. They are categorized as another instance of something familiarly known. Notions of public and private, for instance, have been fundamental to imagining social life in the region for at least a century and a half. But when we trace the changing meanings of public and private—the activities routinely encompassed by each, their positive and negative valences, and their gender codings—we find quite distinct changes between presocialist arrangements, the socialist period, and postsocialism. Sometimes, because the terms remain the same, they create the impression of continuity. At other times the terms shape perceptions so that some changes in political-economic patterns are more noticed than others. Indeed, the systematic ways in which legal systems, state policies, and people in everyday interactions manipulate discursive categories such as public and private to reconfigure, justify, and reinterpret their activities turn out to be important factors in the processes we examine, and a significant form of power. Our goal in analyzing such discursive distinctions is to propose new conceptual tools for scholarly understandings of how institutions and everyday life have changed since the end of socialism.

Each of the following chapters addresses a substantive issue central to a gendered analysis of postsocialism. Chapter 2, "Reproduction as Politics," asks how public discussions about human reproduction, childcare, and sexuality constitute and reconstitute the relationship between states and their subjects. We explore how states exercise power in molding and constraining reproductive practices and sexuality through legislation. But how and why are such laws instituted? Or posed otherwise, what is the role of reproduction—its discourses and practices—in the making of political authority?

In chapter 3, "Dilemmas of Public and Private," we examine how the economic restructuring of the region is constrained by gender relations and ideas about gender difference. But in order to do this we must reach back into the nineteenth century to trace the shifting understandings of public and private that have organized political and economic life in the region. There have been significant changes in the boundary between public and private, with varying roles played by classes, states, and social movements in marking that boundary. We set out the forms of masculinity and femininity that accompanied these imaginings in the socialist period. We use the notion of fractals to argue that a semiotic analysis of the public/private distinction, examined over a substantial time period, enables us to understand some of the currently emerging forms of economic stratification and polarization, and the gendered division of labor in the workplace.

Chapter 4, "Forms of States, Forms of 'Family,'" continues the investigation of the effects of gender on policy formulation and economic processes. The axis of comparison here switches from the past to contemporary welfare states in Western Europe and the United States. They too are responding to the needs of aging populations and to neoliberal pressures to limit spending and benefits. What can be grasped about the gender relations of socialist and postsocialist states if we consider them in relation to welfare states farther west, and examine them in the context of contrasting "Eastern" and "Western" public discourses about states and families? We show how analyses of the postsocialist states of East Central Europe contribute to the ongoing feminist theorization of relations between women and welfare states, and to understanding the costs and benefits of women's autonomy or dependence on states, markets, and individual men.

Feminist theorists have argued that only through active political participation and representation can women organize in their own interests. Therefore, in chapter 5, "Arenas of Political Action," we turn again to politics. Women's and men's differential political participation in East Central Europe calls for a reconceptualization of the gendering of civil society, as well as for a discussion of the effects that international support for nongovernmental organizations has on political action. Furthermore, the example of East Central Europe invites a rethinking of "feminism" as social movement and "woman" as a form of political identity. It suggests an analysis of how such movements are defined, taken up, or rejected by social actors in particular historical circumstances.

There are, of course, many other substantive issues one could examine in trying to understand postsocialism as gendered. We have omitted many obviously relevant ones such as the increase in prostitution and the incorporation of East Central Europeans into the international sex trade; the forms of education for boys and girls; the differential incentives for and consequences of migration. Our aim is not to develop an exhaustive overview of substantive issues, but rather to open suggestive lines of argument and research.

In this extended reflection we maintain that gender is a crucial feature of the postsocialist transformations. In examining discourses of reproduction, the changing public/private divide, the range of current relations between women as clients, employees, citizens, and consumers in welfare states, and the differing political participation of men and women in East Central Europe, we hope to accomplish two goals: to include East Central Europe in some of the major debates of feminist theory, and at the same time, to outline an analytical agenda for examining the ways in which postsocialist change is powerfully shaped by the discourses and practices of gender.

2

Reproduction as Politics

IT IS a striking fact about the collapse of communism in 1989 that abortion was among the first issues raised by virtually all the newly constituted governments of East Central Europe. In Romania, liberalization of abortion was the second decree issued by the provisional government upon the fall of the Ceauşescu regime. Abortion's legality in East Germany and its restriction in West Germany almost derailed German unification. In Poland the question has become virtually a permanent feature of the parliamentary agenda. But abortion was only one of the issues associated with sexuality and human reproduction that have taken center stage in the years since 1989. In the former Yugoslavia, rape was a weapon of war. Because women who had been raped and the children that resulted from rape were ostracized and rejected by their own ethnic groups, rape was also and intentionally a tool of "ethnic cleansing," through its tragic reproductive consequences. Unwanted babies became a political issue in Romania and Germany as well, but in different ways. A private adoption market in babies, not all of whom were unwanted by their birth mothers, emerged in Romania. The rate of voluntary sterilization increased dramatically among eastern German women, which produced a political scandal when it was noticed and labeled a "birth strike" by the mass media.

Throughout the region, as democratic institutions were being created, fiscal and constitutional crises threatened, and legislative politics were being rethought in dramatic ways, the leaders (themselves mostly male) of the new states also heatedly debated questions of "proper" sex, birthrates, contraception, and childcare. In the face of daunting economic and political challenges, the politicians, publishers, and media consumers who constituted the first democratic parliaments and public spheres of 1989 have consistently turned their attention to reproductive issues. Scholars of political transformation in East Central Europe have rarely considered the significance of these pervasive debates. By contrast, we argue in this chapter that the discursive and practical effects of debates about reproduction provide one of the keys to understanding how politics is being reshaped in East Central Europe. Political authority is, in part, reconstituted through arguments about reproduction. The everyday results of such discussion and of reformed reproductive policies contribute not only to changing reproductive practices, but also to the creation of new kinds of political actors and subjectivities, in domestic and international arenas.

In short, the ongoing focus on reproduction, despite the many differences among the countries of the region, is noteworthy and demands explanation. Abortion provides a striking example.[1] In East Germany, Hungary Poland, Serbia, Slovenia, and Croatia, new laws were proposed, often by religious and conservative political organizations, attempting to use parliamentary means to restrict women's access to abortion. There was certainly no surge of popular demand for such restrictions. Instead, in Germany and Hungary, continued conflicts around these laws made it necessary to submit them to constitutional courts. In Serbia and Croatia nationalist and religious groups proposed demographic programs designed to "renew the population." These became a starting point for governmental attempts to restrict abortion. In these latter two cases, as well as in Germany, Poland, and Hungary, women's groups organized protests, and the mass media engaged in sustained discussions about the significance of reproductive practices. In Slovenia, angry debates in parliament and public protest by women's organizations led to the inclusion in the new Slovenian constitution of an article providing women (and men) the right to decide about the birth of their children. In Romania, to be sure, the postcommunist liberalization was, in part, a reaction to the extreme restrictions of the Ceauşescu era. Yet the implications of using abortion as a popular form of fertility control have remained a subject of medical and demographic concern.

But even in those countries where the abortion issue has not been so noisy, public, or protracted, governments were not content to leave reproductive policy alone. In Bulgaria, there was not much discussion in parliament, but a more liberal law was nevertheless put into effect as part of a general liberalizing trend. It replaced communist-era arrangements that had restricted abortion among ethnic Bulgarians while allowing it among Turkish and Romani minorities. In the Czech Republic and Slovakia, despite legislative proposals, there were no restrictions enacted, but a health-care reform resulted in higher fees for "nonmedical" abortions, thereby limiting access. Even in these countries a wide range of elite groups were involved in the debates: not only political leaders and government officials in ministries responsible for health, education, and youth, but also church leaders, nongovernmental organizations devoted to women's rights and population issues, and experts in health, education, and social policy. Childcare and sexuality have also been caught up in public debate and government action across the region.[2]

For liberal political theory and sociological common sense, this interest in reproduction during a period of radical political and economic change appears anomalous because reproduction is generally considered to be part of the private sphere of domesticity and family, and not the public sphere of politics, civil society, and state-formation. But for feminist scholars who have long argued that the private/public distinction is less a straightforward description of social domains than an ideologized dichotomy that produces the appearance of separation between activities that are nonetheless closely linked, such discussion is hardly surprising.[3] It constitutes a salient instance of what has recently been called the "politics of reproduction." It provides further evidence for important relations between supposedly private activities such as childbirth and child-rearing and public activities such as political debate. Studies of the "politics of reproduction" investigate the "intersection of politics and the life cycle" (Kligman 1992:364) and take as an object of investigation the "seemingly distant power relations [that] shape local reproductive experiences" (Ginsburg and Rapp 1991:313). They explore how "state policy and ideological control are experienced in everyday life" (Kligman 1998:3), and how reproduction "provides a terrain for imagining new cultural futures" (Ginsburg and Rapp 1995:2). Indeed, the laws, regulations, and administrative machinery that the new states are installing will have long-range repercussions for the ways in which women in East Central Europe give birth and how people practice contraception, raise their children, and imagine their own and their children's futures.

But studies of the "politics of reproduction" encompass not only how childbirth and child-rearing are affected by distant power relations, but also how political process itself is shaped through the discussion and control of reproduction. The two are closely interrelated, and we return at the end of this chapter to the reciprocal effects between them. We begin, however, by highlighting the contribution of reproductive issues to state-making and other political processes that theorists of "transition" have taken as their domain. We focus on how debates about reproduction "reveal the ways in which politics is being reconstituted, contested, and newly legitimated" (Gal 1994:258). In short, our discussion analyzes how the public debates about reproduction make politics.

Human reproduction is the means by which both individuals and collectivities assure their continuity. It is a ground for political battles in part because states, families, and other social actors all understand themselves as having much at stake in the control of childbearing and child-rearing. Historically constructed and variable, these multiple perspectives or "interests" in reproduction are often at odds. Note that with this observation we move beyond well-worn functionalist arguments about the "need" for human reproduction in sustaining social systems or in providing labor power. We turn our attention to the diverse discourses that shape beliefs and everyday practices of reproduction: We examine their contingency and conflict and the (often unintended) effects on the historical construction, authorization, and justification of political actors and action.[4]

We start with the perspectives of states, as formulated in European political thought. The health of a state has long been linked to the rapid reproduction of its inhabitants; the vigor of the individual body has served as a sign of the health or infirmity of the body politic. In monarchical systems the body of greatest importance, both figuratively and materially, was the king's. His reproduction was central for the maintenance of royal lines, just as culturally defined forms of bodily reproduction were essential for the maintenance of aristocratic families and their power.

In the early modern period, political-economic theory shifted its focus from the body of the ruler to the bodies of the ruled, so that the condition and size of the populace living within the state's territory became a central concern of statecraft. Discussing this shift, Foucault posited a rupture between notions of state power built around the physical existence of the sovereign—his personalistic relations to other sovereigns or to his court—and those built around the territory's inhabitants. He argued that this shift marked a quite different idea of government as a routine management of things and people, an economizing, categorizing control of their welfare and activities. The form of knowledge implied by the first kind of rule is an art based on interpersonal intuition, on the passions, virtues, and vices of rulers. The form of knowledge implied by the second is a more impersonal, systematized "science of state" based on attentive administration aimed at the general welfare. This change has been conceptualized in other ways as well. Some see it as a shift in the goals and dilemmas of governing, which turned from a concern with satisfying or controlling the prince's "passion" for glory to a novel category of political thought: the "interests" of individuals and groups.[5]

Foucault's schematic juxtaposition of two regimes presents a picture of intellectual history that has been challenged by historical scholarship demonstrating more piecemeal and contradictory processes of change in ideas about government between the sixteenth and nineteenth centuries. These ideas often differed across the western European states. Glory and passion were not so much superseded as reorganized and in part redirected to foreign policy and external relations; liberal theories of governance introduced other categories, such as that of "the people." Nevertheless, it seems fair to say that by the eighteenth century, the basis of a state's wealth and power was generally understood to lie not so much in the extent of its territory, but in the size and productivity of its population. Mercantilist thought provides a good example: The amount of bullion in the sovereign's treasury was only one indication of the might of his dominion. Another was the number of people living in his territory. It became a matter of significance that a large population not only increased the strength of armies, but made available increasing supplies of labor. Thus Frederick the Great compared backward Russia with fortunate Holland, which, though vastly smaller in extent, had the dense settlement, wealth, and industrious commercial population that made it, in his judgment, a greater European power.[6]

Not only did a large population make a good, strong state, but the abundance of inhabitants testified to the state's morality: "Every wise, just and mild government . . . will always abound most in people," noted David Hume (cited in Gallagher 1987:83). This link between population and the state's morality became a continuing theme in European politics. In a telling way, however, the equation was sometimes reversed. Hume's optimistic conviction was later shaken by Malthus's thesis outlining inevitable, socially deleterious effects of unbridled population increase. Steadily increasing population came to be seen by some as less a reward and sign of moral superiority than a danger to the orderly state. Nevertheless, when nineteenth-century France experienced a falling birthrate greater than that of the other industrializing nations of western Europe, the response was political panic at what was universally perceived as a threat to France's military and economic might. Crucially, then, whether the project was to increase or decrease population, its control and the question of its "quality" remained matters of state.

The political concern with the quantity and quality of inhabitants took several forms. One was the expansion of state and colonial administration in early modern Europe, with even greater intensity in the nineteenth century. Another was the growing interest of administrators in the precise life-condition of a territory's inhabitants. It was the emerging scholarly disciplines of folklore, geography, and statistics, among others, that produced the notion of "population" as a datum. "Population" became an object of knowledge, one that could be known through the aggregation of detail about the material and behavioral aspects of people's lives. Populations provided the opportunity for administrative and normalizing intervention. In the German context, for example, the *Staatswissenschaften* (sciences of state) evolved slowly from the earlier notion of public finance and justice as functions of government to include the addition of "administration" as a third science of state, one aiming to assure the welfare and prosperity of the state and its subjects. With the help of these disciplines, population could be shaped and controlled through "policing" or regulation. In political theory, the management, increase, and improvement of such populations through education and public health came to be seen as a fundamental justification of states, as important as the maintenance of sovereignty itself.[7]

When viewed within this historical context, the pronatalist activities of the liberal, fascist, communist, and welfare states of twentieth-century Europe have a long pedigree, forming part of what Foucault has called "biopolitics." The tracks of state power are evident not only in these political and disciplinary discourses but in widespread practices such as the legal enforcement of normative (reproductive) heterosexuality, the surveillance of women's bodies, and the attempts to control women's fertility.

For the empirical study of state practices, we caution against any definition of states as reified or personified entities with set social functions and unified goals. Although it is very hard to avoid nominalization—writing about the state as "it"—the objectification of the state as an entity effectively masks the active participation of people in "making" the state. Moreover, the perception that states have unified intents and motives is the effect of familiar political tropes; it is a misrecognition that itself requires analysis and explanation. In everyday politics, the imputation of meaning to particular policies and state actions is a consequential political act. Public perception that "the state" intends something is the result of interpretive work, often accomplished by mass media, and can become the object of conflict and further argument, with significant consequences.

For our purposes here, keeping these considerations in mind, states can best be characterized as consisting of historically particular administrative institutions that have a diversity of offices and officers as well as of organizational levels and departments. These are never entirely coordinated and are often involved in conflict or competition among themselves. Such state institutions are engaged in the exercise of authority, or legitimate violence, over a given populace and territory. They produce policies, regulations, laws, practices, and discourses that address aspects of reproduction in diverse, sometimes conflicting, and often even contradictory, ways. Accordingly, an ethnography of a state through the lens of reproduction proceeds by taking the pronouncements and actions of particular actors claiming to represent the state—or arguing among themselves, sometimes about who best represents it—and examines these to show how policies, practices, and official statements based on implicit assumptions about gender relations together create a constraining context for the reproductive activities of the state's inhabitants. They, in turn, variously interpret this constraining context and respond through acquiescence, diverse forms and degrees of resistance, or subversion.[8]

This brief excursion into political theory has been necessary to reveal the roots of state interests in reproduction. The concerns of families in the regulation of childbirth may seem more self-evident, but these too are embedded in cultural definitions. Social historians, anthropologists, and historical demographers have conceptualized a millennium of changing population pyramids in Europe as the result of "family strategies" that are diverse and variable. Thus, families too understand themselves to have important stakes in reproduction, whether to ensure the inheritance of land, name, and property; to cement social continuity; to provide objects of love and recipients for consumption; or to fill family needs for labor or income. Furthermore, scholars have also shown that within families there are often systematic struggles between men and women, as well as between generations, about arrangements for the timing, gender, and number of their offspring.[9]

Social movements such as feminism, republicanism, labor unionism, eugenics, and nationalism, as well as various religious movements, also have ideologies of reproduction, and internecine arguments over the "correct" view about childbirth, motherhood, and related matters. Certainly communism, both before and after coming to power in East Central Europe, had ideologies of reproduction that we will discuss further here and in chapter 3. Many nineteenth- and twentieth-century feminist movements constructed a broad politics of morality around their concerns for protecting reproduction and children. The point is a very general one. Social movements often define themselves through utopian narratives in which idealized images of reproduction and continuity play a crucial role: they define who should (and should not) reproduce, and how much; who should be responsible for what aspects of reproduction, for what kind of remuneration or return; and how reproduction is related to morality.[10]

Discursive battles among these variously constructed perspectives can be mobilized at any time. But they are unavoidable in periods of political rupture, such as the events of 1989, when new and old elites negotiate and struggle over state forms. At such junctures, not only are the political players reshuffled, but the rules of the political project are being rethought and reorganized, bringing into question the legitimacy of political action and the identities of political actors. We suggest that it is for this very reason, as a grounding for constituting authority, that reproductive policy and ideology are crucial features of such political processes.

We identify four interrelated ways in which reproduction makes politics: (1) public discussions about reproductive issues contribute to recasting the relationship between states and their inhabitants; (2) among such relations nationhood is particularly salient, and narratives of nationhood rely crucially on reproductive discourses and practices to make and remake the category of "nation" and its boundaries; (3) debates about reproduction serve as coded arguments about political legitimacy and the morality of the state; and (4) such debates constitute women as a political group and as particular kinds of political actors.[11]

First, discourses about reproduction contribute to the reconstitution of the relationship between a state and its populace. State-making is in part a process of establishing and maintaining centralized authority over a territory and those who inhabit it. But this relation of authority can be figured in many ways. Whether people are represented in state discourses as "subjects," "citizens," "workers," "brothers-in-nationhood," "children," or "kin and family members" is a matter that is dramatically enacted and demonstrated, in practice, through the implementation and justification of strictures on reproduction and sexuality.

Such relations between the state and its populace imply a structure of sentiment. They can be terrorized, eroticized, enchanted. Here, it is worthwhile to give some indication of the way discourses and practices can shape such relations. By drawing on examples not from the contemporary context in East Central Europe that we will later analyze, but from historical cases, we stress that the processes we are describing are by no means limited to our region and time. For examples of a reign of fear, if not terror, and its broader consequences for interaction and sentiment, one need look no farther than Ceauşescu's Romania, where women's bodies and doctors' activities were under routine surveillance to assure that they did not terminate pregnancies. Fear of such state interference in everyday life was a constant feature of that era. As was also the case in Stalin's Soviet Union, fear was further embedded in social experience through the practice of encouraging denunciations about reproductive matters along with other issues. This allowed individuals to unleash state violence on their neighbors, in the name of protecting ideological rigor. In this way ordinary people had unprecedented access to state apparatuses, and simultaneously lived in ever-present dread of arrest and torture.[12]

By contrast, analysts of Italian politics have repeatedly noted the strong elements of sexuality in fascist leaders' relation to their audiences. But there is disagreement about the exact nature of the appeal. All stress the centrality of "virility" in fascist rhetoric and in Mussolini's self-presentation. But for some authors political rhetoric was pervaded by images of people "falling in love" with the regime and its leader, while others note a "scenario in which the virile leader 'rapes' the feminized masses" (Spackman 1996:xii). Italian fascism can also serve as an odd example of reproduction as enchantment. Mussolini repeatedly invited his listeners to engage in what has been called a "demographic delirium," through which fascists could be born but not made. "Now one can no longer become a fascist," he said as early as 1927. Fascists could only occur "naturally" because children born under his rule would somehow, magically, be physical embodiments of his doctrine.[13]

But thcsc various ways of constituting subjects are not mutually ex clusive. On the contrary, in present-day East Central Europe this is a field of argument. Social actors within the state, competing to control parts of the state apparatus, may take sides on such matters. More broadly, much political debate can be understood as a way of arguing about which of these state-subject relations will take precedence in a particular historical moment, or for particular political purposes.[14]

If reproductive discourse and practices provide a fulcrum for constructing the relationship between a state and its subjects, then constraints on reproduction serve to define who is a proper member of the state's populace. Thus, for example, "citizens" are in many cases implicitly recognized as deserving of that title, and of the set of attendant "rights," by their display of particular forms of state-sanctioned, legally acceptable, usually reproductive sexuality. And conversely, the reproduction of citizens is seen as beneficial, judicious, necessary for the future, while the reproduction of those not recognized as such—for instance, immigrants or stigmatized minorities—is seen, for that very reason, as dangerous, out of control, and polluting. While always linked to images of reproduction, state-subject relations are differently configured depending on the ideology—socialist, welfare, national, liberal democratic, fascist—in terms of which representatives of the state explain and legitimate the state itself. This kind of debate is pervasive in contemporary East Central Europe.

For instance, when Hungarian leaders discussed the abortion issue in 1990–92, a major concern was whether the relevant legal code was a "regulation" or a "law." Some leaders argued that if the inhabitants of Hungary were to be newly treated as citizens of a democracy, no longer the infantilized children of a paternalist communist state that delivered itself of dictates, then matters of importance, such as reproduction, should be legislated by properly elected parliamentary representatives. If under communism abortion policy was a feature of such governmental dictates, they said, then for that very reason it now had to be challenged and negotiated as law, even if its substance was not at issue. What was made an issue, instead, were the forms of acceptable political control, the boundaries of what a state can and cannot demand of its citizens.

In the Germany of the early 1990s, the obligations of the state to its citizens and vice versa were also at issue, but in a different way. For many in West Germany, the rights of the fetus took precedence over those of women. Many East Germans charged that while unification promised democracy and liberal rights, the restriction of the East German abortion laws would in fact be a loss of democracy and individual rights for women. Thus the debate on abortion in the East was very much about what classes of people would be favored for the supposedly universal category of "citizen." The process we are describing is also starkly evident in Poland, where opponents of abortion as well as those who support abortion rights ask: Will Poland become a theocracy, with Christian inhabitants who follow the teachings of the Catholic Church? Will it become the model Catholic state that will reevangelize Europe? Or will the state be secular and neutral, its parliament free to tax the Church, its inhabitants defined as religiously unmarked "citizens" not assumed to be Christians, nor necessarily in agreement with Church doctrine?[15]

Another way to construct the relationship between a state and (at least part of) its populace is through the making and remaking of the nation and its boundaries. Hence we turn to a second way in which debates and policies about reproduction, along with the practices they propose and justify, are crucial in politics. To specify what we mean by this, it is important to note that nations are quite different kinds of entities than states, though both must be culturally imagined. States, as we have noted, are relatively centralized organizational structures with claims to sovereignty over a territory. Nations however are symbolic constructs, categories of identity or systems of social classification that can be used to create horizontal solidarities or "imagined communities." Such imagined communities are generally classified as civic or ethnic in constitution: the former is associated with civic nationhood based on notions of common political responsibilities and rights; the latter, ethnonationalism, based on assumptions of shared origin, culture, and blood.

National identities (civic or ethnic) are made through a semiotic process that classically relies on oppositions and exclusions. National identity is most often created against other categories: against imperial forms of political loyalty; against "natives" already living in a newly claimed territory; against other categories of nationhood understood to be cohabiting in one state. As a result, the category-system that creates nationhood always has within it the logical potential for further splintering, further segmentation, the formation of more (sub)national categories that oppose the ones already constituted.[16]

We take nationalism to be a social movement, or a political position, built around (contestable) claims to such categories of identity. It is a movement that is sometimes directed toward the capture of a state apparatus by those claiming to be members of a particular nation. But whether demanding formation of a new state, or more influence within an already constituted state, or negotiating varying relations with a series of states in which linked (diasporic) nationalist movements operate, nationalist arguments are ways of mobilizing collective action and thus bringing into being the imagined collectivity—the nation—itself. The process is classically "performative." That is, nationalist leaders presuppose a social entity (the nation) in whose name they act, but which is created as a collectivity only as a result of their mobilization efforts. This may occur through the formation of a social movement, through preferential or prejudicial treatment within legal codes or organizations of a state, or by the marking of individuals in censuses or in other sorts of administrative bookkeeping. The process is not a demographic one of "finding" those who carry the traits of some purported national group, nor of bringing groups to "consciousness" or "awakening" them. It is rather a matter of leaders promoting a political position that assumes the existence of the group in question. Such nationalist arguments tend to elide other and competing kinds of identity categories, notably of class and gender, but also of political opinion and region.

What, then, is the role played by narratives of reproduction in the making of such (ethno)national categories? It hardly needs emphasizing that in most forms of ethnonationalist thought biological reproduction and biological continuity over time are the centerpieces of creating and imagining community. Although populations are often enlarged and diminished by migration and assimilation, nationalist ideology commonly ignores or erases these processes, instead highlighting and constructing ties of blood. Although individuals routinely have claims to several national identities, and boundaries between categories are often permeable or fuzzy, nationalist discourse and the ordinary language of nationhood erase such "messiness."

For most forms of (ethno)nationalism, making the members of the nation is not only a symbolic classifying process, but also very much a material, corporeal one: Links between generations must, perforce, be reproductive links, embodiments of membership. One's relation to the future and to history is understood in generational terms, through stories of physical, biological reproduction. And when nations are institutionalized, some forms of reproduction are defined as the sole legitimate, genuine, authentic means of national reproduction. Thus, whether both parents, or only one, were members of the same national group and whether or not the birth occurred on national territory become questions of great moment in individual lives, in legal conflicts about rights and responsibilities, and in making national boundaries.[17]

In the face of these familiar phenomena, it is remarkable that the modern theorists of nationalism—Anderson, Gellner, Hobsbawm, Horowitz, Smith—have had little to say about the role of gender and reproduction in nationalism. But feminist criticism of this omission has produced an important literature on gender and nation as linked cultural categories, a literature in which reproduction is often considered. For instance, feminist writings have explicated nationalism's family imagery that usually casts the nation as female and the state as male, simultaneously eroticizing the relation between men and the nation. It valorizes motherhood, making women the spiritual representatives of the nation. Many variants of this imagery have been identified. Chatterjee, among others, has noted one complex and important configuration that recurs in postcolonial contexts. Anticolonial nationalist movements often differentiate group identity into material and spiritual, assigning to "their" women the burden of representing tradition (if often in some recently invented form), and thus of safeguarding the spiritual essence of the group. Men are thereby freed to be the unmarked, and rational, subjects of "modernity." Ironically, while rejecting colonial domination, such nationalist discourses and movements nevertheless implicitly accept the colonialist judgment that degrees of modernity and civilization are gauged by how men treat "their" women. In an interesting variant of this, in East Central Europe as in postcolonial contexts, the use of reproductive and contraceptive technologies becomes a sign of national success and modernity.[18]

To these insights we add that the focus on motherhood and women as "vessels of the nation/race" also carries other interesting contradictions. Because national movements are most frequently conceptualized as "deep horizontal (male) fraternities," they often implicitly adopt the logic of patrilineal systems in which women are not only the indispensable locus of continuity, but also the outsiders who must be controlled. Through the potential of their unruly sexual behavior, women are seen to pose a threat to the group. Thus, women are blamed for demographic decline, and for being too "selfish" to have children. Women are charged with engaging in "birth strikes"; they are accused of siding with political systems such as communism that are considered to be unnatural or of committing treason if they do not wish their sons to die in wars. Oddly, then, the common narrative of national "victimization" by outside forces, especially by other nearby nations, can also include a narrative of the nation victimized by its own women, who are seen as an internal enemy. This result is often reached as well in the postcolonial narratives outlined above, if women are perceived to be betraying the "culture" whose spiritual essence they are supposed to represent. The control of women thus becomes a logical project of nationalism. A classic means of such control is the regulation of women's reproductive capacity, whether by forcing unwanted births or restricting wanted ones.

It is in part this link between nationhood and reproduction that made the use of rape in the Yugoslav war such a powerful weapon. The irony of ethnic cleansing, based ostensibly on the idea of the intolerability of national difference within a single territory, is that the various sides understood each other only too well. As others have pointed out, the tactic of mass rape was effective because of similarity: All sides were speaking in the idiom of biologized essences in which, as in the narratives noted above, women were the bearers of group identity. This is what made rape and the threat of rape not a crime against particular women, but a threat to the purity and honor of the group. If raped women and their children were later rejected by their own group, the strategic use of rape could materially affect the survival and future of that group.[19]

Fears about the "death of the nation," justified by reference to falling birthrates, are a recurrent theme of nationalist discourse all over Europe. They gain general political significance when the interests of states are assumed to be coterminous with the increase in a single or dominant national group inhabiting the state's territory. Such fears are invariably directed against other categories of people perceived as rivals for territory or for political and economic resources. Warnings about demographic decline are used as political stances by those trying to mobilize what Brubaker has termed nationalizing states against national minorities. For example, to consolidate his power in the late 1980s, Slobodan Milošević skillfully exploited Serbian national ideology by repeatedly playing upon demographic fear: The higher birthrate of Albanians in Kosovo endangered Serbia's "heartland," which would be overwhelmed by these non-Slavs. Largely unsubstantiated accusations about Albanian men raping Serbian women were also employed to further harden ethnonationalist sentiments and to legitimate government action against Albanians. They also served to foreground gender as a marker of ethnic or national identity, and rape as a weapon of war. As the cases of Serbia and Croatia demonstrate, policies that are aimed at increasing the population of one national group within a state's territory are not at all incompatible with policies that simultaneously discourage the increase of another, deemed by those in control of the state to be "dangerous" or simply less worthy or less legitimately linked to the (nationalizing) state.[20]

Thus, within the context of nationalist discourse focused on biological reproduction, state policies that regulate reproductive practices gain importance for a variety of reasons. Indeed, we have come full circle, back to the interests of state agencies in the control of reproduction. But here we see such interests justified not as an expression of a state's relation to its "citizens," but rather as a government justifying its acts as the protection of the "national essence." This distinction is nicely highlighted by comparing Ceaușescu's policies with those of Serbia after 1989. In Ceaușescu's Romania, abortion was forbidden for everyone, regardless of nationality, education, or other characteristics. In Serbia,

laws were framed as a matter of encouraging the disproportionate increase of some subset of the population, namely, those considered the
authentic or "proper" citizens of the state. The two policies are equiva-
lent in demanding a sacrifice from women for the "collectivity" that,
however, is the socialist state in one case and the nation in the other.
They differ in that nationalist policies create a social hierarchy ostensibly
based on the inheritance of biological characteristics. This was not so in
Ceauşescu's nationalism, which was aimed at transforming all co-inhab-
iting nationalities into new socialist citizens of the Socialist Republic of
Romania.

Demographic panic expressed in the motto "The Nation Is Dying"
often hides the fact that population decline is a problem because immigration is not seen as a legitimate way of increasing population. Only
some inhabitants—not immigrants—count as genuine citizens. It also
hides a further embarrassment. Part of the reason for population decline
in Poland, Croatia, Slovakia, and other states is that members of those
nations would rather migrate out, presumably for the sake of higher
standards of living, than stay to "be" the nation.[21]

Many levels and aspects of state organization can be mobilized for the
institutionalization of biologized national selves. All involve reproduction in some way: legal constraints on who may marry whom; regulations on what constitutes "normal" sexuality or the proper work of men
and women; assumptions (often written into tax codes) about acceptable family forms, about who is expected to provide childcare and other
caretaking support; the timing, rate, and ease of marriage and divorce.
Clearly, not only ideas about nationhood, but also about health, respectability, sexuality, and idealized gender are often involved. These
ideas, when legislated, enacted, and so institutionalized, corporeally create the boundaries by which national selves, and ultimately national
groups, are systematically produced.

There is a third way in which discussions of reproduction contribute
to the reconstruction of states. We have found that in case after case,
debates about reproduction can be understood as coded discussions
about claims to political legitimacy. More precisely, the issue of reproduction is one of the means by which the morality and desirability of
political institutions is imagined, and claims for the "goodness" of state
forms are made. This use of debates about reproduction as an allegorical, indirect way of talking about the political future is by no means pe-
culiar to postsocialist tranformations. It is a widespread phenomenon in
other regions and in other historical traditions as well. We argue that the
nature of the politicization and the details of the arguments reveal much
about the particular polity in which they occur.[22]

In East Central Europe, the debates at first involved the attempt to make democratic states out of the population and materials of state socialism. A contrast between the morality of democracy as against the immorality of communism was often highlighted through debates about their contrasting approaches to reproductive policies. Whereas communism, it was claimed, corruptly allowed the killing of fetuses, or equally corruptly cared only about increasing the labor force, postcommunist states could and should make principled, moral decisions about such matters. Or again, if, as many insisted, communism went against nature in allowing women to circumvent motherhood, postcommunist state forms and the governments in charge of them promised to uphold the unchanging forces of a natural gender order. They hoped to rectify the wrongs of the past and gain credibility and legitimacy. In some cases, this worked even for the choice of leaders: Anticommunist arguments in the post-1989 years suggested that leaders who were (reproductively) linked to the populace because of shared origin and ethnicity were more authentically "representative" of the populace—in this special, and also nondemocratic, sense.

But even after the founding of fledgling democratic institutions, there have continued to be profound and potentially explosive disagreements about how states should be run and who genuinely belongs in the polity. Numerous political scientists have recently pointed out that the new democracies are dependent for their stability on basic agreements that democracy is "the only game in town." Free markets go hand in hand with this game. Yet both political and economic transformations require legitimation.[23] How then do social actors characterize a form of politics as "good" or better than others? We argue that discussions about human reproduction have an enormous power to moralize politics because reproduction is already constituted, in the European tradition we are examining here, as a natural, primal phenomenon involving the most fundamental issues of life and death. Legislating reproductive morality for its citizens is one way in which a government can appear as "good," as a moral actor in social life. To constitute democracy rhetorically in this way, reproduction often takes center stage.

More specifically, politicians must appeal to newly constituted publics that are unlikely to be swayed by old arguments about the wisdom of a vanguard party, but that have little experience or knowledge about alternatives among democratic arrangements. Yet, in contrast to state socialism, where voting merely rubber-stamped political decisions made elsewhere, democratic systems call directly on the populace to vote, framing this as an act that decides what policy is best. Debating the legal control of reproduction becomes a substitute for debate about democratic politics. It is a tactic in the everyday struggle among competing elites to legitimate proposals and strategies concerning a wide range of political arrangements, many of which are unrelated to reproduction itself.[24]

Furthermore, by discussing politics through the allegory of reproduction, politicians effectively efface their own ambitions, appearing to favor political strategies and institutional structures not because politicians might benefit, but for an independent moral good: in order to protect the fetus, the mother, the nation, or domestic privacy. Whatever the justifications for particular positions, reproductive debates are one of the few ways in which it is possible to avoid the shadow of self-interest, even in the face of cynical audiences. Such avoidance was particularly important in East Central Europe, where political activity itself has been deeply stigmatized as little more than opportunism and corruption.

But in fact, claiming an apparently disinterested perch above the fray is a very widespread, even classic, method of attaining political authority. Rhetorical analyses of such strategies have, in recent years, identified the ways in which effacing the personal involvement of the speaker produces a "voice from nowhere" that has the effect of objectivity in truth claims. Genres that allow political actors to speak in the voice and name of abstract entities such as social forces, invisible ancestors, or the common good similarly allow speakers to dissociate their own persons from the policies they propose. But in the cases we have examined, there is a further elision or distancing involved. Politicians make claims for the rightness of the political structures and initiatives they favor not by talking about government itself, but by stating their positions on questions such as abortion, sterilization, women's sexuality, or the proper forms of family life. Thus, political actors indirectly demonstrate their own moral credentials through their concern with the reproductive future. Their version of reproductive morality is meant to cast a flattering, moral aura over their other decisions.[25]

The Hungarian debate about abortion in the early 1990s provides an example of reproduction as allegory. Those who argued that personal morality in abortion decisions should not be legislated were liberals who thereby also demanded a minimal state. In this way, the discourse of human reproduction became an integral part of the process by which the desirability of new state forms was constituted. Or, in Poland, for instance, a politician's opinion on abortion continues to be, in everyday politics, a litmus test revealing his opinion on many other issues, ranging from Poland's relationship to the Catholic Church to social welfare questions. In both Hungary and Poland, elites arguing about abortion were also trying to construct the political principles according to which they wished to be judged in routine politics. By which criteria—ethnicity, morality, expertise—should leaders be chosen? Populist politicians, conservative physicians, and lawyers insisted that only they understood the full moral weight of questions about abortion (the liberals, after all, thought private individuals should decide). In this way they implied, and sometimes stated, that only they were fit to govern.

Within this broad process of moralization, however, each case is historically specific. For instance, in Romania after 1989 the immediate legalization of abortion was not only a response to overwhelming popular sentiment, but also a gesture giving the government the moral high ground as against the inhuman and inhumane policies of Ceauşescu's regime. In Poland, by contrast, it was through the restriction of abortion during the same period that politicians attempted to signal the morality of the new government, its opposition to communism, and its alliance with the Catholic Church.

Different from both of these was the case of the sterilization scandal in unified Germany, reported by Dölling and her coworkers. The drop in the eastern German birthrate after 1989 was noticed by the mass media and emerged as a story about eastern women's "refusal" to have children. Various public voices interpreted high sterilization statistics as a "birth strike" in which eastern women were unwilling to support the larger German nation. Other voices, meanwhile, took the sterilization statistics as an index of the lack of sophisticated modernity and enlightened self-interest of eastern German women, as well as, paradoxically, their self-centeredness in not wanting to be mothers. All these comparisons worked to create a more global juxtaposition between the "orderliness" and "humane modernity" of the West with what was constructed as a chaotic, ignorant, lazy, and underdeveloped East. But when Dölling and her coworkers interviewed the women who had undergone sterilization, they found a multitude of reasons why they chose the procedure. Many women had simply reached their desired family size; others were worried about unemployment or discrimination against women with children in the new, unified Germany. None of their motives matched the morality tales about East and West that the media had constructed around their actions. In short, various public and political figures, through the mass media, used women's reproductive decisions to moralize and justify both unification and Western hegemony.

A final example illustrates the odd moralization of reproduction in nationalist discourses. In the Serbian case noted earlier, and following the patrilineal logic already discussed, the representations of Serbian and Albanian women in Kosovo were telling. Serbian women who represented the ideal of socialist modernity and gender equality were exhorted to have more children in the interest of preserving the Serbian nation. In contrast to the relatively "emancipated" Serbian women, Albanian women were seen by Serbs as victims, backward and shackled by their families to lives of relentless childbearing. The high Albanian birth-rate was described as immoral because "primitive" and said to have been achieved at the price of subordinating and demeaning Albanian women. The echoes of Germany's East/West discourse are evident. This also re-capitulates the familiar colonialist narratives mentioned above, in which the civility of a colonized group is judged by "its" treatment of women. As in the German case, Albanian and Serbian women do not simply re-produce; their childbearing is taken as a moral message that justifies the later actions of others.[26]

There is a fourth way in which debates about reproduction make pol-itics. Such public arguments constitute women as a political category, projecting them as political actors of a particular kind. The way women's political roles are constituted varies considerably across social systems. Yet debates about reproduction repeatedly face a fundamental contra-diction: Whether to treat women as producers or reproducers has been a perennial dilemma, differently handled in different historical moments and systems.

Within most nationalist discourses, for instance, women and men are assumed to have quite different subjectivities. Women are understood to owe a special kind of patriotic duty and to have a different relation to time and space than men. As we have noted, women are often identified with spiritual values and are seen to safeguard the morally laden tradi-tion of the past. Motherhood is often viewed as the primary form of female political agency, women's major patriotic duty. In contrast, since the early Soviet period, the production of more workers through moth-erhood was only one of the duties that women owed to the communist state; wage work—"labor" itself—was always another.

To take quite a different historical and comparative example, in East Asian colonial states women were responsible for the hygiene, health, and racial purity of the imperial power. Through the regulation of re-production, colonial regimes attempted to create racial boundaries and thereby contain the political effects of racial difference. And as a final example, we should mention liberal states, where women were often charged with displaying on behalf of their families and male relatives the forms of respectability that, in distinguishing their associated males by class, provided a model of bourgeois *male* citizenship. But in liberal pol-ities women's position reveals a contradiction. Legislation about repro-duction has forced liberals to consider women a group, even though the system itself privileges "individual rights." The notion of rights assumes that for political purposes men and women are alike. However in repro-duction this is not the case; men and women are corporeally, materially different, underlining the inconsistency of the "equal treatment" legisla-tion that is the hallmark of liberalism.[27]

Discussions of reproduction also have a more direct effect in defining women as potential actors in political arenas. Anti-abortion legislation in Poland after 1989 motivated women to organize into women's groups that actively opposed this legislation, and that would otherwise not have materialized. There is similar evidence from Hungary in the socialist period. Signatures collected for an anti-abortion petition by academic women in Budapest and the provinces endangered their jobs but may have contributed to changing regulations.[28]

But politics in East Central Europe, as elsewhere, is not only about policy but is also a career path and work possibility for some segment of the population. In a situation where forty years of communist policy produced women who are at least as well educated as men (sometimes, on average, better), and actually have political experience (in most cases as a result of quota systems), new arguments are needed to justify the claim by men of preferential access to this newly created and often lucrative postsocialist occupation. The Communist Party may be out, but who should go into politics? In Poland, arguments about women's responsibilities as reproducers are often made by politicians who are redefining the work of politics as specially suited to men, that is, as requiring specifically male qualities. Similar discussions about the suitability of men and women for politics are also evident in Bulgaria and Romania.[29]

In outlining these four ways in which discourses of reproduction reconstitute states and politics, our analysis diverges from two other currents in feminist analyses of states. One influential approach focuses on existing state structures, their discourses and practices, arguing that without intentionally or overtly pursuing the "interests" of men, they nevertheless create and support social arrangements that enforce the privilege of some men over most women. In this view, each state is seen to be embedded in wider gender regimes, in unspoken assumptions and taken-for-granted practices of masculinity and femininity that themselves favor particular forms of male dominance. Put another way: "[T]he multiple dimensions of socially constructed masculinity have historically shaped the multiple modes of power circulating through the domain called the state" (Brown 1992). While agreeing in principle with this approach, we note that such work does not consider how policies that subordinate women and privilege men are actually developed and put into practice. This question is in part taken up by another line of research that traces how negotiations and interactions between states, social movements, and other political actors about issues relating to women result in different patterns of state-supported male privilege in different historical moments.[30]

Following neither of these analytical strategies, our own discussion began with the ways in which reproductive issues are customarily used to argue about a wide range of other political questions. They are used in broader political fields as coded arguments that constitute new state-subject relations, moralize positions on diverse other issues, authorize new political mechanisms, and legitimate individual politicians. In this sense, state policies about the linked issues of reproduction, contraception, and normative sexuality are never only about biological reproduction. For instance, turning again to the example of Poland, any Polish politician's position on abortion is a litmus test of his opinions on diverse issues such as church-state relations, health policy, and the national budget. This politicization of abortion means that, at least since 1989, each change of president, parliament, and government in Poland has brought a change in abortion laws, with very real consequences for the everyday lives of men and women.

Hence the instrumentalization of reproductive arguments has an important feedback effect. It shapes the policies and practices of reproduction that states support and that men and women experience. Our approach contributes to understanding the process by which state agencies, even unwittingly, can come to espouse and promote policies that ensure the privilege of some men over most women.

We have thus returned to the classic subject matter of the politics of reproduction: the effect of seemingly distant power relations on local reproductive experiences.

To be sure, between the political arguments we have discussed and the processes that put a policy into practice, there are inevitable compromises, lapses, gaps, and contradictions. In general, the actual processes of legislation, regulation, and enforcement take diverse forms, depending on the particular structures of polities. Policies are rarely implemented fully as intended. Furthermore, the laws and regulations that result from a political process never entirely determine action. In any polity, men and women also ignore, flout, reinterpret, and deflect explicit state actions and maneuver around them, creating alternatives outside the purview of legal regulations and state structures. But laws do nevertheless restrict the range of actual practices of reproduction that are possible for ordinary men and women. They define the boundaries of legality, the official expectations and imagery against which people must struggle, and which they may on occasion resist.[31]

As a result, routine forms of everyday reproductive practice that have emerged in each of the countries of East Central Europe have been importantly shaped by the framing of issues and the range of discursive patterns on which we have focused here. In addition, they are influenced by broadly economic processes and international pressures that may be well beyond the domains of state agencies. In Poland, for instance, some doctors have set up private abortion clinics where they make healthy profits performing the abortions that are apparently morally offensive to them when done in hospitals during customary working hours. Or, some East German women who have themselves sterilized are acting in part to improve their chances in a newly hypercompetitive job market that rewards women who can prove they will have no reproductive responsibilities that might interfere with work. Noting these factors, a number of scholars have argued that the invocation of reproductive responsibility is being used as a way to get women out of the labor market in a time of rising unemployment.[32]

There are also important international dimensions to reproductive policies and practices. States that legislate against abortion within their boundaries often do not interfere with women traveling abroad for "abortion tourism." This has become a popular strategy for women who have the money to do so, which produces an income stratification in reproductive practices. The increased availability of contraceptives has had a similar effect, since they are not affordable for many. The influence of the Vatican on Polish parliamentary discussions of abortion has already been mentioned, but the Vatican is only one of the many transnational organizations that pressure East Central European governments. However, external influence is not always in the form of direct pressure. Some have suggested that the Hungarian abortion debate was in part a kind of mimicry of the way American and Western European politicians had so effectively used this issue in the years immediately before. The rhetoric of Croatian, Hungarian, and other nationalist discourses about "national death" recall and reiterate interwar debates. Certainly, in reproductive matters, as elsewhere, leaders in East Central Europe have actively watched each other, and have been influenced as well by models to the west in planning their political actions.

Such activity itself has repercussions not only on domestic but also on international politics. How governments react to the International Monetary Fund, World Bank, or UN advice on social benefits or reproductive health and family planning strategies, how reproductive policies are seen to intersect with minority politics, or how the criminalization of homosexuality in Romania is seen to violate democratic rights all contribute to the way the states of East Central Europe are evaluated and treated by supranational organizations, and in international forums. Accordingly, such policies are carefully considered. The governments of East Central Europe are particularly sensitive to their images abroad. But the watching and weighing also work in the reverse direction. Abortion has become a subject of legal debate in the European Union, not on moral but on economic grounds. The European Union's Court of Justice was brought into cases where the economic aims of the EU—free movement of labor, capital, and information across state lines—seemed to be violated by the anti-abortion laws of some of the states that restrict the movement of information about abortion.[33] These and other precedents concerning human and fetal rights are being watched and invoked by lawyers arguing abortion cases in the constitutional courts of the East Central European states, where at least some leaders hope to preadapt to EU regulations in order to more easily gain admittance in the near future. We have again come full circle: Representations about reproduction make politics, not only at home, but also on the international stage.

3

Dilemmas of Public and Private

REPRODUCTION is complexly linked to political processes and state policies. But reproduction, and gender relations more broadly defined, are
no less intertwined with the economic changes occurring in East Central
Europe. In this chapter and the next, we examine how the region's
newly expanding market economies are producing different outcomes
for men and women and new patterns of relations between them. At the
same time, we also pose the converse question of how ideas and expectations about men and women are among the factors shaping economic
change.

Gender relations include the routine ways in which men and women
interact with each other in social institutions: the division of labor in
households, in sexual relationships, friendships, workplaces, and within
different sectors of the economy. They include, as well, the kinds of life
courses produced by such organization of work and the characteristic
structures of feeling that orient what men and women expect out of life.
In East Central Europe, change is simultaneously occurring in the institutions and routinizations of work, in images of masculinity, femininity,
and marriage, as well as in narratives about life course and life strategy.
The resulting patterns of gender relations, we suggest, are not only diverse, but hardly resemble the patterns in the past or present with which
they are customarily equated. To understand these changes, we turn
from the earlier focus on discourses about reproduction to the links between state policies, market forces, and the broader organization of intimate life.

But what, after all, is "intimate life"? Where are the boundaries between "public" and "private"? And how do these cultural categories
change? As we have already noted, the public/private distinction is an
aspect of ideology—both for analysts and for East Central European social actors—that requires historical contextualization. Two kinds of
comparison seem crucial. First, by considering the current postsocialist
changes in the light of earlier, presocialist shifts in the understanding of
public and private, we show how gender relations and political economic change have been interrelated in the course of two centuries. Second, by comparing postsocialist arrangements of work to those in the
contemporary welfare states of Western Europe, the two sides of the
continent can be seen as parts of a single, interacting system, connected

through increasing economic relations, a shared international climate in social policy, and migration patterns. In this way, we integrate the evidence from East Central Europe into debates within feminist scholarship about the effects of markets ("private") and welfare states ("public") on the relations between men and women. This chapter considers the historical comparisons; chapter 4 takes up the links between East and West.

For each kind of comparison, we start by analyzing current assumptions about families, markets, and states according to which politicians and scholars—ourselves included—make judgments and advocate action. These assumptions often rely on historical narratives. Our own reconstruction of East Central Europe's place within the historical context of Europe as a whole argues against recent assessments that have characterized postsocialist patterns of gender relations as a return to "age-old, traditional forms" or "natural" arrangements between the sexes. It similarly opposes those who advocate (or fear) returning to an idealized "nineteenth-century European bourgeois norm" that supposedly resulted from capitalist social relations, and thus can be expected to reemerge in East Central Europe's new capitalism.[1] Instead we sketch how the gender patterns of nineteenth-century Europe were themselves innovations, less a reflex of industrial capitalism than a product of class formation, labor union and feminist activism, and state action. Their relation to postsocialist gender arrangements is complex. Because in Europe the relations between men and women have so long been ordered around a public/private dichotomy, this cultural opposition provides a crucial point of departure.

Current discussions of public and private rely, sometimes only implicitly, on the political criticism mounted against patriarchal monarchism in France and Britain in the seventeenth and eighteenth centuries. These Enlightenment critiques posited a new form of political life governed not by natural hierarchy in the form of heredity and family loyalty, but by universal, impersonal criteria of achievement, rights, equality, and property. But as feminist theorists have argued, political life so defined, and based on the contractual agreement of free individuals, has always required constituting and then "forgetting" a domestic sphere where "natural" hierarchy—now expelled from political life—continued as a legitimate organizing principle for the relations between men and women, parents and children. Women were relegated to this "natural," more emotional, domestic, reproductive, and still hierarchical private life. What emerged as the public, the "social," power-laden, and historically determining sphere, was a world of men equal before the law.

Significantly, a further distinction was also at work. Using the same dichotomy of public and private, the male public was itself divided into a public, which included the state and political activity generally, and a private, understood not as a domestic sphere but as private property, the market, and civil society. This produced the cultural understanding that politics (public) was different from economics (private), yet allowed both to be coded as male domains. Women—long lacking control over private property as well as their own persons—were not included in this "private."[2]

These terms have continued to be the focus of philosophical discussion among liberal, Marxist, and conservative thinkers. They have been a central and abiding concern of feminist theory. While agreeing that the public/private distinction is crucial in understanding relations between families, political structures, and economic processes, scholars advocating various political and theoretical positions have differed considerably on how exactly to characterize the dichotomy and its historical development. Is this a contrast between different spaces and actual locations of interaction such as homes, salons, and legislative assemblies? Or between institutions such as states, markets, and political parties? Or perhaps between different forms of criticism and debate about the state and political action? Philosophical positions have varied along other axes as well. They differ in their positive or negative evaluation of the public and private, and in their vision of which is the more dynamic and changeable, which the more natural or static sphere. They argue whether the public legitimates the state, is in conflict with it, or justifies political action separate from the state. At least three dimensions or senses of "privacy" have been distinguished in philosophical writings: the realm of moral and religious values; economic rights; and domestic, sexual, reproductive matters. There have also been arguments about which idea of the public is most conducive to mass politics, to the representation of minority or stigmatized groups, and to ideals of democracy.[3]

In the wide range of recent writing about public/private, most discussions have adopted one of two approaches. The first of these is historical and attempts to follow the changing definitions of the public and the private over time in different national and political traditions. It considers public and private as philosophical responses to political and economic conditions produced in the concrete historical situation of emerging capitalism. For example, Habermas's influential rethinking of the category of the bourgeois "public" traced its transformations in English, French, and German social thought of the last two centuries. He explored how ideas about truth, morality, property, freedom, and reason were differently configured around these notions by writers such as Rousseau, Kant, and Hegel, who took "public" as a central term in their work. Although, as Habermas goes on to show, critical Marxist and liberal thinkers questioned how the "public" would be affected by the inclusion of additional categories of people into political participation, they nonetheless retained the public/private distinction.[4]

The alternative approach has been to typologize the different forms that the distinction has taken. For instance, one can compare Arendt's writings with liberal theories and with Habermas's discourse theory, examining how each understands the category of public debate and the role of debate in an ideal democratic politics. Arendt borrowed the classical Greek notion of a political "space" that is the ideal locus—or form of association—for agonistic, heroic, and competitive display that results in leadership for the group. In the liberal and bourgeois tradition, by contrast, public dialogue ideally entails restrained, reasoned discussion, assuming a fundamental deliberative process that, by its rational form, legitimates decisions. But such debate engages only those matters which can be points of compromise, while basic conflicts about values are off-limits, relegated to the private. Different yet again is Habermas's thesis that public discussion is a way of debating ideas about value and "the good." In this view, no topic is off-limits, and as new political groups form, they are expected to redefine and often extend what are considered the proper subjects of public deliberation.[5]

Building on the results of such historical and typological approaches, we propose, in addition, a broadly cultural or semiotic perspective. By "semiotic" we mean an approach that considers how signs and their relationships contribute to the meaning-making properties of this dichotomy: how ordinary social actors, as well as social theorists, use and change the idea of "public/private" as they order and understand their social lives. We take from the historical perspective the assumption that the public/private distinction is an aspect of ideology, closely related to the historical circumstances that it is trying to explain and shape. Accordingly, most of this chapter relies on historical studies that have shown how the boundaries and definitions of public and private have shifted. We take from the feminist typological approach the important insight that, like any structural opposition, public and private always define and constitute each other. It is the very exclusion of women and the domestic that produces a bourgeois public sphere.

But we depart from earlier structuralist views by arguing that the apparent constancy of the opposition itself requires explanation: The "effect" of continuity results from a subtle communicative process. It is not only that the definitions of what is public and what private change, even within a single national or philosophical tradition. As feminists have emphasized, the placement of the boundary has itself often been a matter of contention. The ability of a social actor or social institution to fix the boundary has invariably been a source and sign of power. Similarly, the ability of a movement to shift the boundary—introducing new topics or institutions into public debate—is also an emblem and result of its power. Given the protean nature of the dichotomy, then, it is important to consider public and private not as some ubiquitous and constant structural opposition, but as a field of disagreement and conflict in which the very facts of constant use, discussion, and contention produce and reproduce a sense of continuity.

From a semiotic perspective, the repeated use of the categories, in the face of their constantly changing content, is possible because, contrary to customary scholarly parlance, "public" and "private" are not particular places, domains, spheres of activity, or even types of interaction. Even less are they distinctive institutions and practices. Rather, the public/private dichotomy is best understood as a discursive distinction that, once established, can be used to characterize, categorize, organize, and contrast virtually any kind of social fact: spaces, institutions, groups, people's identities, discourses, activities, interactions, relations. Public and private are indexical signs, or shifters, always dependent for part of their referential meaning on the interactional contexts in which they are used. Thus, the exact distinction between public and private is relative to the interactional situation in which it is applied.[6]

Furthermore, the public/private dichotomy, like many similar cultural oppositions, is a fractal distinction. This means it is recursively applicable—like self-similar fractal patterns in geometry—and therefore can be nested. That is, whatever the local, historically specific content of the dichotomy, the distinction between public and private can be reproduced repeatedly by projecting it onto a narrower context or a broader one. Activities, identities, and interactions can be split into private and public parts, and each of these parts can be split again, by the same public/private distinction. The result is that within any public one can always create a private; within any private one can create a public. Which "level" of contrast and context is invoked in any interaction or instance of use is a matter of positioning and of the perspectives of social actors and institutions. Public and private can also be signaled through momentary changes of gesture, spatial distance, and "voicing." Or the difference between public and private can be made more explicit, lasting and binding through arrangements such as legal regulation. Another way to say this is that everyday public and private distinctions—whether of activities, spaces, or social groups—are subject to reframings and subdivisions in which some part of the public is redefined as private, and vice versa.[7]

The nested categorization of spaces and practices can also be detected in philosophy and social theorizing. The fractal divisions to which the public/private distinction has been susceptible within social theory are readily illustrated in the examples we mentioned earlier. For instance,

Pateman's rereading of the classic Enlightenment theorists can be understood as a critique of the nested structure of their arguments. She shows that for Rousseau and other thinkers, the distinction between private property and the public state rested on a previous (and unacknowledged) dichotomy between a more general private (the domestic) and a more general public (the social). What makes it easy to forget that the original distinction excluded women, Pateman suggests, is the fact that the same distinction applied again, seeming to replace the first because so similar to it. As we will see, erasures like this often result from such fractal distinctions.

In a somewhat different example, Habermas's own argument about the structure of the early bourgeois public sphere depends on a first distinction between the private realm and the sphere of public authority, made up of the state and the court. But, he writes, "[w]ithin the realm that was the preserve of private people we . . . distinguish again between private and public spheres. The private sphere comprised civil society in the narrower sense, that is to say, the realm of commodity exchange and of social labor; embedded in it was the family and its interior domain" (1989:30). Here the nested quality of civil society as a public within a larger private sphere does not have the effect of erasure, but rather gives the state and civil society a kind of closeness or compatibility: They are both the public sides of the dichotomy, but at different "levels" or contexts of distinction. A semiotic approach, we suggest, allows us to highlight not so much the particular distinctions that theorists have proposed, but the process by which they have constructed their theories.

Far from being a sign of imprecision or confusion, then, the shifting applicability of the public/private distinction, as well as its changing alignment with other dichotomies—male/female, us/them—is a quite systematic and fertile feature of communication, and not an uncommon aspect of ideologies. It will have different specific features in different historical periods and social formations. But once the dichotomy is established, the semiotic logic forms a backbone or scaffolding for change. Rather than trying to settle once and for all what public and private have meant to some theorist or social movement, we ask instead how people—drawing on familiar materials—use these oppositions as flexible cultural resources that enable new imaginings of social action.[8]

The remainder of this chapter briefly traces the historical permutations of public/private in Europe and particularly in East Central Europe, showing that alignments of this distinction with male/female, masculinity/femininity, us/them, and social class have been much more labile than is usually recognized. Higher value and privilege have most often been accorded that which is coded as masculine. But publics, for example, have not always been seen as male and the values, sentiments, and subjectivities associated with public and private have shifted significantly. By following these changes, we examine the implications of such semiotic processes for historical change: How do various social actors, states, social movements, and families employ the nested possibilities of public and private and their changing valences and gender codings to understand, shape, and justify their circumstances?

A fully established public/private distinction allows such semiotic acrobatics. How did the opposition itself emerge as a cultural category? As many have noted, its elaboration and transformation in Europe over the last several hundred years has been a complicated process, one linked to changing ideas and practices concerning gender, work, sexuality, and politics. The description of its vicissitudes has produced an impressive scholarly literature. We can hardly attempt to present a complete picture of that development here. Nevertheless, a brief outline is necessary to the goal of this chapter, to chart the ways these distinctions have defined and constrained economic and political arrangements.

We started this discussion with the philosophical discourses of the Enlightenment, as critiqued by feminist scholars. But the ideas that defined women as naturally tied to a "private" and to reproduction, and men to "public" politics, distinct from economics, were not only academic. They were simultaneously a more general response to the arrangements of work and family life in European capitalism and industrialization that the philosophical debates helped to conceptualize and legitimate. Moreover, these ideas were elaborated as a commonsense understanding of the social world by Western European middle classes over the course of the nineteenth century. Amplified into the doctrine of "separate spheres" for men and women, they were eventually adopted in modified form by the working classes as well. They prescribed a separation between men and women in which men were "breadwinners" and women the specialists in reproduction, household labor, and in the emotional support needed against the perceived evil effects of the market and industrial work. When the first welfare states emerged in Europe, they were aimed at providing insurance for men as workers who supported families, and thus reinforced this ideal of the division of labor.[9]

But historical investigations suggest that the work of men and women was not so separate as the ideology would have it. Industrial production, while quite differently organized than preindustrial production, was not always and strictly independent of the household. Indeed, household and workplace were tightly bound together, even when different sorts of work were performed in them. Each supported and allowed for the operation of the other. Rather than the creation of two distinct "worlds"—reproduction in the household and production—there was a simultaneous change, all over Western Europe, in the organization of both households and production, occurring in tandem with class formation.

For the emerging working classes, the gendering of various types of industrial and artisanal work—their cultural coding as suitable for men or women—was a process fraught with conflict. It took the spreading ideal of separate spheres and the demand for a "family wage" to define the category of "worker" as male, despite the broad diversity of paid skilled work and waged occupations in which women were engaged. In the case of middle classes, too, despite important national differences, a striking overall pattern can be discerned. Household work was systematically redefined as lacking value, in contrast to wage work. And within the ideology of separate spheres, it was notions of properly rational and sexually restrained masculinity and soft, sensitive, emotional femininity that signaled middle-class identity, in contrast as much to the libertine habits thought to characterize the aristocracy as to the practices of peasants and the emerging working classes.[10]

In the Habsburg lands, the Balkans, and Russia, where the mechanization and capitalization of agriculture were spurred by the food demands of western industrialization over the course of the nineteenth century, variations of the same gender ideologies were evident. By the turn of the century, for instance, there were growing urban bourgeoisies in Berlin, Budapest, Prague, and Vienna. In all these cities, bourgeois women were charged with the management of households, using the labor of servants who migrated from the countryside for work. It is telling that these servants posed a vexing problem for the new cultural construction of domesticity and privacy. The household could not operate without them. Yet because servants demanded payment in the impersonal form of wages, they were seen by bourgeois men and women as impudent, disloyal, and dangerous to a domestic sphere ideally based on love, kinship, and hierarchical loyalty. This implies that despite the pronounced tendency of the middle classes in East Central Europe to mimic gentry and aristocratic practices in many respects, middle-class households also provide evidence of a distinctly bourgeois mentality in the handling of public and private. Visions of masculinity and femininity in this period are also suggestive. It was in East Central Europe that bourgeoisies produced the infamous fin-de-siècle flowering of art celebrating private female sensuality, decadence, repression, and neurosis, in contrast to hard-won masculine rationality and civilization, as in the work of Gustav Klimt, Otto Weininger, and Sigmund Freud.[11]

Turning to other social strata, we note that industrialization was weak and uneven in the East at the turn of the century, and the relative number of industrial workers was small. However, the landless agricultural proletariat was very large and growing as agriculture was increasingly organized by capitalist logic. Male agricultural workers experienced labor for the manor or employer as a theft of their masculinity, a quality defined in accord with earlier peasant norms as the prerogative to control their own and their wives' and children's labor. The interests of the household were defined against the interests of the manor. In contrast to domestic/private demands, those of such public work could be rightfully resisted. Thus, here too, we find a class-coded gender distinction linked to public and private that helped to organize economic relations.

Only relatively self-sufficient peasant households failed to participate in this version of the discursive formation that distinguished public from private life. The older patriarchal and patrilineal systems of the region assumed that men represented families in village forums, while women were understood as strangers to the patrilineal families they entered at marriage. Always viewed as outsiders, potentially threatening, they were nonetheless indispensable to the perpetuation of their marital households. But in these noncapitalist family economies—typical of many parts of the region, especially the Balkans, well into the twentieth century—the gendered division of labor did not resemble bourgeois arrangements: Women often took a large share of agricultural production, within which they sometimes managed the distribution of work and resources.[12]

In broad strokes, then, public and private were linked to ideas about masculinity and femininity; fundamental legal and economic arrangements fixed the boundary itself, and assured the dependence of women upon husbands, fathers, and sometimes sons in a range of gender regimes across nineteenth- and early-twentieth-century capitalist Europe. Even when the state intervened through early welfare schemes, it supported these arrangements.

For our purposes these patterns are important not only as precursors, but because it was in the context of these images and arrangements that European communist movements emerged. These were among the circumstances to which communist theorizing responded in the process of framing programs of reform and revolution. Marxist theory was in concert with liberal thought in seeing production (public) as the main site of historical and revolutionary change, with much less attention paid to those activities not ordinarily called "work" in that period, such as tasks surrounding reproduction. Nevertheless, many leftist theorists since Engels have considered changes in the situation of women, reproduction, and sexuality as crucial to changing the world. They criticized bourgeois marriage as the source of women's financial and personal dependence, and thus of inequality between men and women. Socialist revolution would recreate ideal love and male-female partnership by eliminating the bourgeois distinction between public and private. The equality of men and women would be brought about through re-education, public (waged) labor for all, easy divorce and by socializing the burdensome (female) tasks of reproducing labor, thus liberating sexuality as a positive "social force" independent of marriage.[13]

In the years after World War I, communist parties and some feminist groups were joined in these utopian visions by a wide range of leftist political organizations all over Europe, including those committed to sexual reform. They were reacting to the contradictory effects of the war. In part, women's work experiences during the war contributed to a novel feminine image, the "new woman" of the 1920s—active, slender, athletic, sexual—a far cry from the delicate, protected, and passive "angel in the home" of the later-nineteenth century. On the other hand, the war brought enormous loss of life and narratives of damaged masculinity. Demands by the left for women's access to equal work, to abortion, contraception, education, and (nonreproductive) sexual experience went directly against nationalist goals to increase population and reinvigorate male pride. In support of national goals, many feminist movements of the period also advocated for the protection of motherhood. In this confrontation, communist utopias were compromised at a very early stage: European communist parties, which were usually in opposition, nevertheless went along with the reproductive policies of the leading parties in their countries.[14]

From the perspective of women in East Central Europe, the results of communist and leftist activism varied a great deal between the wars, and depended in part on the levels of economic development. While the Czech parts of Czechoslovakia, some parts of Poland, and Hungary embarked on relatively successful industrialization that engaged some percentage of women, the rates of women's literacy were low virtually everywhere. The more southeastern and northeastern parts of the region remained overwhelmingly agricultural, with high fertility rates compared to the West and even to western parts of the region. Often the attempts at industrialization and the effects of the economic depression undermined women's sources of influence in peasant households. In cases where interwar leftist and peasant parties survived the increasingly authoritarian political climate, their organizing among rural and urban women was relatively conservative, focused on reinforcing women's roles as mothers and guardians of the home. Women in most of the region—except Czechoslovakia, Poland, and Germany—did not gain the franchise until after the Second World War.[15]

In the Soviet Union too, an early moment celebrating the politically liberatory possibilities of sexuality and equality between men and women was replaced, by the 1930s, with Stalinist pronatalism and the ubiquitous image of woman as mother (even Mother Russia) or as the agricultural and thus lesser feminine (sickle) to the industrial masculine (hammer). Tellingly, Stalinist policy declared a "solution" to the "woman question"—that is, to the problem of how women were to be integrated into a communist system. The considerable gender inequalities in Soviet life increased but became "unsayable."

The "gender regimes" of state socialism in East Central Europe were built out of these ideological critiques and failed utopias, as well as out of the preexisting arrangements of capitalist gender relations that structured male dominance in households, politics, and workplaces. After the Second World War, the new communist states tried to erase the existing institutional forms of the public/private dichotomy. Many of the distinctive characteristics of state socialism derive from this ideological rejection. Once again, this suggests the ways in which ideas about gender—and its long-standing linkage to the public/private—shaped political economic arrangements. Ironically, however, new and subtle configurations of public/private emerged in the course of four decades, as state socialism succeeded in producing another system that, though quite different in institutional organization from capitalist gender regimes nevertheless was equally effective in securing an altered form of male privilege.[16]

Two complementary and interrelated conceptualizations of these processes have appeared in recent feminist scholarship. One focuses on the question of how gender "difference" itself was handled by state socialism; the other, on how public and private were redefined and revalued, their links to masculinity and femininity reconfigured. We review and integrate these approaches in order to show how state socialist systems tried to manage the hierarchical power relations between men and women that they inherited. Then we discuss the contradictions and tensions that these new gender relations created for men and women. The postsocialist transformations of public and private, which are our ultimate subject matter, are comprehensible only if seen as partly shaped by socialism itself.

In most of the communist states of East Central Europe, women were at first defined primarily as workers, a dramatic revision of pre-war imaginings. This was part of the broader commitment to the homogenization and equalization of the populace that intended to eliminate all social distinctions, including gender, in order to construct the "new socialist man." The 1950s marked a period in which this ideology, along with the need to increase the labor force in the face of war losses and in the interests of industrialization, produced a wholesale, and sometimes coerced, entry of women into the ranks of paid workers. Similarly, women entered higher education in numbers that eventually equaled and exceeded those of men. The attempt to revalue and thus equalize all work by making it "public"—that is, the attempt to view it as a form of production—went to extremes: In some eras, women who had many children were rewarded on the model of Stakhanovite workers.[17]

The private was simultaneously targeted for fundamental change that went well beyond the elimination of "private property" and included that embedded, nested sense of "private"—the domestic household. In a nice example of the kind of competition and mutual watching that characterized the Cold War, postwar Western trends resanctified the nuclear family as a symbol of the "free world," while the East moved in the opposite direction. New regulations eased divorce, set up at least rudimentary childcare facilities, socialized laundry, cooking, and other household tasks, and even pressured men to participate in household labor. But these latter changes were expensive to construct and maintain, resisted by the populace, and difficult to enforce. Some of them fell by the wayside and others were inadequately developed. Women became a numerically important presence in the public, that is, in the lower rungs of state-owned paid work and state-run political activity. But they retained almost sole responsibility for household work and childrearing. Thus, despite early efforts, the division of labor in the household was never fundamentally transformed by state socialism. Socialization of housework was not fully realized; housework remained publicly invisible and devalued.[18]

Nevertheless, the intrusion of state institutions into what was formerly a private sphere of family and reproduction produced a much-remarked and fundamental change. While wage work—not only possible, but virtually compulsory for all—made both men and women dependent on the state as employees in state-owned enterprises, policies toward families made women and children less dependent on husbands and fathers. In contrast to the earlier bourgeois pattern, women were no longer restricted to the private nor exclusively linked to it in discourse. And their relation to the state was not always mediated by relations to (private) men. In contrast to any previous peasant or worker pattern in the region, women were, instead, more directly dependent on the state, and often perceived to be in an uneasy alliance with it. Schematically, the fundamental distinction between household and public remained in everyday practice, but the outlawing or appropriation of the independent press, voluntary associations, independent unions, and civic organizations radically transformed the parameters of what had been the bourgeois public.

By the 1960s, threatened with a decreasing birthrate, nationalist outcries, and popular resentment of many of these changes—not to mention a series of armed revolutions—worried planners reinstated motherhood as a crucial responsibility of women to the state. Indeed, they tried to use policies toward women to manipulate both birthrates and the size of the active labor force. Here we see the actual operation of the politics of reproduction discussed in chapter 2. The emphasis shifted from policies that would homogenize the labor force by demanding changes in family life to policies that identified women as "different" from male workers, with special obligations and relations to the state. Across the region, state policies varied from generous childcare payments to maternity leaves, to increased access to housing for mothers and families with children, to the invasive control of women's bodies practiced in Ceausescu's Romania. Only in a superficial way did the welfare provisions of Western Europe emerging at this time resemble such policies.

In creating the corporate category of "women," who required special policies, planners relied on preexisting gender stereotypes. They defined women's work as primarily in the caretaking and service sectors rather than in the politically favored, higher-waged domain of heavy industry. Even while instituting quotas that would increase women's participation in politics and the party, they saw women as politically "backward" and therefore unreliable. Ironically, gender-specific policies such as maternity leaves themselves produced an image and reality of women as less dependable workers, and so reinforced their subordinate position in the labor force. It was in part this treatment of women as categorically "different" that allowed the re-creation of gender hierarchies in work and in political authority. This maintained male monopoly of top positions despite the ideology of equality and the quite new context of centralized economic and political institutions.[19]

These manipulations of the labor force also marked one common state response to the increasing economic crises of the centralized economies. To varying degrees and in various periods, most of the socialist states retreated from their attempts to regulate families directly. Several of them started, instead, to tolerate if not encourage the development of "black," "informal," or "second" economies that participants labeled "private" or "familial," and that included extensive nonstate production at first in agriculture, later in a wide range of industries and services. Such household (familial, secondary) economic activity relied on goods and time from state enterprises. In turn, wages in the state sector were set so low that for most people activity in the second economy was virtually indispensable. State planners then relied (if only tacitly) on the second economy to satisfy consumer demands that the official economy had promised but could not deliver.[20] With the notable exception of Romania, the states of the region over time generally loosened their hold on direct regulation of reproduction and everyday life. In at least some of the countries, various forms of officially forbidden cultural and political activity—samizdat, union organizing, contact with Western colleagues and relatives—were nevertheless allowed to occur.

From our perspective, the most important point about these developments is the striking way in which they further changed and even reversed the familiar public/private distinctions of the bourgeois world. The household, far from being a site for only reproduction and consumption, was transformed for many into the place where the really intense, productive, and rewarding work of their lives was accomplished. Extreme housing shortages, on the other hand, made sex relatively public, as several generations often shared a single room and young people were virtually forced to use parks, forests, and beaches as venues for sexual activity. And, although production/consumption as well as production/reproduction continued to be opposed to each other in official pronouncements, such distinctions were complicated in practice, since the major activities of production, consumption, and reproduction were often located in the same spaces of the home, depended on the same social relations of kin and family, and were seen by participants as opposed to a "public" (state-owned and controlled) sector.

Complex interdependencies developed between the state sector and familial efforts. One might say that time and work were fractally subdivided, the private nested inside the public. For instance, in building private houses with the labor of family, kin, and neighbors, people often used building materials stolen from public, state-owned workplaces. The informal barter economy relied on the access to machinery and materials provided by the particular location of families within state networks and enterprises. And by the end of the communist period, in some of the countries of the region, the public economy was similarly subdivided. Groups of workers within state enterprises organized private businesses or "work groups" that independently sold their expertise or took subcontracting jobs, sometimes from the very company (state-owned) inside which they worked. The private businesses operating inside the public enterprise were also not entirely private, since they were dependent on the machinery and materials of the public enterprise itself. In some countries there was, in fact, a private/public dichotomy at every level of institutional structure and practice.[21]

Nevertheless, people perceived a fundamental distinction between the state, understood as a powerful "they" who ran the country, and the family, the private "us" who sacrificed and suffered. The private/public distinction was mapped onto us/them in a way that departed from bourgeois logic. The world of official politics, censored communication, and registered jobs was seen as directly opposed to private plots and other kinship-based endeavors in the second economy. The two kinds of work called on different principles of motivation and reward. People loafed in official jobs, but in the second economy practiced extreme overwork ("self-exploitation"). Furthermore, the private "us" and the public "them" were understood to operate according to different moral principles. The cultural imperative to be honest and ethically responsible to those who counted as the private "we" contrasted with distrust and a tolerance for duplicity and interpersonal manipulation in dealings with "them."

Yet these distinctions hid a profound irony. As everyone implicitly knew, the "we" of the private and the "they" of the public were often the very same individuals. The nested interdependencies of work, time, and materials, as well as the ever-present bureaucracies of state social- ism, assured that everyone participated to some extent among the "they" who ruled as well as the "we" who suffered. The possibility of denunciation, the necessity for barter, bribes, "connections," and flat- tery to acquire the basic staples of daily life, and the incentive to lie that is built into soft-budget plans created an instrumentalization of inter- personal relations. Rather than any clear-cut "us" versus "them" or "pri- vate" versus "public," there was a ubiquitous self-embedding or inter- weaving of these categories. Everyone was to some extent complicit in the system of patronage, lying, theft, hedging, and duplicity through which the system operated. Not surprisingly, intimates, family members and friends informed on each other. Nevertheless, people insisted on this distinction between "us" versus "them" and "private" versus "pub- lic"; they took seriously the popular description and scholarly explana- tion of their societies as bifurcated. Here, we are especially interested in the mechanisms that allowed people to find this separation of spheres persuasive and believable, thereby misrecognizing the interdependen- cies in their everyday experience.[22]

The contradiction between everyday practices and the theoretical dis- cussion of public and private depended on a general property of commu- nication. As we have noted, in everyday life, ever-changing boundaries between public and private were most often signaled implicitly and in- voked indexically within interactions. But when people stepped back from such ordinary practices and discussed their actions abstractly, the shifting, mundane uses of public/private, us/them became fixed labels that appeared to represent a stable reality to which they referred. Thus, fleeting, inhabitable roles (us/them) came to seem like immutable, bounded social groups, and shifting categories of activity (public/pri- vate) came to seem solid and distinct. This semiotic property of abstract descriptions—as ideological constructions—succeeded in hiding the embeddings of public/private, us/them, even from those who most viv- idly experienced its everyday complexities. It enabled people to differen- tiate between a trustworthy, private, familial "we" who could rely on one another and an untrustworthy, public "they" who were in charge of the state.[23]

In the socialist period, the specifically gendered meanings of public and private were also transformed. Both men and women participated extensively in the socialist "private" world of nonstate, often household production. Yet the household was the "private," and thus was "feminized" in relation to the state. Indeed one can argue that the family did the unrecognized productive work for the state that women have traditionally done for the family. But within the private realm of the household, further divisions implicitly exploited the logic of the public/private distinction. For example, dissident writers (in Hungary, Czechoslovakia, and Poland) constructed a "public" inside the household as an implicitly male realm in which men could exercise political authority and imagination. This may be viewed as a discursive move to reclaim for men a patriarchal authority over the household that the state had in many ways usurped. But this newly defined (domestic) public was a realm made possible by the private dimension of the divided household, where the work of women was indispensable as a support not only for the material well-being of its members but also for their political engagement. Women's work was made invisible because it was doubly privatized as the household (private) was split into political activities (public) and basic maintenance. Thus, despite the necessity of women's work to maintain the household, this fractioning produced a seeming paradox: When the household became idealized as the locus of political activity, honest work, and sometimes even "resistance," its public aspects were highlighted and its discursive links to women could be made to seem weak. In Hungary and the German Democratic Republic women were increasingly accused—as much by system critics as by system supporters—of being unfairly advantaged, denatured, and perverted by their alignment with the state.[24]

Although many of these broad patterns are familiar to students of state socialism, what has been much less recognized are the structures of feeling within gender relations, the subjectivities created, and the images of masculinity/femininity that were produced in response to these arrangements. Though these varied considerably from country to country and between different strata, there are nevertheless many common themes. Most striking, perhaps, and most frequently noted in even casual descriptions, was the sheer drudgery and endless work of women's lives. Where second economies flourished, men also worked multiple jobs. But the hardships of combining the provisioning of a family in a shortage economy with household labor, childcare, and waged work fell most heavily on women. In some countries this was increased further by their obligation to do volunteer political work and to bear children. And because the state never provided enough of the support services families required, women's responsibilities extended well into old age, as grandmothers continued to help younger generations, providing household support that husbands would not.[25]

A telling aspect of the reorganization of labor is the way this labor was conceptualized by participants. Women generally saw themselves as courageously and unselfishly coping with very difficult demands, which brought not only exhaustion but two other and contradictory results. On the one hand, women gained a sense of gratification, moral superiority, and power in the household from their centrality and apparent indispensability. They also gained a somewhat different, more autonomous sense of self-worth and self-esteem from participation in the labor force. Despite discriminatory wages that were considerably below those of men and despite excess hours of labor, many came to take seriously a communist ideal of equality between men and women. On the other hand, the conditions of work, the low wages, and the magnitude of demands on them produced a sense of victimization and perennial guilt at their never being able to do enough of anything, especially mothering.

Centrally controlled women's magazines contributed to shaping these dominant, paradoxical images of overly powerful yet inadequate womanhood. They presented unattainable images of women who could effortlessly be "engineer, pretty wife, mother, fashion plate, and political activist." These were "superwomen," filling the expectations of socialist womanhood without exhaustion. But many older religious and nationalist ideals of feminine self-sacrifice were also called upon and echoed by the magazines. Occasionally, media campaigns blamed a host of societal ills—from demographic decline to lapses in public morality—on women's supposedly inadequate mothering and supposedly excessive "selfishness." To be sure, other modes of femininity coexisted with the dominant one. For instance, some women saw themselves more as crafty "tricksters," provisioning themselves and their household, than as martyrs to their family. In either case, however, there was an obvious gap between images of the "superwoman" and women's actual experiences. Literary representations suggest that women deeply resented official media's projections of effortless female perfection. But letters to the editor, opinion polls, oral testimonies, and literature also give us a sense that the paradoxical combination of excessive power and inadequacy was not only an imposed image. It was also actively embraced by many women themselves, as well as by their families.[26]

But this image of the female "brave victim" was only one term of a relation. As in any gender system, the female image had its male counterpart. The brave, supercompetent victim was defined in contrast to the image of her husband, the socialist man who might be better paid and dominant at work but who acted as the "big child" in the family: disorganized, needy, dependent, vulnerable, demanding to be taken care of and sheltered, to be humored as he occasionally acted out with aggression, alcoholism, womanizing, or absenteeism. We note the contrast between these images and the forms of masculinity and femininity in the earlier bourgeois world, and in the contemporaneous West, where masterful male aggressivity and the breadwinner role remained hegemonic, and second wave feminism battled with middle-class women's sense of incompetence and disempowerment. Although media provided images of unattainable perfection in both East and West, they differed substantially in content.[27]

Certainly, paternalist communism infantilized its citizens, in part by insisting that the state should explicitly dictate what people ought to think and believe. But it seems broadly true that while communism over the years produced for women a surplus of newly configured tasks and images—mother, worker, helpmate, manager—it usurped "head of household" as a masculine image and produced very few alternative pictures of masculinity. What it did offer—Stakhanovite worker, the physical prowess of the popular athlete, the loyal party member, or, as a less dominant form, the careerist opportunist—was not linked to men's roles in families and households. In this system, male dominance took the form of men's virtual monopoly of leadership positions and prerogative to be served within the household. The extreme fragility of marital ties accompanied this complex of gender stereotypes, which were reinforced by the relative ease of divorce and the guarantee of state support for single women and children. In many countries, since laws favored women's retention of children and housing, divorce brought more damaging results for men than for women, adding to men's sense of vulnerability.

Images and practices of sexuality and the body were also transformed. The interwar communist discussions of sexual liberation and search for pleasure by women were replaced by a communist puritanism that focused on reproductive sexuality; the existence of same-sex sexuality was simply denied. German, Polish, Bulgarian, and Hungarian women's magazines concentrated on presenting images of women as competent workers and mothers, but the pursuit of sexualized beauty was not a conspicuous aspect of femininity. Problems of women's sexuality and autonomy were hardly addressed at all in official discourse. Recent interviews suggest that in Romania sex could not be discussed even among women themselves or with their own daughters, let alone in the media. In the spirit of brave victim/big child imagery, Polish women's magazines of the 1970s listed sex as yet another burden, a part of women's household work, and charged teenaged girls with the responsibility for resisting and controlling the sexual urges of boys.

The tensions between the brave victim and big child were not merely matters of communist propaganda but aspects of experience. In interviews and letters to the editor written in Poland, Hungary, Serbia, and Romania a sense of hostility between spouses repeatedly surfaced. In Romania women cautioned their daughters to regard boys as "of another species"; working class Hungarian women rarely made long-term plans with their husbands, and tensions were especially high in those many households where women held more prestigious jobs than their husbands did. In Romania the outlawing of abortion and the dearth of contraception transformed ordinary sexual contact between husbands and wives into moments of enormous risk and dread for women. Attention to the care and enhancement of the body was considered suitable only for those not yet married. By their forties, working women perceived their bodies to be irreparably worn and deformed by years of hard labor. That this was indeed the hegemonic or default form of femininity is supported by the observation that for those urban women who tried to attend to their appearance—in Prague, Budapest—the lack of products and the shortage of money and time made the effort difficult, one requiring enormous ingenuity, which then became a point of pride.[28]

Thus, socialism radically reshaped gender relations, producing distinctive (though far from homogeneous) forms of male privilege. The public/private dichotomy itself did not disappear but was fundamentally reconfigured. It was aligned with a discursive opposition between the victimized "us" and a new and powerful "them" who ruled. The longstanding association between women and the private, men and the public was partly dislodged and revalued. In everday life, people used the complex subdivisions we have described as a means of gaining a measure of strategic flexibility in a system of apparently rigid social structures. At the same time, we have tried to show how preexisting gender relations constrained and channeled the directions of social change. For instance, socialist planners' beliefs about women's political unreliability shaped the policies that they implemented about women's party membership. Or, as another example, changed understandings of men's and women's relation to households helped underwrite the emergence of the second economy.

Since 1989 the withdrawal of the state from the support of prices, services, and health care and the more general marketization and privatization of the economy have transformed virtually all the institutions—states, schools, workplaces, households—through which socialist gender regimes were constituted. A large scholarly literature has documented the sharp decrease in production, rapid increase in unemployment, deterioration of public services, and fall in real wages accompanied by inflation and a steep rise in the cost of living. The result, however, has not been a uniform immiseration of the populace, but rather a marked and rapid increase in social inequality, indeed, a restratification of society. New elites have formed alongside the old, who now often appear in different ideological garb. And there is also a change in the principles by which stratification is ordered and justified.[29]

Current observers have carefully documented how these economic changes are differentially affecting men and women. There is widespread agreement that in most of the countries of the region, women have been experiencing more unemployment than men. Similarly, it has been women who have most directly suffered from the reduction, elimination, or reduced value of social welfare provisions, including child-support payments and maternity leaves, which have resulted from the lack of state funds, inflation, or requirements by international lenders such as the IMF and the World Bank. To compensate for these losses, women—who continue to be responsible for the work of caring for children—must earn supplementary income to pay for childcare at the very time they are losing their jobs. This adds to their already burdened care-work at home.

But the result of these changes has not been a uniform impoverishment of women nor the formation of a single new gender regime, even less a recapitulation of earlier gender relations. Instead, there is a wide range of trajectories—opening up possibilities for some groups, closing them off to others. In chapter 4 we describe some of the ways in which postsocialist family and marital arrangements mediate upward and downward mobility. In the rest of this chapter we focus on observations about the gendering of the workplace and labor market. Both of these contribute to our central analytical question: In the context of past arrangements and continuities as well as current influences from outside the region, how are gender relations and the widespread understanding of a transformed public/private dichotomy shaping economic change? How are gender relations mediating the increasing disparity in wealth, and the polarization of incomes, that have accompanied marketization of the economy?

To date, the study of postcommunist economic change has concentrated on economic units and sectors where men are overrepresented, thereby inadvertently ignoring gender differences. Until very recently, most research has focused on large-scale privatization, the selling of state enterprises, and the effects of large-scale foreign capital investment.[30] Most feminist commentators, by contrast, have highlighted unemployment statistics, noting women's greater loss of jobs in most countries since 1989. We suggest, instead, that examining the distribution and location of men and women in the economy will show the relations between these as well as other relatively unremarked yet important changes such as the expansion of small-scale services and manufacturing; the role of unregistered, irregular, and secondary employment; the changing wage structure and social influence of occupations. Broadening the field of vision in this way will point to the continuing, yet problematic, significance of a public/private dichotomy. A brief discussion of patterns of gender segregation in the labor force and of their relationship to social mobility illustrates this.

East European state socialism produced a segregation of the labor force by gender but one that, in keeping with state socialist planning, was not entirely structured by labor markets. It differed in its specifics from gender segregation found elsewhere in the world, despite evident similarities. For example, women were overwhelmingly employed in agricultural, clerical, administrative, sales and service, light industrial, and caretaking occupations, including medicine, while men were overrepresented in managerial, skilled, craft, technical, and heavy industrial work. Even within these gendered occupations there was further gender segregation, so that in agriculture, for instance, women generally did the nonmechanized work; men used the machines. In heavy industry, a privileged sector of the socialist economy, women generally held clerical positions. Because women and men were thus concentrated in different occupations and men tended to occupy the leading managerial and executive positions everywhere, differing rates of unemployment for men and women after 1989 depended, in part, on which industries were targeted for privatization, streamlining, or retrenchment in the different phases of transition. Since the sequence was not identical across the region, this approach to the questions of unemployment also helps to explain differences between countries in unemployment patterns.[31]

Such occupational segregation is always based on culturally defined ideas about the kinds of activities suited to each gender and the differential value given to men's and women's work. The definitions are changeable, however, and have for centuries been a site of gender conflict in Europe, played out within guilds, later among unions, capitalists, and state agencies. When there are labor markets, they are shaped by the culturally and legally constrained preferences of employers for workers with different skills and specific characteristics, which often include gender, race, or nationality. In general, markets have also been structured by the choices of workers as changing conditions of work across industries make some occupations more attractive because they offer higher wages, benefits, security, mobility, and good working conditions, while others are deskilled by technological change or reorganization and thus offer worse working conditions and lower wages.[32]

Since 1989, and in several countries well before that, the distribution of labor across jobs and occupations in East Central Europe has been more thoroughly marketized. Workers have become more mobile and often have been forced to change their positions and livelihoods. Jobs too have been revalued, as financial services, marketing, and various branches of tourism have gained an importance they did not have in socialism. At the same time, many forms of heavy industry and administrative work have disappeared or been devalued. Entire industries, and the occupations within them, have been restructured; some, eliminated. New industries have opened up, drawing workers away from other fields, which then became available to workers who have not had a chance in those fields before. Although these kinds of fluctuations are constant features of capitalist labor markets, the recent changes in East Central Europe have been extreme in scale and astonishing in their speed. We suggest that the resulting shifts in the pattern of gender composition and segregation of the labor force—along with the concomitant reshuffling of "public" and "private"—are important to consider, for they structure social stratification. Although current changes may well not last, they will nevertheless set the direction of change in the labor force for decades.[33]

For instance, studies from Hungary and East Germany indicate that as banking, insurance, and the entire financial sector have become privatized, increasingly central to the economy, and significantly more lucrative, men have streamed into jobs there. Men started to occupy leadership positions even though women had dominated banking for decades before, when it consisted largely of routine accounting. This shift was possible in part because new criteria were used in hiring for top positions, privileging the qualifications gained mostly by men through reeducation programs such as management training.

It is not only that occupations, professions, and whole industries have contracted and expanded, but as Szalai and Fodor have pointed out, the skills, education, and resources of workers have also been revalued and reinterpreted in the new economic context. Here "skills" must be defined broadly to include such factors as network contacts and relative degrees of time flexibility. While the continuing value of communist party membership and management networks for middle-aged and older men's retention of leadership positions has been extensively noted, the effect of revaluing women's long-standing resources is only now being examined in scholarly research. Forms of work that women increasingly occupy draw on experience and expertise they gained through the educational advantages and second economies of state socialism or in household responsibilities. Women have been systematically involved in marketing the services—catering, childcare, counseling, computer-related skills, travel and real estate information—that were earlier part of a barter economy or were forms of women's volunteer labor. Thus many women have become small entrepreneurs, usually so small as to have to take subcontracted work from a very wide range of businesses, some of which are still state owned. They do bookkeeping for larger firms whose bookkeepers are temporarily overburdened or catering for enterprises that used to have their own in-house kitchens. Often they use equipment that is part of their own households, such as computers or kitchen machinery. In such ways women's skills have been given new value in the market environment and provide novel opportunities for employment.[34]

Social work is another example. It is a field newly expanding in East Central Europe around the claim to expertise in dealing with homelessness and poverty. These are social problems that have increased in the course of privatization and reduced social assistance. Although far from lucrative, social work is a form of upward mobility for working-class women. In contrast to the case of banking mentioned earlier, this is becoming an overwhelmingly female profession, commodifying and thus revaluing supposedly female qualities of caring and empathy.[35]

Another aspect of social work is also significant. Like teaching and large sections of the health care industry, which were feminized under state socialism, it is largely a "public" or state-funded profession at a time when public funds are being withdrawn from many such services. In the newly emerging pattern of gender segregation, the heretofore feminized occupations and professions remain largely in the public sector, where labor discipline is lax, allowing an easier compromise with household obligations. In contrast, men's relatively greater time flexibility, due to fewer domestic obligations, becomes a valued resource in the labor market. Young men are moving rapidly into the newly expanding, more demanding, higher-paying private sector.[36]

Thus, there is a suggestive link between women and the public and men and the private. This is not only a matter of occupational segregation, but of cultural expectations as well. Despite the proliferation of female small-scale entrepreneurs, it is men more than women who are increasingly associated with the idealized and even romanticized private, the dynamic, capitalist sector of the economy. Indeed, the aggressivity, initiative, and competition that are identified with the market are becoming new representative forms of masculinity. Younger generations are more effectively influenced by such images than older ones. Marody and Giza-Poleszczuk report that in Poland some wives have started to complain to psychologists about the passivity and lack of initiative of their husbands. It is not that these men have changed, but that they have remained in the "big child" mode of state socialist manhood, one no longer widely desired. As a Polish women's magazine wryly put it: "[C]apitalism is usually an enterprising man who tries to either dispossess you of your apartment or your land. He knows best, knows that he deserves it, and that everything can be arranged."

Although such public/private patterns and their gendering are readily discernible at the level of work stereotypes and the labor market as a whole, it is instructive to look more closely at the working lives of women. This allows us to see once again the many kinds of subdivisions and combinations of public and private that we have already noted in earlier institutionalized versions of the dichotomy, but this time with changed relations to gender. That is, although women are generally associated with public employment, the public and private seem to be more complexly nested in the occupational lives of individual women than the cultural stereotypes would suggest. Szalai has shown that in addition to an official job, usually in the public, state-owned sector of the economy, many Hungarian women have taken on one-time or part-time contractual or subcontractual irregular forms of employment in the private sector. The combinations of work often sound odd by socialist as well as bourgeois standards: for instance, (public) schoolteaching in the morning and (private) housework for wages in the afternoon. Public sector jobs offer health care and other benefits but are low paying; jobs in the private sector, however irregular, often pay very well.

The strategies of Hungarian women, while not equally applicable across the region, nevertheless reflect widespread patterns. Parallel strategies have been described for rural Romania and for Germany. It is possible to understand the increase in prostitution and other sexual services in the region as in part related to these same structural patterns. The sex industry is recognized as one of the expanding areas of employment that has newly opened to workers displaced by unemployment or attracted from other jobs by higher wages. Many women engage in sex work as part of strategies that include other jobs. As family finances require, women try to move back and forth between work that provides social benefits and more lucrative, illegal sex work.[37]

Combining these different forms of work—and, if possible, gaining maternity benefits and child allowances as well—enables women to straddle or exploit the new legal and discursive divides between public and private. Returning to a fractal imagery, we can say they make divisions in their lives on a day-to-day basis that recall the distinctions between public and private workers. Importantly, such mixtures of public and private are also evident in other domains of postsocialism. In this sense women's strategies resemble the unexpected nestings of public and private ownership ("recombinant property") described by economic sociologists for large corporations in the postsocialist era.[38]

We have argued in this chapter that by attending to the location of men and women in the labor market, it is possible to trace a number of features of the new economies that are otherwise obscured. Entire occupations are being regendered as male or female, in part as a result of their changing importance in the new economic environment. In some countries, for instance, the small-scale service sector appears to be largely female, while men are better represented in large-scale private enterprises. We also see a division of the labor force into part-time workers who take many jobs and full-time workers whose salaries and wages are enough to support them without further employment. There is, as well, an increasing difference in the level of wages between low-paying, public employment and a demanding, high-paying private sector; within the private sector workers who do not need or want time flexibility are more valued than those who do. The way gender differences shape these emerging distinctions is hard to ignore.

Moreover these distinctions rely on cultural assumptions and new legal and economic arrangements concerning public and private. The public/private opposition itself, with its semiotic properties, has clearly been a long-standing feature of European discourses and practices. Yet there have been considerable shifts in the valuation and gendering of the dichotomy. The apparent continuity is, paradoxically, a flexible resource for actors in envisioning, creating, and adjusting to social change.

The current understandings of public and private in the region no longer match the arrangement—specific to state socialist systems—in which the powerless, victimized "us" could be understood as a private realm arrayed against the powerful public "them." The salient increase in visible forms of social inequality and the proliferation of diverse public voices make it more difficult to envision a unified "us" against a monolithic "them" controlling the state. Nor is there a continuation of the socialist practice in which the private worlds of domesticity included production as well as, in some countries, a masculinized "public" political component. Yet postsocialist patterns also fail to match the earlier bourgeois ideals of separate spheres. Nor do current gender alignments of public and private mirror patterns of workplace gender relations in contemporary Western Europe or the United States. A close look at women's strategies reveals that the labor market is bifurcating in multiple ways: into public and private, to be sure, but within this into regular and secure jobs, coded as male, and into unstable, part-time work and multiple jobs occupied mostly by women. While equally a part of the private sector and potentially lucrative, these latter jobs offer neither security nor social benefits.

Debate about social policy in the region continues to be structured around a choice between a market ("private") and a state ("public") economy. This choice simultaneously encodes different political orientations and erases the nested private/public relations contained within each "choice," which have been discussed throughout this chapter. Invoking the most general level of the public/private opposition has the ideological effect of hiding the linkages between these two categories of practices, activities, and institutional organization, even though what is hidden varies historically. These days, emphasizing the public/private distinction also makes it possible to draw tempting parallels with other systems such as Western welfare states, where such dichotomies are also in play. It is to these possible parallels that we now turn.

4

Forms of States, Forms of "Family"

WE HAVE TRACED the historical permutations of "public" and "private" as cultural categories that inform gender arrangements and are imbued with gender meanings. This chapter continues to explore the ways in which gender relations are changed, especially as states have increasingly withdrawn from production and from many forms of social provisioning. Of equal interest, as before, is the reciprocal effect: Gender relations themselves shape economic processes such as the upward and downward mobility that have created a much remarked restratification of society in the region. Our task in this chapter is to turn from historical considerations to a different axis of comparison: to place the socialist and post-socialist cases of East Central Europe in the context of debates about contemporary welfare states and their effects on gender and on social stratification.

During the Cold War, political stances on both sides emphasized the differences in systems and thus generally precluded comparative approaches that would recognize parallels between Western welfare states and communist systems. Direct comparisons were rarely made. Yet, in their ideals at least, the socialist states of East Central Europe were a form of "welfare state." Heavily subsidized foods and rents, full employment, relatively high wages for workers (as compared to other strata), and the provision of nominally free or cheap health, education, child-care, maternity benefits, and cultural services would have warranted classifying them as welfare states, if these services had in fact been adequate in quality and quantity, and generally available. The structural similarities to Western welfare states are striking. Although the social provisioning was characterized by shortage, inefficiency, unfairness, and in some cases coercion, the recent reduction, reorganization, or elimination of that deeply flawed system of social support has nevertheless caused considerable hardship for many. Rapid and increasingly visible class differentiation has exacerbated the plight of those hit hardest.[1]

The restructuring of social policy in all postsocialist governments has been directly affected by budgetary and fiscal constraints, as well as fears of political instability. Neoliberalism, promoted by international advisers and lenders such as the World Bank, the IMF, and EBRD, among other agencies, and embraced by most domestic experts in the region, has been one driving force behind the reformulation of social policies. Indeed, some scholars have claimed that social and labor market policies have rarely before been so heavily shaped by international financial institutions. Accordingly, East Central European states—like Western welfare states within the European Union to which they aspire—have been strongly encouraged to reduce social spending and privatize social services.[2]

In East Central Europe, however, social spending by states has not declined significantly since 1989. According to World Bank reports, the proportion of the gross domestic product spent on social provisioning has instead increased, and remains a higher percentage than in the welfare states to the west. Nevertheless, the absolute amount of expenditures on social services is considerably lower than in western Europe, and high inflation in the east has further reduced the value of the money that is spent. Services have consequently deteriorated even further at the moment when they are most urgently needed. Although social budgets have not been reduced and some programs from the socialist era remain in place, the restructuring of social spending has been profound. Instead of the earlier subsidies, most expenditures now go to unemployment programs, poverty assistance, and pensions. Decisions and responsibility are often devolved from the center to municipal and local governments. Increasingly, state funds are granted to nongovernmental, nonprofit, or even private agencies that provide and administer the necessary services. Whereas pre-1989 arrangements were ideologically grounded in the prevention or denial of poverty and income differences, new programs are often intended as emergency measures to offset the impoverishment and visible economic inequalities that have arisen since 1989.[3]

In contrast, the historical situation of welfare states as they developed in the West was at first eased by a more positive political economic context. The postwar period in which welfare states grew significantly in Western Europe was one in which strong economic expansion allowed the peaceful coexistence of relatively full employment and income equalization. But this no longer seems possible. The ideals of economic equality and social citizenship that were the impetus for some of the European welfare states of the postwar era now seem utopian. Nor is there broad evidence anymore for the stability of the single-earner nuclear family, on which the plans of many welfare states were based. Rather, there is much controversy about "welfare." One line of thought announces the "crisis of the welfare state" under the pressures of aging populations and increasing wage competition in globally integrated markets, suggesting that policy makers must choose: either expensive state-sponsored provisioning that works toward income equality but brings lower competitive advantage in international markets and therefore results in unemployment; or minimal state involvement, flexible labor, and free markets that reward winners and punish losers and that promise to prevent dependent populations and long-term unemployment.

Others, however, claim that this conundrum is illusory: Welfare arrangements and institutional structures vary tremendously; comparisons between the highly industrialized countries suggest there is no necessary trade-off between labor force flexibility and competitiveness on the one hand and welfare provisioning on the other. It is sometimes forgotten that policy decisions about such matters address more than economic issues. They simultaneously engage moral commitments, ideas about justice, demographic patterns, and gender relations—all of which are up for grabs in East Central Europe.[4]

Politicians across the political spectrum in the region are in a bind. Despite the great diversity of welfare arrangements and funding schemes outlined or recommended by experts, there seems to be only a narrow field of choice. Public opinion generally supports maintaining most of the benefits received in the communist era. Leaders fear large-scale dissatisfaction on the part of newly enfranchised voters and are therefore reluctant to cut transfer payments in a time of economic hardship. Yet, like their Western counterparts, politicians in East Central Europe are told that the lack of fundamental change in social spending endangers the prospects of economic growth, which is seen by many as the only long-term remedy for the increasing problem of poverty.[5]

There are important differences between countries; policies concerning social provisioning are very much in flux. Among elites, decisions about the proper courses of action are subject to extensive political negotiation and manipulation. In several countries constitutional courts have become involved in arbitrating solutions. Our own necessarily brief discussion touches on some of these details and their implications, but cannot follow the ins and outs of the political processes that constrain the decisions taken. We aim instead to outline some of the basic issues, and sketch the dilemmas involved, hoping to spark further discussion and research. It is certain that comparisons between East and West are now indispensable, as much to make arguments about the future as to understand the past.

For those who consider the gender dimensions of welfare states to be crucial, a large feminist literature of the last decade provides important insights about how states—through policy effects on the domestic division of labor, on access to waged work by men and women, on levels of remuneration and protection, on access to social benefits—regulate and even construct gender relations, including relations within the family. Such feminist thinking has helped us understand much about gender relations under communism and postcommunism, as was evident in our discussions in chapters 2 and 3. Yet, at first sight, it proves less useful here. Ironically, the greatest obstacle to conceptual integration across regions is the striking divergence in public discourses about the state and the family in "East" and "West."

In Western scholarly and popular discourse a proliferation of models exists for categorizing welfare states. Despite the reign of neoliberal ideals in international policy circles during the last two decades, it is taken for granted by scholars that there are many kinds of states and many kinds of welfare arrangements. This is as true of feminist analysts as of others. Depending on political perspective or the particular state with which they have had the most experience, some scholars have argued that welfare states are or can be "woman friendly." Hernes, for example, suggested some years ago that the Scandinavian democracies could potentially be transformed into woman-friendly societies; that is, into states that would not force harder choices, greater sacrifices, or more limited opportunities on women than on men, nor create other forms of inequality, as between different groups of women. Under the right historical conditions, then, there is the possibility and perhaps even the reality of a "state feminism." With women's acquisition of citizenship rights and political participation, states can be made to appropriate the goals of feminism, enabling women to become important bargaining partners in matters concerning basic values and the form of benefits.[6]

Others, by contrast, call welfare states "public patriarchies." Walby, for instance, argues that by becoming dependent on the welfare state, women merely trade in a subordinate relation with individual men in households for a similarly subordinating and exploitative relation with state bureaucracies. Britain serves as her point of departure. She shows that "women's work" such as cooking, cleaning, and caretaking have all been commodified, so it is no longer women in patriarchal households who are solely responsible for it. Such work is still undervalued, however, and done almost entirely by women, though now mediated by the state. The relative advantage for women of one over the other kind of dependence hinges on forms of control, levels of surveillance. It is, for Walby, a matter of choosing between two evils. Brown, starting from the American case, has gone even further, arguing that states have four "dimensions" of power—legal, capitalist, bureaucratic, military/prerogative—and all of them inevitably support male privilege in one way or another. States create dangerous dependency for women, and constitute them as subordinate and powerless subjects in multiple ways. Therefore, the sorts of women's subjectivities necessary for political action are unlikely to emerge. For this reason, feminist movements should rarely if ever enlist the help of states in the interests of women. Such efforts are destined to backfire, only increasing male control of women and of the state itself.[7]

Other scholars avoid these extremes and emphasize the significantly different gendering effects of different welfare states, and even of particular policies. Thus Siim, for instance, acknowledges both pro-state and anti-state positions, deriving respectively from Scandinavian (as opposed to American and Western European) experience and from social democratic (as opposed to liberal and Marxist) political commitments. It is undeniable that states have become crucial factors in influencing women's lives in Western Europe in the second half of the twentieth century, not only because women are among the main consumers of state social services, but also because they are the major category of state claimants and state employees. Yet even in Scandinavia, the home of the most purposively gender-egalitarian welfare states, men are more likely to be the framers of social policy affecting women. Moreover, those states continue to uphold the privileges of men in the labor market, and women's caring work continues to be devalued. Nevertheless, women do have citizenship rights, and through work they have a role in the economic public sphere as well. Thus, the modern welfare state, Siim and others argue, has a double meaning for women: on the one hand it gives women access to power as workers, mothers, and citizens, but on the other subsumes them under a bureaucratic, public hierarchy.[8]

In East Central Europe public discussion is differently focused. There debate centers on the contrast between state and market, between "public" and "private" support of social provisioning. In view of the radical institutional transformation underway since 1989, this is hardly surprising. However, the effect of this stark contrast between states and markets is to flatten distinctions between states and between differently regulated markets. Thus there is relatively little public discussion in East Central Europe of the *different* sorts of state arrangements, and the *different* possible effects of welfare schemes premised on, say, conservative versus liberal versus social democratic ideals, or on different definitions of citizenship, or on the different positions of a state within the global economic system. Nor is the involvement of NGOs in social welfare critically assessed. To the extent that such issues are discussed, the terms of debate rarely draw attention to the explicitly gendered effects of policy choices.[9]

One little-remarked reason for the near exclusive focus in public debate on the choice between market versus state solutions to combining productive and reproductive labor is, we suggest, related to the role of the family—in practice and in discourse—during this period of dramatic societal restructuring. To be sure, the legacy of fear and distrust of the communist state runs deep and is shared by odd bedfellows—liberals and nationalist anticommunists—who otherwise oppose each other in the postcommunist world. For many, distrust of the state provokes a virtual allergy to state regulation of any kind. But there is also much nostalgia, especially among the less fortunate sectors of the population, for the security of the late-communist era. The family, however, offers a context in which everyone—rich or poor—participates in one way or another and through which they therefore feel they can gauge the effects of current changes. Although discussions of the family are everywhere ideologically loaded, they are different enough in East Central Europe to provide an instructive contrast to parallel discussions in other Western countries.

In the United States, neoconservative and centrist discussions have for several decades emphasized the "crisis" in family life. They have labeled the family "sick" and have called for churches, local and state governments, and individuals to "re-create" it. They decry the breakup of the family, blaming all manner of social problems on immoral abandonment of "family values," on out-of-wedlock births, the increasing public visibility of homosexuality, the supposedly increasing irresponsibility of men, and the detrimental effects of second wave feminism. Feminists have insisted on the importance of changing family forms and relations so that women can enter the labor force, achieve autonomy, and not be dependent on individual men. Whatever the actual causes of new family forms, neoconservatives can indeed point to statistical changes, including increased divorce rates, declining birthrates, increases in single parenthood, and the statistical decline of their ideal household consisting of a breadwinning male, a dependent housewife, and two children. Similar changes in family composition have occurred in parts of Western Europe, often in response to or buffered by welfare state legislation. For instance, in Sweden 63 percent of all households consist of a single person only; the rate of divorce is high, fertility is also relatively high, and half of all births occur outside of marriage. But despite continuing debate about the future of the welfare state and women's political participation, family forms do not seem to be a major cause for concern in Swedish public debates. This is in part due to welfare arrangements themselves, since income replacement and parental support policies have decreased the importance of "family forms."[10]

The family in East Central European public discourse differs from both these patterns. In the face of massive social change, the family is popularly considered the one institution that provides continuity with the past. Both men and women idealize the family in ways similar to the familiar romanticization of the peasantry as "authentic." Many observers have suggested that women are better equipped to deal with postsocialist changes because their identities are closely linked to the solid foundation of the family, a site of familiarity and normalcy in a time of general upheaval and in some cases war. Even the steep rise in the morbidity and mortality of men since 1989, compared with these statistics for women, has been attributed to women's lower stress levels, due to the continuity of their family roles. The general assumption seems to be that it is the "public" that changes, not the "private" sphere. In this respect the current discussions echo Marxist precedents as well as modernization theory, both of which located significant social change mainly in the public or productive sector of society.[11]

While the state and other institutions are questioned and viewed with suspicion by large segments of the population, the family is generally sacralized, and not only by nationalists. To be sure, in East Central Europe, just as in the United States, women's changing roles within families were sometimes blamed as the source of social evil, when this was politically convenient. But today, nostalgic memory often constructs the communist-era family as autonomous from the corruption of the state and politics. The private household continues to be valued as the place where people live their honest, authentic, and meaningful lives. In the communist era the danger was understood to be the intrusiveness of the state; now it is more often the uncertainty and untrustworthiness of state action and the insecurity of markets and employment. The image of a stable, autonomous family survives, despite the fact that in East Central Europe too, over the last several decades, there have been profound changes in household composition, dramatic increases in divorce rates and in single parenting, as well as decreases in fertility and in the public subsidizing of childbearing and child rearing.[12]

The idea of the East Central European family as an almost isolated, reassuring constant in a world of social uncertainty must be understood as a discursive construction, at least as much a product of political ideology as the American notion that changing family forms and gender relations are themselves the causes of all social problems. Ironically, standard communist propaganda in many East Central European countries before 1989 echoed Western neoconservative views of the family. Both stressed that decadent capitalism and "feminism" destroyed what people valued most—namely, the family. On this score official communism claimed to be better than capitalism, and for once the "party line" dovetailed with people's everyday experience for, in a further irony, the family—the private, the second economy—often felt like a place of refuge from the very state that claimed to protect it. These days, when people recall socialist-era antipolitics, many remember the family as a "site of resistance" to communism. Given this discursive context, combined with fiscal pressures from international funding agencies to reduce costs, it is perhaps not surprising that few politicians are discussing the ways in which the state in postsocialism should use social provisioning as a means of changing family life or creating egalitarian gender relations within the household. Pension schemes and unemployment insurance receive far more sympathetic political attention than parental or child support arrangements.[13]

But this is not the only way to conceptualize the family in East Central Europe. Another line of evidence and opinion, espoused by some analysts both within and outside the region, argues for an alternate understanding of the "family" during socialism and postsocialism. Far from being independent of the state or directly opposed to it, the family economy (second, household, private) under socialism was parasitic on the state, and vice versa. Private production generally operated with goods and time taken from the public sector. The inadequacies of the public sector, in turn, virtually forced people into other sources of income, which then provided the services and commodities—such as new housing, for instance, or auto repair—that the state had promised but was incapable of producing for the populace. This is the perspective we took in chapter 3. Further, we found that public-and-private constituted a system in which there was embedding of practices considered public inside those considered private, and private ones embedded inside public, with many further, similar subdivisions. Thus the ideological opposition between state and family (public and private) and the valorization of the family as authentic and honest that are so common in public discourse in the region contradict the much more complex set of practices that linked families, households, and states.

Starting with this less popular and less heroic picture of the family and state in socialism, a brief comparison of social provisioning in East Central Europe with other models of welfare states proves illuminating. Communist states legislated social rights for their populace and took responsibility, at least in principle, for securing the basic needs of citizens with the aim of easing the economic consequences of inequality. They made relative income equity an ideological goal and a source of political as well as moral legitimacy. Furthermore, they at least planned for the social rights of women by attempting to integrate women into the waged labor force, to provide a system of childcare, and to socialize other household tasks. Though the historical development of East Central European states diverges considerably from the models constructed for the rise of Western welfare states, these countries constituted a kind of (failed) welfare state, if only by the classic definition that a welfare state aims to secure the basic needs of its populace.

Nevertheless, among the many typologies for distinguishing such states, several are clearly inapplicable to state socialism. For example, liberal, corporatist, and social democratic ideals rely on the "social arenas" of market, family, state, and voluntary sector in different ways and to different extents, producing quite different structures for social provisioning. These structures reflect divergent assumptions about the aims of welfare and its varying effects on income distribution and hierarchy, especially in the family. As Esping-Anderson has noted, in the early 1990s, the United States was perhaps the best example of the liberal model that encourages the market and helps only those residually excluded from it. Germany, by contrast was a good case of the corporatist welfare state that maintains status differentials, relies on the traditional family, but stands ready to displace the market in general provisioning if families are forced into destitution. Sweden exemplified the universalist welfare state, based on social democratic principles, that goes furthest in treating men and women alike, decommodifying services, and bearing the costs not only of possible market failure but also of family-making itself.[14]

Communist states did not fit any of these models. Over the years, practical and political considerations superseded any consistently thought out and distinctively communist social and welfare ideology. As labor demands and birthrates fluctuated, so did the reactions of central planners to women's labor force participation, to maternity and childcare leaves, and to the distribution of resources to families with many children. In spite of similar ideological commitments and political systems, policies and policy outcomes regarding "welfare" provisions diverged among the countries of East Central Europe as well. Nevertheless, if one is to follow a typologizing strategy, then a new category is needed for the communist case. Some have suggested "bureaucratic state collectivist systems of welfare."[15]

We do not intend to propose another typology, still less to locate different countries on such a grid. Our purpose in the rest of this chapter is a three-way comparison among socialist arrangements, postsocialist ones, and those characteristic of various welfare states in the West. Most useful for such an attempt are five dimensions of comparison suggested by the large feminist critique of welfare state typologies.

The *first* such dimension is the relative strength of the ideal of a male breadwinner or family wage in the structure and ideology underlying particular welfare state policies. In their influential comparative work, Esping-Andersen and his colleagues neglected the ways in which states can help in women's reproductive and household responsibilities. Within their otherwise useful theoretical perspective, pensions and income maintenance schemes, the welfare goods most utilized by the male worker as recipient, gained attention; childcare and parental leave were slighted. Even in their attention to decommodification—how welfare policies free recipients from dependence on the market—

Esping-Andersen's studies failed to note that men's independence from the market sometimes simply means they receive free services from women in their families. Recognition of this point exposes the assumptions made about gender relations in the more conventional analyses of welfare policy. Thus, the conservative, male-dominant policies of Germany and Britain, which support the family wage and do not make childcare a high priority, can be contrasted with those of the Scandinavian countries in which the vast majority of women hold jobs (many of which are part-time) and public childcare is plentiful.[16]

This dimension of comparison—the relative strength of breadwinner ideology—is revealing for state socialism as well. The communist countries embraced an ideological commitment to gender equality through full wage employment for women as well as men. All benefits were linked to labor force participation, which in practice became an obligation. For women this meant a decrease in dependence on individual men and an increasingly direct dependence on the state. Furthermore, benefits accrued to mothers universally, and not on the basis of need. In some countries maternity leaves and the related compensation were augmented by further benefits pegged to the mother's previous income.

In trying to assess the socialist period, it is important to consider not only the ideological commitments of the various countries, but also the actual policy effects. Despite the apparent commitment to gender equality, the policies of the communist states never confronted the contradictions of encouraging both childbearing and full-time wage work for women. Supposed solutions, like maternity leaves, were structured in such a way as to produce disadvantages for women as workers, making them seem less reliable and thus increasing the gender stratification of wages and work. Throughout the communist period and in most countries of the region, women systematically earned as much as 30–40 percent less than men. And by the last decades of communism, women were systematically absent from most managerial ranks, even in those sectors and occupations (e.g., teaching) where women predominated. In other words, the issues raised in the large Scandinavian literature about the need to recognize and value the unpaid work of women and to theorize the relationship between waged and unpaid work were never addressed. Policies were generally aimed at altering the behavior of women, not men. And, as we noted in chapter 3, the sexual division of labor in the household changed very little over the course of the communist period. As is well known, although women entered wage work in large numbers, and in many countries participated actively in the second economy, they also retained primary responsibility for childcare and housework.

In the postsocialist period, policies have not been systematically linked to a "breadwinner" ideology, but have nevertheless had gendered effects, with implications for the value of "carework." Most benefits have continued to be tied to participation in the labor force. This presents problems for women, who are disproportionately represented among the recently unemployed in most countries of the region. The new unemployment policies, meanwhile, have often been indexed to previous earnings and time in the labor force, thereby slighting women. Pensions, the largest social expenditures in current East Central European social budgets, are similarly indexed. Earlier retirement age for women is still the norm. Women also "lose" years of work through childcare leaves. Thus, women pensioners are everywhere in greater danger of falling into poverty. Pension policies, and their disadvantages to women, reached crisis proportions when post-1989 policies encouraged even earlier retirements so as to mitigate the unemployment of younger generations.[17]

Maternity leaves and family allowances that provide cash payments to families after the birth of children constitute a different category of benefits. Designed to support children in all kinds of families, they have been universalist in coverage and in effects. They assume that children are to some extent the direct responsibility of the state. Where attempts have been made to abolish or restrict these benefits, there have been serious negative reactions. The 1995 Hungarian "Bokros austerity package" is a telling example. In addition to instituting fees for health care and higher education, this set of laws required means testing for child support and maternity leave. The argument was that in a time of federal budget deficits, such payments should go only to those most in need of them. But when challenged by opponents through the Constitutional Court, many restrictions of the bill were struck down. Neoliberal critics charged that the court was illegitimately interfering with economic reform: The constitution clearly states that Hungary is not a welfare state. Yet to the satisfaction of large segments of the public, a concept of "material justice" was used by the court to support many of the earlier welfare measures. Similar battles have occurred in Poland as well. Such debates make emerging social fissures particularly visible.[18]

More broadly, there has been a withdrawal of state subsidies from already underfunded and overburdened health care and from early childcare facilities in favor of unemployment and pension payments that generally benefit men more than women. This raises the question of who will do the work of caring for children, the sick, and the elderly. For instance, Czech policy makers, like those in Hungary and elsewhere, have explicitly adopted the conservative principle of "subsidiarity," arguing that the state is to create the conditions for a good life, but should help directly only if the family fails. Thus, the communist illusion of free care is to be eliminated by making visible the links between what people pay to insurance and taxation schemes and what they can get back in support. Individuals are to be "actively" responsible for their own lives and the welfare of their families through work and savings. Once again, ironically echoing communist attempts to create the "new man," East Central Europeans are to be "re-formed" as people.[19]

Notable for our perspective is the increased role of the "family" in this rhetoric. As women lose jobs or enter into the informal and part-time economy, they—and not some abstract family—are likely to be the ones who take up even more of the slack in sick care, elder care and childcare. The withdrawal of subsidies is intended to relieve state budgets while encouraging privatization of such services. And carework is often commodified, as when women take on small-scale service-sector entrepreneurship involving such services. But policies based on such principles can as easily decommodify (or refamilialize) the work of women, by increasing the demand for their unremunerated carework within relatively cash-poor families.

By contrast, proposals for cash payments from the state to those who care for elderly relatives call on an unusual combination of principles, crosscutting a "breadwinner" ideology. Such a plan would give monetary value to carework, something Western feminists have long been demanding. But since such work is clearly gendered, it would also funnel women away from the pool of those seeking more lucrative employment. Finally, popular acceptance of a newly minted "breadwinner" ideology seems to be emerging in the region, and might well vary by social stratum and generation. Ethnographic evidence suggests that men and women alike are beginning to consider dependent wives as desirable signs of masculinity for professional or managerial men.[20]

A *second* dimension of comparison between Western welfare states and the communist/postsocialist states is the rate and means of women's entry into the labor force. It is useful to recall that in the Western welfare states, as in state socialism, women's massive incorporation into the labor force occurred after the Second World War and was linked to the expansion of the service sector, especially services in the fast-growing welfare state itself. The reasons for the state's expansion were quite different in the East and the West. There is no scholarly consensus in explaining the postwar growth of welfare states. Some argue that as capitalist relations eroded traditional forms of social security, and as workers became both organized and vocal in their own interests, democratic politics enabled an airing of their redistributional demands. Depending on theoretical perspective, then, pension, unemployment, and other benefits could be seen as ways of easing class tensions, exercising control and surveillance of populations that threatened capitalist or broader elite interests, or as the expansion and, finally, universalization of full, social citizenship. As employees, women simply constituted an untapped pool of labor that could be called upon in this expansion of state services.

In contrast, the entry of women into the labor force in the East was a major ideological commitment of the state. As we outlined in chapter 3, full employment through the centralized control of production (and reproduction) and state provision of basic social benefits for all citizens formed the backbone of the socialist modernization strategy, while simultaneously legitimating state socialism as a system that would allow workers to enter modernity in a more just and egalitarian way.

Crucial to this dimension of comparison is the observation that only in communism was women's labor force participation coerced. Many scholars have argued that employment dictated by the state did not necessarily translate into women's emancipation. East Central European women felt overburdened and frustrated because for them labor force participation was a state-mandated obligation. They felt guiltily unable to meet the demands of their everyday lives, especially with respect to mothering. In the West, by contrast, it is argued that employment brought women a sense of achievement and autonomy because women themselves struggled on their own behalf to gain entry into the labor force.[21]

There is no denying the coercive aspects of communist states. Nonetheless, in the case of women's employment we believe it is worth reconsidering the fundamental distinction outlined above. No direct evidence exists of the desires of women in the 1950s, when such policies were introduced. As Ferge has argued from historical data as well as her own experience, the reactions to women's incorporation into the labor force must have depended at least in part on women's life stage and their political views about communist ideals, as well as the economic and social background from which they entered the labor force. However resented by some, for other women (from poor or working-class families) labor force participation was already the norm. For still others (young and ambitious) it may well have been experienced as an opening of possibilities.

Behind the coercion thesis also lie assumptions about women's natural place in reproductive work: No one asks men if they "want" to work, and men's right to work is usually seen as a liberation from market forces. Another approach to the same question is to more closely examine the experience of other welfare states. Descriptions of Sweden indicate that in the 1970s a government decision tied parental benefits to labor force participation, with tax law favoring double-earner households. This created structural constraints that made it very disadvantageous for women to remain outside of the paid labor force.[22]

The broader point here is to explore what one means by "coercion," that is, how people experience forms of state and market control and their rights as citizens in a welfare state. Problematizing the definitions of such fundamental analytical concepts is very much in the tradition of recent feminist work on the welfare state. Similarly, a key characteristic of the postsocialist period is this kind of redefinition. For example, as we noted in chapter 3, women in Hungary are more likely than men to remain in the poorly paid but stable public (state) sector. Because such jobs are far from lucrative, however, women engage in a strategy of also taking multiple, informal, irregular work that pays well and that provides time flexibility but no security or benefits. What is striking about these strategies is their partial continuity with state socialism. These kinds of "irregular" work used to be the loophole through which women and their families, by self-exploitation, satisfied their consumer desires in a shortage economy. Despite the changed circumstances, these same strategies are now the equally self-exploitative hedge by which women (and their families) survive and satisfy their consumer desires in a form of peripheral "developing" capitalism. The strategy dovetails with the interests of private firms by providing forms of labor that have relatively low labor costs.

Significantly, the earlier need for this strategy was routinely understood by social actors as the consequence of a corrupt and immoral "system" that was unable to provide what it had promised. It was experienced as unfair coercion, forcing people to work too hard. Since 1989, however, the multijob strategy has been redefined as an individual problem. Its structural and gendered characteristics, what might be called market coercion, have been rendered invisible. For many, a sense of insecurity about work, as about much else, has become a routine part of everyday life. Yet all this appears to be no one's fault, not part of any visible system—in fact, not coercion at all, just what flexible workers must do to survive in a postsocialist, post-Fordist world. Our point is the recontextualization and political significance of such definitions. The question of what counts as "coercion"—in a particular historical moment—parallels, of course, the question of what counts as "choice," and is in part dependent on the perspective of those who make the judgment, as well as on discourses and political circumstances.

A *third* dimension of comparison between Western welfare states and the communist/postsocialist cases concerns the changing and changeable bases on which claims can be made against states. Fraser's influential discussion shows how "needs" are malleable and constructed; they contrast with "rights" invoked as legally binding claims on states. Both are made and modified through discursive and political conflicts. Welfare claims provide yet another case of the way relations between states and their inhabitants are created through discourse and policy, quite parallel, in this sense, to the reproductive politics we described in chapter 2.

Whether women (and men) receive aid and support as mothers, parents, workers, or citizens is crucial in shaping the form of the aid, as well as its broader social consequences. As many have noted, policies and indeed whole welfare regimes vary significantly as to what social roles and relations have been constituted—through political and philosophical debate, legal procedures, or struggles such as labor strikes and pacts among corporate groups—as grounds for persuasive and efficacious demands on the state. What part of the aid is paid by which agency of a state, and how, has also been a point of contention. Historical accounts have described how categories of "deserving" and undeserving poor were deployed in Western welfare states. The relative merits of children, soldiers, the disabled, women, and men as recipients of state aid have also changed over time. Aid that is understood as a return on previous contributions of money or service by recipients is usually judged differently from aid that has no such visibly active counterpart. Many forms of state aid more often received by men—veterans' benefits, retirement benefits, or income support—are not even viewed as "welfare" in some countries.

Universal cash transfers that make no distinctions within the relevant population of recipients have often been, in the history of Western welfare, less stigmatizing than aid for which recipients must reach some criterion of minimum income or ill health. Even the temporality of programs has made a difference in their popular acceptance and effects: Programs that aim to rectify what is seen as a short-term problem such as unemployment are often judged differently from general poverty assistance. In sum, justifications for state spending are based not only on the assessments of economic experts, but on moral commitments and political goals about matters such as: the morality of large or small income differentials; the necessity for pronatalism as a route to larger populations; the acceptability of various levels of unemployment, poverty, and minimum wages; the desirability of women's presence in the labor force.[23]

For most of the socialist period, state support was characteristically much less visible as such, and more omnipresent than the forms of aid listed above because it took the form of subsidies that compensated for "compressed" wage differentials. Employment was a constitutionally protected "right." Relatively cheap food, housing, and services could not be "claimed," since they were more likely to be experienced as taken-for-granted entitlements or as "gifts" from a paternalist state. But often these gifts could be accessed only through "connections" and bribes, or they had to be supplemented by informal barter arrangements in the second economy. Accordingly, experts within the region voiced persistent criticisms of socialist "welfare" systems even before 1989. Because industrial policy (jobs, wages) was combined with social policy, enterprises and trade unions served as both production and provisioning facilities. Social problems were difficult to target as separate from production, making it hard for individuals to relate benefits to their own actions and needs. Services were undemocratically and often arbitrarily delivered. Party committees or other local political organs could act capriciously in deciding who would get how much of what, creating particularized forms of inequality. And finally, there were very few ways of directly addressing social problems ignored or denied by the state. Poverty or unemployment were not supposed to occur, so they were simply omitted from any kind of ameliorative plan.[24]

The current period of restructuring provides the opportunity to observe how claims on the state are newly constructed and debated. The precise way in which the state is withdrawing from social provisioning—best analyzed through case studies—goes a long way to explain the possibilities and limitations on claims. In one detailed study of a Hungarian town, Kovács and Váradi reported on the situation of women cannery workers. During the socialist period, the paternalist factory supplied so much of the infrastructure of its workers' lives—work, leisure, political activity, childcare, provisioning, haircutting and other grooming—that it replaced the support of husbands and also of other family ties. Life history interviews revealed that the women in the factory had virtually no relationships outside of work. Privatization of the factory led to the end of most of these services. The foreign corporation that had bought the cannery did not continue such social provisioning.

As a result, the factory women found themselves without services or other resources, including human support to replace what they had lost. Their wages did not increase enough to offset the loss of services; competition due to layoffs intensified social tensions within the factory. Kin were preoccupied with their own parallel problems. Importantly, the emergency measures of unemployment and poverty relief that had been instituted to combat the harsh depredations of "the transition" did not benefit these women. They were not unemployed, nor were they legally or technically destitute, that is, living below a minimum wage. In short there was no basis on which they could make claims on the state. Yet these working women were sliding into poverty and despair, their situation a direct legacy of communism that encouraged their dependence on state provisions and services that have since disappeared and are not addressed by postsocialist "welfare."

Another case study, by contrast, shows the effective formulation of claims. Goven describes how local discourses in Hungary along with the directives of international lending institutions proved powerful in constructing "needs," identities, and hence novel claims on which to base new policy of parental leaves. This was accomplished in part through the definition of categories of worthy and unworthy citizens, and justifications for different forms of state obligation to them. The Hungarian Parliament's debate about parental leave in the early 1990s occurred in the context of competition between political parties vying for legitimacy, wary of the expansion of people's political rights of expression and opinion. Social policy provided a way to differentiate political membership and assign different sets of entitlements, rights, and dispensations to persons in different social structural locations.[25]

The Parliament's discussion and final action went beyond the neoliberal recommendations of the World Bank. Everyone agreed that the universal maternal support of the late-communist era must end; the parties argued rather about who should get the limited support available. The terms of the debate in Parliament followed those of many earlier Hungarian debates about social difference, rather than those of the World Bank per se. The ruling (Socialist) government's minister argued for aiding the poor, and the populist opposition argued for direct support of ethnically Hungarian middle classes in order to assure national continuity and prevent demographic disaster. "Mothers" were everywhere present in the discussion, along with their "need" and "right" to choose to stay home with their children. "Women" and their right to work or to have childcare as a state-supported option were conspicuously absent. As Goven acerbically put it:

> In this case, the need for mothers to stay home with their children was recognized . . . ; the need (of both mothers and children) for access to extra-domestic childcare was not. Intertwined in this discussion was recognition of men's—but not women's—need for (and right to?) autonomy; the nation's need for middle-class children; middle-class families' need for (and right to) compensation and autonomy (e.g., non-means-tested benefits, paid in cash, with neither restriction nor supervision over how such benefits were spent); and "other" families' need for supervision and discipline. (2000)

The case demonstrates how the pared-down welfare system of a neoliberal state is discursively made and how different categories of citizenship and privilege are produced and reinforced by welfare policy.

In another instance from the postsocialist period, a change in the structure of claims turned reproduction into a mechanism of social differentiation. As we noted earlier, in state socialism, for better and for worse, policies concerning motherhood applied across the board to all women who became mothers. Thus, socialist stratification was not based on reproductive relations. Those high up in Romania's communist party, for example, were often more able than others to get (illegal) abortions under Ceauşescu's pronatalist policies because they had the connections required. But they remained vulnerable to blackmail and charges that they had had abortions. On the positive side, making use of maternity leaves carried little stigma, since they were available to everyone.

The austerity packages instituted or proposed since 1989, however, have helped to create differentiation and inequality in this sphere. For example, poor Hungarian women and Romani women in Hungary who used to be able to claim state aid on the basis of the prestigious category of "mother" were threatened with the surveillance of social workers, who would decide whether their material circumstances rather than maternal skills were deserving of public assistance. In East Germany women have opted to be sterilized in order to make themselves more attractive to employers seeking "reliable" workers to whom they will not have to pay maternity benefits. In various ways, then, stratified motherhood has been institutionalized. Families that can afford it are pulling their children out of state-run nurseries and kindergartens, which are in any case understaffed due to budget cuts and layoffs. Claims on the state, in the form of public assistance, have become stigmatized, equated with poverty and inadequate skills; private care and private education have gained cachet.[26]

These cases of newly emerging stratification bring us to a *fourth* dimension of comparison between Western welfare states and the communist/postsocialist cases. Scholars who create typologies of welfare states have long noted that such states vary in their handling of income differentials and inequality. "Liberal" and "corporate" welfare states accept and maintain inequalities of income, designing social provisions in a manner that keeps social hierarchies in place. Only the "social democratic" states are ideologically committed to relative economic egalitarianism and in practice attempt to foster policies that will produce such an outcome.

In East Central Europe the early communist states embraced a commitment to relative income equality; in postsocialism there is no such official commitment. Indeed, all economic analyses of the region report that income inequality has increased dramatically, rivaling that in Western Europe. These reports do not consider the contribution of the thriving informal economies to these growing differences. For instance, in Poland, increasing income differentiation has come through the rise in wages of a small minority of the well educated and the downward mobility of many with less or different types of education. It is important in this period of postsocialist restructuring to examine this dimension with gender in mind, for gender relations are crucial in the making of upward and downward mobility. Several examples will illustrate how gender is, in this way, mediating and thus shaping economic processes. New forms of families and new kinds of gender relations are emerging as a result.[27]

Women and men in East Central Europe face different sets of employment conditions. Although wage work is no longer obligatory, regular work is almost always full-time. Even if exit from the labor force in favor of full-time mothering were preferred by women—in part because it seems a privilege that women were denied under socialism—it is not financially possible for many. Two incomes are indispensable to maintain most households. State-supported childcare facilities have become rare; private ones are expensive. Women's diverse strategies of combining irregular and informal employment with regular jobs in the state sector are the response to the constraints produced by postsocialist state policies. Men by contrast are more likely to take full-time jobs with benefits in the growing private sector. Because in most countries men engage in multiple employment less frequently, since 1989 gender has become a key to the stratification that separates secure, regular work from insecure if often lucrative opportunities. For example, Hungarian research suggests the relative disadvantage of women vis-à-vis men in this regard, but Szalai also notes a deeper irony. Women who have many such small, part-time, one-time, subcontracted work tend to get more of it, thereby earning even higher incomes. Those who do not may either become unemployed or fall into poverty, producing another and more drastic kind of polarization.[28]

There is evidence for this pattern of irregular informal employment all over the region. The benefit system itself is in part responsible for the process of economic informalization that has become endemic in East Central Europe, a process in which employers are actively involved. In the Czech Republic in 1990–91 many employers opted to hire only those workers who possessed a self-employment business license, thus avoiding social security contributions. Most observers suspect that, although made illegal a year later, the practice continues, if in veiled and hidden ways. The arrangements are mutually beneficial; employees can thereby avoid payroll taxes. In view of the widespread informal economy of Poland before 1989, it would be hard to imagine that these practices are less than pervasive there as well.[29]

This kind of evidence, though necessarily partial, provides a glimpse of the structural situation of many women in postsocialism, with marked contrasts in gender stratification from what is apparent in the welfare states to the west. It suggests a future recipe for a new kind of female vulnerability in East Central Europe. This is in part a legacy of the communist period and in part a result of the current circumstances. Women's wages in regular jobs have generally been lower than men's throughout the socialist and postsocialist periods. The marketized economy makes their household and childcare responsibilities more privatized, less a matter for public concern than they were during state socialism. Women's survival strategies, though creative and often ingenious, reflect their continuing structural inequality in the labor market. The result is a particular kind of gender arrangement: not primarily a dependence on men in households, a pattern that, though possible for a few with very successful husbands, is not feasible for the large majority; nor dependence on the maternalist welfare provisions of the state, which are increasingly available only to the destitute on a "needs-tested" basis. Rather, women are combining bits of these strategies with dependence on the exigencies of those parts of the market economy that are least regulated and secure, and in which they have very little bargaining power. Given these developments, the feminization of poverty in the region deserves further research.

Yet not all women in the region are so vulnerable. Income stratification and social mobility are mediated by gender and gender relations in more complex ways as well. The ethnographic study of a Hungarian town by Kovács and Váradi that was mentioned earlier provides close-up examples of several contrasting trajectories in women's lives. These are linked to quite divergent ideas—emerging in recent years—about the proper form of relations between spouses. Such views involve new images of self and of masculinity and femininity. They range from a model of male breadwinner/female consumption specialist to the ideal of cooperative, sharing "partnership" between spouses, to a form of hostility between men and women that presumes women are often better off raising their children without men. This variation belies the homogenized, ideological view of "the family" discussed above, that is widespread in the region. Implicitly, all three forms hinge on assumptions about state benefits and how much (or little) one can and should rely on them. Thus here we consider not so much state policies as the presuppositions about them on which social actors rely.

The gender ideologies that Kovács and Váradi documented are themselves emblems of emerging class distinctions. Only the most elite families in town, those in which the men held leading positions in newly privatized companies or who were devoted on religious grounds to a subordinate role for women, espoused the breadwinner/housewife model. The wealthiest could actually live out such a pattern; the others advocated it while acting otherwise. For this whole stratum, the ideology itself demonstrated their elite standing. The ideal of marital "partnership," on the other hand, was characteristic of upwardly mobile, highly successful women entrepreneurs. In contrast to both, it was factory workers who most often felt that life without men was possible and sometimes even preferable; these women had the weakest emotional bonds with husbands.

Because Kovács and Váradi's research included life histories, we know that entrepreneurial women did not differ only in their beliefs but in their behavior as well. They often divorced the men who they decided had ideas about gender relations incompatible with the women's own expectations and ambitions. Women described systematic decisions to divorce men who insisted on what seemed to them a subordinate role for the woman. The question was not one of equal divisions of household or waged labor: these women, like all others in East Central Europe, retained primary responsibility for childcare and housework and worked for wages. Rather they rejected husbands unwilling to provide emotional support and small amounts of practical help necessary in achieving the women's economic ambitions. Quite literally, then, for these women choice of spouses who would be adequate "partners"—the term used by the women themselves—was a central and often partly conscious mobility strategy.

These Hungarian entrepreneurial women provide a lesson in the paradoxes of continuity with the state socialist period, if we compare them with the cannery women of the same town, discussed earlier. While the cannery workers relied in practical matters on the state-owned enterprise and its supportive provisions, entrepreneurial women had very little to do with the total institutions of state socialism. They often relied from early in life on the second economy instead. Yet, ironically, both sets of women are the heirs of state socialism. For the workers the practical legacy is one of dependence. For the entrepreneurial women it was state socialism's ideology of gender equality and its practice of educating and employing women that gave them a way of thinking about themselves as potentially self-sufficient, and in some respects equal to men.[30]

The mediation of mobility by gender relations and gender ideologies is not limited to spouse selection, however. It also involves subjectivity, a sense of self, uses of the body, and ideas about sexuality. Here the continuities disappear; we note sharp ruptures with the past, not only in practices but also in representations. Perhaps the most striking change is in the mass media's images of what constitutes successful, and thus hegemonic, masculinity and femininity. Having been bought by international media conglomerates, magazines in the region increasingly resemble in their messages the other products of the same companies.

Marody and Giza-Poleszczuk point to a new emphasis on individuation in the recent magazines, and the sexualization of femininity in Poland. Dölling notes parallel processes in Germany, as does Băban in Romania and Daskalova in Bulgaria. Women who structured their sense of self around the "brave victim" persona discussed in detail in chapter

3, and thus on the gratifications and power available through self-sacrifice for a familial collectivity, feel profoundly demeaned by imagery that derives ultimate value from the decoration and enhancement of the self and the body. It is age that is the great divider here. Sacrifice for other, larger, collectivities—nation, religion—is congruent with this socialist (as well as postsocialist nationalist) form of femininity, and might well be attractive for older women, as many commentators have remarked. In any case, older women's sense of failure and disappointment parallels the problems of passive masculinity that is a counterpart to the "brave victim." Both of these images rely on a different conception of the relation between the state and its populace from that of active citizens.

The new, sexualized individualism is also destructive of self-esteem for women interviewed by Băban who grew to adulthood in Ceauşescu's Romania. There, antiabortion policies helped produce a contempt for one's own body and fear of sexuality. A similar contempt emerged in Kovács and Váradi's interviews with cannery workers who rejected as laughable and futile the cosmetics favored by their entrepreneurial neighbors. For these workers there was a moral question involved, and redefinitions of work. They asserted that not everyone is cut out to be an entrepreneur. Their own sense of self was based on regular and often manual labor, which is increasingly difficult to find and rarely valorized in public. It is the entrepreneurs and the trophy wives in Kovács and Váradi's sample whose body practices and senses of self were affirmed by mass media. They exercised and went to spas, saunas, and cosmetologists to improve their bodies and appearance. For the housewives, this was the "work" they offered in return for their husbands' financial support. In the case of the entrepreneurs, the well groomed body was understood as part of a business strategy, a mobility ploy, a signal of the entrepreneur's success.

In discussing the fourth dimension of comparison—how welfare states handle income inequalities—we focused on ethnographic examples that illustrate some of the ways in which, within the context of increasingly neoliberal state policies, gender has mediated economic restratification in East Central Europe. Our goal has been to show how women's strategies in the new circumstances—multiple jobs, spouse selection—as well as their body practices, self-definitions, and ideologies of marriage contribute to shaping economic inequalities.

Another ethnographic example from a long interview conducted by Gal in Hungary offers a further glimpse of how self-images and gender relations are intertwined with economic strategies and state benefits in the thinking and planning of men and women. This interview highlights a *fifth* dimension on which to compare the gendered dilemmas of Western welfare states with the communist/postsocialist cases: the "dependency" and "autonomy" issues that have been at the center of feminist analyses of the welfare state.[31]

A Budapest journalist, age fifty, long divorced from his first wife, invited his new woman friend, age forty, to move into his two-bedroom apartment. She agreed, deciding to rent out her smaller apartment for extra money as she continued in her poorly paying, dead-end, make-work job as an accountant for an agency of the Ministry of Health. They managed to make ends meet on the two salaries; her love of cooking and cleaning, they explained, dovetailed well with his love of eating, and the lax requirements of her job allowed her to handle all of the household labor. This, therefore, was never a matter of contention between them. But when the journalist's newspaper was bought by a large German conglomerate, he received a special five-year assignment that doubled his salary. This still made him a relatively low-level earner by the standards of Western journalists or the wealthy new entrepreneurs of Budapest. Nevertheless, it enabled the couple to start rethinking their arrangements. She announced that since she had long hated her workplace, she would prefer to quit her job and be a stay-home "wife." They would not marry, they said, because that would just invite the state further into their private lives. But he promised informally to pay her health insurance from his own salary. The cost of this, he reasoned aloud to her, would be no more than the cost of a housekeeper. Her friends at work were shocked, but for two different reasons. The older ones, who came of age before 1989, were frightened for her. They warned her not to become so dependent on a man or trust him to supply her financial support and indispensable health and pension benefits. The younger ones frankly envied her for having "landed a rich one." On her side, she explained that staying home made her feel pampered, something she had long craved. She would go to saunas and health clubs, shop in the afternoons. And it would allow her to cater with greater energy to his needs as "he deserved" for being such a masculine man. Serving him, she said, made her feel more feminine.

He enthusiastically endorsed the idea, because it matched so well what he had seen of bourgeois arrangements in his many trips to Western Europe during the communist era. He freely admitted there was an element of mimicry in his actions: A stay-home wife was a status symbol that he had long wanted and richly deserved. At the same time, familiar with American struggles over gender, he teased the American interviewer that his woman was no nasty feminist who wanted to compete with her man. But what would happen when his special assignment was over, in several years, and his salary fell again? After the extended paean to bourgeois arrangements, they were a bit sheepish, as they together explained, bit by bit in the course of the interview, her plans to establish an accounting practice at home, without registration, and with the quite realistic hope that it would grow enough by the end of his five-year assignment to allow her to pay her own health benefits. She laughed as she revealed that she actually expected to get really rich by the time his salary dropped.

Just as with the examples in Kovács and Váradi's work, the conventionally cited models of historical gender relations in the literature do not adequately describe the emotional and economic strategies of this couple; nor does their situation readily match the current Western models from which they think they are, in part, borrowing. We do not wish to generalize from a single case, of course. Rather, we note how mixed feelings about gender images, the ambiguity of meaning in "stay-home wife," reservations about trust between partners as well as the dilemmas of "dependence" and the ambivalent wish for "autonomy" from workplaces, states, state benefits, and spouses are cast into sharp relief by this couple.

As we have noted, in feminist scholarship the classic liberal pattern of women's dependence on individual men in households has been contrasted with a more direct dependence on state provisions characteristic of welfare states. And many have pointed out that rejection of both of these leaves women dependent on unpredictable market mechanisms. There has also been discussion of the differential weight, in different polities, of the range of roles women play vis-à-vis states. In Western welfare states women are not only clients and consumers of services but also employees, citizens, and policy makers. Their activities in nongovernmental or voluntary associations may mitigate other forms of dependence. Often there are separate procedures and corporate groups (unions, political parties), attached to the different roles—client, policy maker, employee, voter—so that individuals can use the organizations against each other and against the state if necessary. It is this diversity of roles that has prompted some to predict optimistically that women can balance welfare dependence with political activism. Perhaps welfare recipients can come to realize common interests and organize around these. Similarly, although women are disproportionately dependent on the state as employees and clients, they are more parallel with men as citizens and politicians, and may therefore have a chance through those roles to influence the political process. Thus, recent analytic schemes focusing on women's various roles and forms of citizenship in welfare states attempt neither to reject the idea of dependency nor to valorize autonomy.

Moreover, as Fraser and Gordon have observed in their historical deconstruction of "dependency," the notion itself is conceptually complex—simultaneously emotional, political, and economic. "Dependence" has been highly stigmatized in Anglo-Saxon countries since the nineteenth century, and now lacks the earlier positive meaning of "working for wages." Along with the emphasis on individualism and political rights, independence has become a virtually unquestioned positive value. The use of "dependence" "autonomy" and "choice" in discussions about welfare—whether by feminists or others—draws on this history. Having excavated the sources and connotations of "dependence" and "independence," Fraser and Gordon reject both and recommend the notion of "interdependence" as a way of recognizing, in an unstigmatized vocabulary, the inescapable and positive social supports of everyday life.[32]

We suggest that the somewhat different definitions and histories of "dependence"—its discourse and practice—in East Central Europe may lend further nuance to these feminist debates. "Dependence" has not been a positive concept in East Central Europe either. The struggle for independence from one or another imperial power in recent centuries has been a crucial (if sometimes censored and tacit) theme of national historiography. Critics of communism complained about dependence on paternalist states and characterized the populations of East Central Europe as "infantilized"—forced into tutelage, fearfulness, and passivity. Most importantly, relations to the state were effectively centralized. In contrast to welfare states in the West, the parts of the state could not be so easily played against each other. Thus, for any public act of disobedience, complaint, or protest, socially atomized individuals with "one-dimensional" relations to the state could expect retaliation from any aspect of the state not only against themselves but against their extended family members, and sometimes in ways unrelated to the initial infraction. The retaliation for illegal abortions in Romania, for instance, could be the denial (or threat of denial) of university entrance for the child of the doctor involved. This provides further evidence that far from being autonomous of the state, families in communism were often the means by which people were controlled. Here "dependence," simultaneously on the family and state, was again negative, a source of danger.[33]

Yet, for the postsocialist period, the examples we have marshaled suggest that "dependency" is a highly ambiguous concept, and in multiple ways. Although the "dependence" of the communist era is generally decried, there is considerable nostalgia for the material security, sense of "community," and relative egalitarianism that the communist system supposedly fostered. Furthermore, even a decade after 1989, opinion polls in East Central Europe continue to show that reliance on state support is socially acceptable. Indeed, in Europe more broadly, and in East Central Europe in particular, many believe it is in keeping with the role of government to provide directly for the well-being of the populace. There have been numerous popular protests against the threat to remove social benefits. In the current hard times, when family allowances make up as much as a third of family incomes in some parts of the region, many value such "dependence."[34]

Furthermore, as ethnographic examples suggest, people seem to resent not so much the state's support as the terms in which it is or was provided. Hungarian and Romani mothers earlier relied on their ability to mobilize the agents of the state for their own interests inside families and did not want their value as mothers reduced to levels of "neediness" alone. Hungarian cannery workers insisted on the dignity and right to work, and resisted the injunction to become entrepreneurs. The women entrepreneurs, in turn, rejected the notion of women's independence, requiring instead the active support and partnership of their husbands. Similarly, East German women wanted the state to provide abortion and sterilization cheaply and on demand, as they tried to balance motherhood and careers.

Since 1989, the alternatives for women in East Central Europe seem not to be readily characterized as a choice between the increasingly influential but unfamiliar and unreliable market, as opposed to reliance exclusively on individual men or on masculinist states. Rather, ethnographic and survey materials suggest that it is "balance" that is the most salient cultural category. Women's current strategies revolve around creating and sustaining multiple, complementary and counterbalanced dependencies. These provide not "independence" or even "choice" but rather backup resources, including some security in an environment where this is increasingly scarce. This alternate understanding of what has been labeled "dependency" in everyday life may further refine analyses of Western welfare states as well.

We have been arguing in this chapter that the dichotomy between "state" and "market" that still often frames discussions of the region masks the complexity of their interrelatedness. There are many types of "welfare" states, and many sorts of relations between market and state that have quite different implications for families and gender relations. In East Central Europe, public discourse that assumes the autonomy and historical stability of the "family" distracts attention from the ways in which the family has changed, and from how changed circumstances have affected the life chances of households, despite surface continuity. This parallels the way in which the American public discourse that laments the death of the family ignores the emergence of new household forms and the way these interact with other social changes. The public discussion of families is quite different in Eastern Europe, Western Europe, Scandinavia, and the United States, even though demographic trends are more similar and the current attacks on welfare provisioning across the continent as well as in the United States are similarly motivated.

Our comparison of Western welfare states with East Central European cases—both in the communist and postcommunist periods—has highlighted five dimensions on which we evaluated the similarities and differences between them. For several dimensions, this comparison helped to clarify the cultural and discursive processes through which changes have been occurring. (1) We discussed "breadwinner ideologies," which are gaining importance at least for some strata in East Central Europe. As state subsidies of health care and education are reduced and social services deteriorate further, such services will increasingly become the responsibilities of families. For some, high wages may pick up the slack; for others "decommodification" of such work, and thus unpaid care by women in households will doubtless be the result, whether or not state policies themselves explicitly promote breadwinner ideologies. We have noted other ways in which state policies facilitate and constrain the definitions of men's and women's "work," shaping differing opportunities and obligations. (2) A comparison of what scholars have said about the labor-market participation of women in East and West led us to consider the changing meanings of "coercion" and "choice," and women's changing experience of them over time and in different societal contexts.

Such revaluations and recontextualizations are a salient feature of postsocialism. (3) Also reconceptualized are the grounds for making claims for support and assistance from the state. Claims are made through the construction of new identities—of worthy and unworthy citizens—and of "needs." It is thus part of the larger issue of how social differentiation and inequality are being discursively created and institutionalized in the region. (4) Inequality is in part mediated by gender. Our examples suggest that this is true not only for workers who have found themselves without access to services when their factory was privatized, but also for entrepreneurs whose marriage choices and forms of consumption establish and represent forms of successful upward mobility. Such changing life circumstances necessarily alter relations of "dependency" and "autonomy," and recast ideas about such relations. (5) Dependence on and independence from the state and market are relativized through the multiple ways in which persons of different generations and identities are linked to such institutions—for example, tax evasion, reliance on child allowances, parental leave. We explored how the meanings and experience of dependence in East Central Europe are being transformed and regendered.

As the schematic comparison outlined in this chapter suggests, the newly emerging relations between men, women, markets, and states in East Central Europe are not homogeneous, nor are they recapitulations of forms evident elsewhere or in earlier historical periods. On the contrary, gender relations are being remade and renegotiated in the face of the redistribution of state allocations and economic restructuring. Gender relations are actively involved, in multiple ways, in shaping the economic restratification of the region.

European welfare states—East and West—are currently confronting intense internal and external pressures to reform. But reform, in democratizing environments or those espousing democratic ideals, must contend with public opinion and political activism. Thus we now turn to women's and men's perceptions of politics and their political participation in East Central Europe.

5

Arenas of Political Action

NEW FORMS of political participation in East Central Europe have received considerable scholarly attention in the last decade. Whether described as the establishment of multiparty systems, of political culture and self-organization, or of a free press and public opinion, the vastly expanded possibilities for political activity and expression have been a salient aspect of postsocialism for participants and observers alike. Within this scholarly work, the role of women in politics has also been discussed and documented. We build on this foundation and point to some of the paradoxes and contradictions of politics in the postsocialist period when viewed from a gendered perspective. Hence we ask whether and how gender categories are relevant to "civil society" and activism; whether and how social problems that might form the impetus for mobilization are framed in gendered terms. As in previous chapters, we consider the way East Central Europe is embedded in cross-currents of ideas and organizations that transcend the region itself. The cases discussed here are instructive for rethinking the forms and logic of political activism, including "feminism," and for exploring the transnational circulation of political discourses.[1]

In the communist period, the policies, politics, and parties of the region were dominated by men. The command economies, single-party states, and state-controlled media precluded popular participation; conflicts between enterprises, social groups, regions, and levels of the bureaucracy were the subject of closed negotiation, subversion, and subterfuge. Since the end of state socialism, however, differences of interest among social groups and enterprises have often involved intense and more open political conflict. Institutional change since 1989 has been analyzed as a building of contexts in which conflict is formulated, expressed, and negotiated. Such contexts include representative legislatures, mass media, and the organizations of civil society.

But "civil society" itself has proven to be problematic as a concept. Here we wish to highlight the ambiguity of the term and the diverse uses to which it has been put. In the 1970s and 1980s, dissident groups and those in "democratic opposition" in Poland, Czechoslovakia, and Hungary used "civil society" as a rallying cry. In the interests of reconstituting democratic practices in the region, but without directly challenging the socialist state, groups such as Solidarity, KOR, Charter 77, and later the Union of Academic Workers and various cultural forums of Hungary knowingly borrowed the term from each other, and ultimately from the history of European political thought about democracy. They presented their opposition to communism as a kind of "bargain," a brave fight not so much for the destruction of the entire system as for the reinstatement of a space for independent activities. For outside analysts as for East Central European activists, the term became a form of hopeful thinking about the political future. Early on, however, commentators also registered skepticism about the euphoria around the concept, noting the incoherent combination of ideas and idealizations that were gathered under this rubric within the region.[2]

The lines of European thought on which the dissidents and their allies drew were themselves multifaceted, complicated, and even contradictory. This is no doubt in part due to the fact that "civil society" has never in its history been a politically neutral, purely theoretical idea. We hardly need rehearse the history of "civil society" here, given the ample literature on the subject. But some indication of its various forms in early democratic theory will help to ground our argument. One strand of thinking understood civil society to be part of the economic realm, separate from the state. Another emphasized the independent self-organization of the citizenry as both a sign and guarantee of democracy, a bulwark against state power. Others in the European tradition supposed that the complex labyrinth of voluntary, professional, and cultural organizations that they defined as civil society was separate from both state and market, able to create social forms that could foster a politically critical public opinion. Still others understood civil society as a protection for the state, a peaceful forum for complaints against it. For East Central Europeans before 1989 the notions of free association and self-organization were perhaps central, as was that of an antipolitics separate from state power. Activity in the second economy was often also included. Indeed, it was this flexibility and ambiguity that contributed to the power of the idea in the region, and its ability to inspire hope and action.[3]

The activist use of the concept in East Central Europe revitalized interest in the idea within Western social science. Since the early 1980s there has been a lively, contentious discussion in American and Western European social theory about the concept's history, and permutations. There has also been a continuing debate about its role in political organizing. For leftist intellectuals in Western Europe it has been a way of reinvigorating political thought in a tradition ravaged by disillusionment. For others in Western Europe it has been an extension of concerns about civic rights, citizenship, and the legal status of immigrant populations. In the United States the idea of civil society has been involved in discussions about political apathy, the need for citizen participation in a "strong" democracy, multiple public spheres, and the dilemmas of multiculturalism. The term has in addition been taken up by those writing about the "transitions" of Latin America, Africa, and other parts of the globe. In East Central Europe, meanwhile, the earlier focus on civil society has abated somewhat. At first invoked as a panacea for the political cynicism, apathy, disaffection, and overcentralization of the region, it has now been partially replaced by political discussions of democratic institutions and practices such as parliamentary procedures, constitution writing, party platforms, and voting.[4] Wherever it has been proposed, civil society has more often been effective as a utopian imaginary that inspires diverse sorts of action in the face of increasing bureaucratic centralization, weakened states, and global capital than as a concrete program derived from theory.

One general lesson of this global circulation of "civil society" as term and idea is that concepts with similar names do not always mean or describe similar things. Ideas from one historical and political era are routinely decontextualized by theorists and activists, and then reinserted into structurally and historically different circumstances in a general form of meaning-making that can change their significance and effects. "Democracy," "civil society," and, as we shall see, "feminism" are exemplary of this process. Careful attention to this aspect of political and social activity—which can produce gaps, slippages, and difference between ideas that purport to be the same, as well as the invention of unexpected unities and common origins for diverse movements—is useful for understanding the way political mobilization and cooperation across regions and over time become possible.[5]

Today's invocation of civil society in East Central Europe and the many organizations that have formed since 1989 are best seen in the context of a wider political field. Women and men in the region have been drawn to a diverse array of new associations independent of the state. These include foundations in the nonprofit sector, nongovernmental organizations (NGOs), charities, self-help and voluntary organizations, and social movements. Throughout the region, many still view national politics with suspicion. In contrast, smaller, noncentralized, more local initiatives—whether organizations of entrepreneurs, health providers, self-helpers in the face of disease or crises, supporters of the arts and local culture or of reforming education—promise to make a real difference in everyday life. Organizations of this kind are not altogether new in the region, although their public legitimacy surely is. It is true that the socialist state worked to eliminate systematically any potential competition for central power by outlawing, infiltrating, co-opting, or otherwise diminishing institutions that might have mediated between the state and family. But these processes of undermining interstitial structures should not be interpreted too literally to mean that there were no forms of organization at all between the state and family.

On the contrary, in many countries—Hungary, Poland, Bulgaria—some part of what is presently understood as civil society is the practical, now legalized continuation of "second society," or informal aid networks, organizations of local patriotism, or even oppositional associations from the state socialist era. In some countries, civil society endeavors today are continuations in another sense as well. If they were sometimes subversive of the official mechanisms of state socialism, they now often provide ways to subvert the fiscal rules of capitalist accounting, since their legal standing as nonprofit organizations provides a means for those professionally involved in them to raise money while evading taxes. In other countries the watchful eye of state regulation continues to keep them in check, and makes their operation more difficult by skimming resources away.[6]

Such interstitial structures and organizations have not only burgeoned in size and number, but have enjoyed a revitalization, renaming, and reconceptualization. They are no longer seen as unfortunate but necessary, often clandestine ways to survive. This transformation is noteworthy. We should understand civil society in the region not primarily as a determinate set of institutions and organizations, which it also is, but as an ideological formation that produces the quite real social effect of newly perceptible boundaries between state organizations and what can now, as a result of such boundaries, be called voluntary, independent, or "nongovernmental organizations."

The making of such boundaries is relevant as well to the gendering of politics, which becomes evident only if we view the organizations of civil society in relation to the governmental arena. It is well known that all over East Central Europe the number of women in national politics dropped considerably after 1989. These lower rates are not, of course, directly comparable to those in state socialist governing bodies, since women's earlier participation was by and large obligatory, and such national assemblies had, at best, a rubber-stamping function. Furthermore, even the lower, post-1989 rates of women's participation in national politics are higher than those in the United States, very close to those in the western European welfare states, though lower than those in Scandinavia. Thus, when situated in an international perspective, the representation of women and the rate of women's participation in national politics in East Central Europe are not as alarming or divergent as is sometimes suggested.[7]

A telling pattern emerges, however, if we consider the entire political field since 1989: The trajectory of its development bears striking resemblance to the shifting valuations, gender alignments, and subdivisions of the public/private distinction we discussed in detail in chapter 3. During the socialist period, when oppositional movements first articulated the importance of civil society and stressed the heroism of their own dissident actions, it was men who took the most visible roles. Women were active in oppositional politics in Czechoslovakia, Poland, and elsewhere, but were very rarely the frontline spokespersons. But when parliamentary politics became a forum for asserting power and influence, civil society came to be seen as less attractive to men and relatively weak. In the years since 1989, civil society has increasingly become an arena of women's political action; national politics, the realm of men. For instance, some statistics suggest that by the mid-1990s, and with variation across the region, a majority of NGOs have been headed by women. But further subdivisions by gender are evident even within the organizations of civil society, as well as those of government. Within civil society, women are more likely to be involved in associations oriented toward public service, education, and local self-help, and less in those with more conventionally political agendas. Meanwhile, women in government tend to work at the local level. Indeed, numbers of women increase steadily as one moves from national to regional to local offices. Thus, from the point of view of centers of power, organizations made up of women—whether or not they are devoted to matters defined as women's issues—are marginalized.[8]

For women's NGOs, as for most others, access to resources has been a major problem. In addition, their status as significantly new in some countries, yet continuous with past activities elsewhere, contributes to the paradoxical nature of these organizations in relation to governments. They are both less effective in democratizing the states in which they operate than theorists had hoped and yet susceptible to influences that make them agents of change. Although nominally independent of states, many in fact get their money from government grants. As a result of this dependence, a number of NGOs, including ones run by women, orient their activities to the state as redistributor. In a study of NGOs in Romania, Grunberg noted that far from having democratizing effects or organizing and representing interests external to the state, these NGOs instead responded to the government's priorities and rhetoric. There is a clear resemblance here to earlier patterns of political activity during communism. Grunberg underscores that in some cases the NGOs have no constituency at all, existing mainly to support their increasingly professionalized staffs.

Other NGOs orient their activities in the same way to foreign agencies. For the Romanian case these range from the Mormon Church to the United States Agency for International Development or the British and Danish Embassies. The European Union has also been a major contributor to women's organizations in recent years. The donor organizations have their own ideologies that motivate and shape their activities. The agendas of Western European funding agencies are most often set by their own concerns about "dangers" from the East such as migration or agricultural dumping. In addition, in Western Europe, as in the United States, the support of "civil society" is often seen as an end in itself, the funding of NGOs (regardless of their goals) considered a way of missionizing for liberal democracy. It is conceptualized as an intrinsically positive objective, whose realization will produce a democratic political culture. This oversimplified view has increasingly been tempered by empirical evidence on the operation of such organizations.

For example, people working in such organizations in East Central Europe quickly learn to produce whatever "language" and "interest" the foreign funders are willing to finance. Of course, not only money and rhetoric, but also techniques of organization, definitions of problems, and even personnel are exchanged. But the result is not always the intended effect on the problem or the people who are the purported target or beneficiaries of the NGO's efforts. Just as the notion of "civil society" circulated throughout intellectual circles in the 1980s, so various ideas and terms such as "project," "assessment," and "training" as well as practices such as filling out application forms and being evaluated by review boards, move around the NGO circuit. These are promoted by Western consultants or the staff of international agencies, and appropriated, reworked, and reinterpreted by local participants in their own contexts, and often for their own purposes.[9]

Even though NGOs may be fraught with problems, they nevertheless have brought important resources into the region and have had significant impact in numerous ways: building infrastructure, importing ideas and practices. One example is provided by Mršević's portrait of Belgrade's SOS Hotline for domestic violence. The Belgrade Hotline was modeled after similar organizations in Ljubljana and Zagreb, which in turn were inspired by models farther to the west. Women from Yugoslavia saw Western hotlines in operation or heard about them from Western European friends and former colleagues, whom they met in study trips abroad. These same foreigners, along with other women, provided initial funding. But it was the Yugoslav war and the heightened awareness of violence that made it possible, indeed imperative, within the local context to focus attention on domestic violence, and that made the organization viable. (The rise in street crime has often had a similar effect in other cities of the region.)

Among the important successes of the hotline was the impact it had on public awareness of the problem of domestic violence. The organization used radio and television interviews, talk shows, and the like to redefine as crimes and "social problems" the beating and sometimes murder of wives, mothers, other female relatives, and children. What had been a regrettable but accepted practice became, in an astonishingly short time, a "social problem." The redefinition contributed to support for the hotline. This occurred not only in Belgrade, but in a similar way through hotlines and their publicity in many cities of the region. In some countries, it was Western women who directly introduced the idea and insisted on the need to attend to it. The construction of "domestic violence" as an acknowledged social problem is exactly the sort of reciprocal relationship between organizations in civil society and the creation and change of discourse in the public sphere that has been theorized by feminists and other social scientists. This illustrates one way in which multiple and decentralized public spheres can replace the state-dominated publics characteristic of the communist era.[10]

Yet, despite the Belgrade hotline's successes, the dedication of its volunteer staff, the change in public discourse that it initiated, and the hundreds of people helped over several years, the hotline virtually disintegrated after the war. The reasons for this reveal a telling continuity. The necessary experts—legal, medical—expected recompense for their services, refusing the voluntaristic model out of which civil society grew. The volunteers themselves splintered into factions on issues of ideological purity that echoed political fights in the communist past. Finally, the hotline failed to survive the end of the war because it needed an external threat or common enemy, in this case military violence, to produce internal unity. This process mirrored the dissolution of the early civil society initiatives that survived as long as there was communism for them to oppose.

These examples make evident the importance of the relationship between civil societies and the international arena. The impact of foreign contacts made possible by the region's great variety of NGOs parallels the more widely investigated and recognized influence of international lending agencies or of religious institutions on the region's governments. In the case of NGOs interested in women's issues support comes from international foundations devoted to health, population issues or reproductive rights, human rights, and education, and from political and religious organizations and smaller feminist groups. There is also the phenomenon of ethnic diaspora organizations for women. Some of these have been in operation serving coethnics dispersed in Europe and North America throughout the communist period. They can now organize "at home," sometimes eclipsing local efforts.[11] Exchanges between

East Central European women, foreign activists, and scholars interested in women's rights are complex and shed further light on the relationship between gender categories, civil society, and the ironies of globalization. The case of "feminisms" will provide an extended example.

Western feminists expected women's groups to be among the first independent organizations to emerge after 1989, in view of the new freedom to associate combined with what was known about women's systematically lower wages compared to men's, and their simultaneous burdens of housework, wage work, and required political work in the region. More recently, observers within East Central Europe have noted that given the withdrawal of many state-sponsored services, independent women's organizations in a strong civil society are the best hope in fighting for retention of women's social rights and benefits. This line of argument certainly makes sense in light of recent research on the active role of women's political organizations in transitions from authoritarian politics in Latin America. And it echoes the findings of historical research about the influence exercised by women's movements on the social policies of Western European states throughout the nineteenth and twentieth centuries. Women's groups put pressure on states to provide social provisioning, sometimes by redefining public discourse and sometimes more directly, by engineering legislative changes.[12]

Yet, as many have remarked, there is no large feminist movement anywhere in East Central Europe. Vocal and effective women's groups in East Germany and the former Yugoslavia that were active at the time of the most dramatic political changes in the late 1980s and early 1990s have been largely demobilized. In contrast, influential Scandinavian women's organizations have been successful in putting their issues on the political agenda; in other parts of Western Europe and the United States, small groups and a few national organizations have kept a discussion of problems labeled "women's issues" alive in the public sphere. In East Central Europe, there appears, at first glance, to be very little explicitly feminist activity. On the contrary, the term "feminism" is treated with ridicule and derision in public forums, often by women as well as men. Feminism is not just controversial; it is stigmatized.[13]

Under these circumstances, perhaps it should not have been surprising that the first encounters after 1989 between Western feminists and women in East Central Europe were emotionally fraught and disillusioning, full of mutual misunderstandings. Sensitive descriptions of these interactions have provided thoughtful analyses of the issues involved. Despite the many differences among "Westerners," and among those Westerners identifying themselves as "feminists," there was a generally shared disappointment at the lack of interest in feminism in East

Central Europe. Westerners reproached East Central European women for being apolitical and not understanding their own oppression and interests. Western feminists seemed to have forgotten that far from being an exception, the case of East Central Europe is fairly typical: large feminist movements are rare in the world. At the same time, in the United States for instance, encroachments on abortion legislation are increasing and attacks on welfare for minority women point to a backlash against feminism. Many feminists from the United States and Western Europe seemed, ironically, to share the "paternalistic" assumptions of their own societies, according to which they were bringing "freedom" and "democracy" to "isolated" and "underdeveloped" easterners. And even though academic feminism in the United States had come to recognize the justice of minority and Third World women's demands to be heard within feminist scholarship, and hence the importance of diversity when it came to East Central Europe, most white, middle-class American feminists nevertheless expected replicas of their own concerns. For many this expectation was in part a product of their family backgrounds as the descendants of East European immigrants, and a consequent, unintended essentialism. On the assumption that "the past is another country," they unconsciously expected the women they encountered to be versions of their own grandmothers, and therefore more like themselves as women and feminists.[14]

On the other hand, the women of East Central Europe who were participants in these encounters were deeply ambivalent about Western feminism and feminists. Diverse in political commitments, as well as in social origin and education, those who were attracted to feminism embraced it as part of the West that was idealized and often imitated. They were nevertheless offended by what they felt to be the missionizing and even imperialist attitude of many Western feminists, who tried to impose their own truths, solutions, and expectations without knowing or trying to understand the specificity of women's situations in the countries of the region. Women in the East looked on incredulously as Western feminists, assuming global solidarity among women, ignored the great differences of wealth and power between themselves and women in East Central Europe. These differences, due to the geopolitical positions of their regions of origin, were felt by Easterners to be of great significance. They resented the patronizing laundry lists of "must-do" activities that Westerners brought with them, as well as the ignorance of many Western feminists concerning the recent history of the region. Some East Central European women have since begun to create their own forms of feminism. Whatever their relationship to Western feminism, there is a general lack of interest in non-Western feminist forms. Other women in

East Central Europe have questioned the primacy of "gender" or "women" as categories of analysis or for mobilization, especially given the new importance of the ideal of gender-blind and rights-based citizenship to which they aspire.[15]

The attempt to understand and theorize the difficulties of cross-national communication among women and the apparent dearth of feminist activism in the region has produced a small but important literature. Written by women from many countries and political positions in East Central Europe, as well as by Western feminists representing various positions, this literature has drawn on feminist theory in order to rethink "civil society" and the nature of women's political mobilization more generally. We suggest that like earlier conflicts within U.S. feminism along racial, class, and ethnic divides, and between American and non-Western feminisms, this encounter is not only about East Central Europe, but is contributing new understandings of "feminism" itself, and its possibilities as an international social movement in a post–Cold War world.

Four major points have emerged from the analysis of these encounters. One of these is a structural factor, the other three relate to discursive and communicational issues. First, socialism produced a quite different structural position for most women in East Central Europe from the situation of middle-class women in the United States and Western Europe. In earlier chapters we have discussed in detail many aspects of these structural differences. Here we note more generally that as a result of these differences, the political program of American and Western European feminism often rang hollow for East Central European women. For instance, the high rates of employment characteristic of women in the East made it hard for them to sympathize with the Western feminist focus on incorporation into the labor market as a means of achieving autonomy. Instead, the liberating effects of waged work sounded to them like a naive replay of discredited socialist tenets. Furthermore, in questions such as abortion and reproduction, autonomy from men and families was not the highest value for women in many Eastern countries. Rather, in domestic decisions they often wanted the increased participation of male family members whose roles, they felt, had been diminished or usurped by the state. The most sustained analyses of these structural conflicts came from those participating in and observing the arguments between East German and West German feminists in the 1980s and early 1990s. West German women understood their major problem to be dependence on individual men who exercised domination inside families, albeit with the aid of state regulation of domestic arrangements; East German women analyzed their situation as the intrusion of the state into their families, often seen as the only site safe from the state for everyone, not just women.[16]

Discursive differences associated with this fundamental structural divergence were no less serious. Women in East Central Europe pointed out that "isms" of all kinds were delegitimated after 1989, and that the communist state's explicit sponsorship of "official" women's organizations—no matter how little they did in support of women—made it difficult to take the project of women's "emancipation" seriously. Some women who espoused liberal principles, in the best tradition of the early democratic oppositions, pointed out that women wanted to be considered citizens like all others. Given communist histories of "policies for women" and Ministries for Family Policy or Institutes for Mother and Child, women in East Central Europe often wanted to avoid any form of special consideration as or inclusion in a socially marked category. Moreover, they pointed out that when nationalist discourses emphasized the difference between women and men, anyone who wanted to argue against nationalism would virtually have to avoid a politics based on gender difference.

A related discursive difference hinged on the different meanings of what might have seemed like the same terms. The American feminist slogan "the personal is political" was particularly alarming to many East Central European women. In its American context the motto was intended to call into question the liberal principle that patriarchy and hierarchy, though considered illegitimate in public politics, could still be the just basis of family life. Feminists pointed to domestic exploitation and violence as proof of the need for political (assuming, of course, democratic) principles in the private sphere as well. But in the East, "politics" meant something quite different. Instead of importing democracy and fairness into the family, bringing "politics" into the family sounded like inviting surveillance, corruption, and humiliation into the home, destroying the only social arena that, despite its actual problems, seemed to many a realm relatively free of state intrusion. Within the dominant discourse on families in East Central Europe that we have discussed at length, this kind of politicization implied that women should criticize their families, and perhaps even give up devotion to this one institution that many felt should, ideally, be safe and constant in a changing and highly politicized world.

A fourth point is more properly communicational and strategic. It calls into question the very "sides" of East and West according to which the encounter between women has been framed so far. The forms of second wave feminism that have been most strongly represented in East Central Europe focus on women's individual rights, on employment, autonomy, and questions of sexual and reproductive freedom. But there are other forms of feminism as well. In the West, "feminism" is neither unified nor monolithic. Hence, it should hardly be surprising if women in East Central Europe differ in political opinion from some of their American and Western European counterparts. It is particularly important to emphasize the multiplicity of ideological shadings present now, and also among earlier movements—only some of which called themselves "feminist"—in order to remind ourselves that feminism is a highly contested term. "Western feminists" are currently embroiled in a range of controversies relevant to East Central Europe. [17]

For instance, there are strong disagreements on how to understand and act on women's relation to states. As we noted in chapter 4, some American and Scandinavian feminists are convinced that the state can be made "woman friendly," with women clients and employees of the state recruited for joint political activism. Others in the same countries argue that the state is unreformable, always masculinist and incapable of constituting women as anything but dependent and subordinate. Pornography and free speech have produced similar acrimonious discussions. The role of motherhood in women's lives has also been debated. Maternalist organizations have been important historically, as the recent recuperation of the history of women's movements makes plain; they have stressed the special value of women's caring capacity in the private sphere, or used this value to argue that women should inject the ethics of care into the public as well. Other women's movements have deemphasized motherhood and focused instead on issues of fairness in assuring women the right to work or have appealed for women's equal citizenship.

This diversity of feminisms suggests that advice and influence do not go always in the stereotyped direction of Western "adviser" to Eastern "recipient." As Olsen has recently noted, the experience of women in East Central Europe with communism should be enlightening for American feminists grappling with the question of legal solutions and their efficacy in solving social problems. We suggest this observation can be broadened to include the postsocialist experience of East Central European women. Their dilemmas about the state, prostitution, and motherhood could all be instructive for feminists elsewhere struggling with parallel issues.[18]

Indeed, if we look farther than Europe and the United States we see that feminisms all over the world run the gamut from essentialist to rights-based, from ecologically sensitive to development-focused. Thus, the controversies among women in East Central Europe, and between them and feminists based in Western Europe and the United States, are hardly exceptional. They are part of the contemporary range of opinion about issues relating to women on the world stage, among international policy makers, funders, and activists. The focus on women by international organizations such as the U.N. and I.L.O. has in part created these discourses. They have been dispersed by these organizations, as well as through the globalization of nonprofit, charitable, and other activist associations. Those involved in such organizations must negotiate the varying and mutable meanings of terms. These shift significantly between their use in conferences and related venues where coalitions are formed, and their use at more local meetings among those familiar with the actual practices the terms are assumed to denote.

Historical studies of women's movements have repeatedly noted that significant differences in approach and perspective have not hindered cooperation among disparate groups working on issues they define as women's concerns. The active making of cooperation and coalition often depend on reinterpreting the past so that it gives warrant for unity, and in defining spheres of agreement and contention. In the face of what seemed like insurmountable differences, for instance, international women's organizations at the turn of the century managed to create coalitions and continuities. No less than "civil society" or "democracy," "feminism" and its cognates are terms that have made their way around the world in the last century, gaining different meanings in the national liberation struggles of the Third World, in the liberal and rights-oriented versions dominant in the United States, and in the maternalist versions common everywhere. We find it useful to think of such terms more as foci for debate and political coalition than as "contentful" essences with determinate origins.[19]

Yet, this broader geographic, historical, and communicative context is often forgotten in an overemphasis on the term "feminism" itself in East Central Europe. The focus has been on the negative stereotypes associated with the term, and the derisive, dismissive response to it in public forums. These reactions have sometimes blinded observers to the actual and diverse political activity around gender issues since 1989. Importantly, this activity is usually not understood or represented by women themselves as "feminist," nor are the problems addressed always seen as the problems of women. For activists interested in social reform and improvement of life conditions, there is the inevitable question of strategy: How to use rhetorical means to form constituencies, to formulate problems in such a way as to claim and garner the support of the greatest number of people. Is a focus on the category "woman" the best way to accomplish this? Certainly the label "feminist" seems, at this historical juncture, more a social and political liability than an advantage. Given the discourses from which political organizing in East Central Europe necessarily starts, we believe that insistence on the word itself is not crucial. It might also be more productive to build on aspects of mother-hood and on citizenship—definable in many ways—than on wo-men's autonomy and individualism. These latter have to date been the strands of second wave feminism most commonly heard in East Central Europe.

Viewed from this wider perspective, it is clear that there has indeed been political activity in East Central Europe around issues being re-defined, at least implicitly, as related to gender. Differences between countries are significant. Nevertheless, as we have noted, there are now hotlines to fight domestic violence in a number of cities of East Central Europe. In fact, the redefinition of domestic violence as a "social prob-lem" in relations between men and women dates entirely from the postsocialist era and counts as a triumph of organizing. There have also been important actions in defense of abortion rights in Poland, Hungary and Germany, as also in defense of the fetus in organizations funded and run by the Catholic Church. Women have organized as mothers for and against the war in the former Yugoslavia. In an interesting contrast, while prostitution has been considered a problem of overly speedy social change in the Czech Republic, in Hungary there have been efforts to see it as a matter of women's relation to men, to entrepreneurship, to work and the control of women's labor. Church-based relief of poverty has also been taken up by women in some areas and defined as particularly suited to their concerns. Self-help associations, organized around cancer care, alcoholism, and other ailments, are also gender coded, with very high rates of women's participation and leadership.[20]

Publishing books, magazines, or pamphlets is also a notable form of political activity, whether initiated by women or by men, in newspapers, or presented on television. Questions of women's employment, its sim-ilarity to work patterns in Western Europe, the possibility of sex dis-crimination, the status of sexual harassment, and issues of reproductive freedom and infertility are being discussed much more readily and self-consciously than ever before—if not always without ridicule. In a study of media representations in Belgrade before the Bosnian War, Lukić provides evidence that the images of men and women in the press be-came a "war by different means." Newspapers and magazines controlled by the central government used rhetorical strategies to convince readers that there was impending danger in order to create an atmosphere of panic and paranoia that set the stage for popular willingness to wage war. Oppositional media, on the other hand, not only told a different story, but used rhetorical devices to make explicit and thereby under-mine the strategies of government media. But none of these media re-ported what women's organizations themselves wanted to express about their own anti-war actions. For this, groups such as Women in Black had to create their own publications. If the women's organizations had existed in greater strength, such variation in media representations would have been an ideal example of public spheres expanded and diversified through the organizations of civil society.

The controversies among women with which we started, and the analysis of which we have summarized, suggest several general points about the logic and dynamic of political participation and activism. The expectation that feminist movements would necessarily emerge when free association became possible in East Central Europe was not only overly optimistic, but a misreading of civil society as a sociocultural phenomenon. It has become clear that there is a tension between the reified types of association described in political theories and the "actually existing" practices and contexts of social action in the region. Recall that the classic liberal ideal of civil society rests on a separation of the abstract (rights bearing) individual who can freely associate and act politically from that individual's actual social characteristics. It thereby presents the image of unfettered possibility for action, while masking the fact that action of any kind depends on resources such as money, connections, time, and even cultural categories such as gender that—unlike abstract rights—are unevenly distributed and differentiate actors of various kinds. In the communist era, and especially in those states where there were only limited second economies and people were minimally self-organized, social differences did not matter in quite the same way. Party membership was of paramount importance in political action. In civil society, by contrast, social characteristics such as gender or ethnic identity can become politicized when their effects are palpable enough so that at least some women come to experience themselves not simply as individuals but as members of a sociopolitical category that is treated differently and which therefore can formulate "interests" in common. The case of East Central Europe allows us to recast assumptions about political mobilization. In this sense, "civil societies" do not so much respond to already existing groups, categories of identity, and interests as create the context in which identities and interests can form.[21]

But they do not form automatically. The terms and ideas for political mobilization are embedded in discourses that provide the ground on which they are understood and from which they gain their power to move people. There are always effects on meaning and use when terms and practices are transferred from one sociohistorical context to another. "Feminism," for instance, is a movement and a set of practices—such as protesting, marching, holding meetings and conferences, lobbying, and consciousness raising—whose history shows it to have been actively made in a variety of specific historical circumstances. And, as we have been arguing, what those who consider themselves feminists see as their interests clearly varies—like those of other social movements—by social location, by historical moment, in some cases by ethnic or national group, and in accordance with their other political commitments.

Indeed, taking this a step further, political solidarity cannot be assumed on the basis of shared "womanhood." The cultural category of "woman" is a practical, everyday form of subjectivity, called up by innumerable mundane activities and practices. It is not the same as the politically significant category of "woman" as a mobilized identity, a self-conscious social collectivity. In order for social categories such as "woman" to serve as the basis for mobilization, they must first be constituted as politically relevant. This is done through public discussion and by social movements themselves that presuppose the existence of a constituency in the process of actually making one. Not all historical circumstances are auspicious for such mobilization. Furthermore, once the politically charged category has been created, it is very much in the interest of social movements to obliterate the distinction between "woman" as subjectivity and "woman" as a politically relevant identity, to make this linkage seem natural and unquestionable.[22]

It follows that a commitment to advance women's interests—and the definition of such "interests"—is never merely the reflex of a politician's or a group's subjectivity as women (or as men, for that matter), nor even their experience of discrimination and oppression. All of these might well be understood through quite different categories, as they often are in East Central Europe. And there are numerous examples from East Central Europe as from elsewhere in the world, of women in high political positions who do not consider their own gender or gender issues relevant for their professional lives.[23] Politicized identities are themselves a result of public arguments and activities that allow individuals to redefine their own sense of self, and redefine events and social processes as, for instance, "problems" rather than circumstances to be endured, as fixable rather than immutable, as caused by gender arrangements rather than other social forces and processes.

One of the sites for creating such changes of definition in East Central Europe, as we have noted, is the mass media. They are important not only as a source of images from which people gain models for personhood—masculinity and femininity—and around which they weave the details of their intimate lives, but even more as sites of political socialization and ideological conflict. But the apparently spectacular increase in the diversity of media in East Central Europe since 1989 is a complex phenomenon. As the newspapers and magazines of the region were bought by various domestic political parties and Western conglomerates, they became the vehicle of political party ideologies and market processes. Often, pornographic materials flooded their pages. Once the organs of Communist Party propaganda, with explicitly didactic and exhortative functions, magazines and newspapers in East Central Europe, as elsewhere in the capitalist world, now engage in forms of seduction, aiming to create and expand consumer desires. For instance, magazines no longer give advice about how to control sexuality, but rather how to use it to get a job and get ahead. They now instruct readers in methods for achieving "success" and create models of consumption that often invite frustration. Questions of consumption—and shortage—have had political significance of one kind or another in the region for decades. Although varied in their target audiences and special subject matter, magazines now contribute directly to transmuting the idea of political freedom into that of self-realization through consumer choice, and vie with each other to redefine the meanings of political actions.[24]

Another important site for creating changed definitions of political problems in East Central Europe is intellectual life. Ironically, despite the disagreements and even emotional turmoil we have summarized above, international contacts between scholars and NGOs over the last decade have been fruitful. They have resulted in a number of women's studies centers, feminist organizations, and small nonprofit feminist newspapers across the region, as well as in collaborative research.[25] Western feminist works have been translated into many languages of the region and published in scholarly and intellectual journals. This has contributed, in some respects, to moderating the derision with which feminist ideas have long been greeted by the scholarly and popular press. However, it has also contributed to the accusation that women's movements are foreign imports (if they are not communist fronts), and thus alien to the region as a whole. This in turn has spurred an investigation by scholars in most of the countries of the region into women's politics in the nineteenth century and interwar era. They have uncovered active bourgeois and socialist women's movements that were in close communication with movements farther to the west, and engaged in parallel or coordinated actions.[26] Thus, not only "feminism" but also "Western" has emerged, in this scholarship, as a contingent and historical label. For in the nineteenth and early-twentieth centuries women's movements in what is now considered East Central Europe included a wide range of political positions that were not simply "eastern" but very much part of international networks and organizations.

The history of women's movements in the countries of East Central Europe is now beginning to emerge. This work resembles that of American and British historians who in the 1960s and 1970s unearthed women's histories. But we doubt this is the major inspiration. Rather, even if sparked from abroad, the recovery of women's activism is itself nevertheless a recognizable local product: it parallels the rediscovery of other aspects of the past in which virtually all the region's historians are actively engaged. The results, like those of other recuperative efforts, will doubtless influence other arenas of political action. Depending on the strategies of scholars and other activists, the term "feminist" might also be (re)legitimated, at least for scholarly use. As with the retrieval of other aspects of the East Central Europe's past, this history of women's movements will have an effect on the mass media, on further political activism, as well as on the everyday self-understanding of men and women.

6

Gender and Change

OUR REFLECTIONS on gender after socialism have been inspired, in large measure, by recent empirical studies—especially those completed in the framework of the collaborative research project we codirected—as well as by our ongoing engagement with feminist theory and the literature that explores the political and economic changes that have followed socialism. In the preceding chapters, we have examined postsocialism in East Central Europe from a gendered perspective, sketching the ways it has been differently experienced by men and women, and has produced new forms of relations between them in the workplace, in households, and in politics. Gender relations are in flux. They vary among the countries of the region, and in their new forms they do not entirely match gender relations elsewhere in the world.

We have also argued that the ideas and practices of gender have shaped many of the political and economic changes that have followed the collapse of communism. We considered four kinds of changes. Chapter 2 took up questions clustered around the interdependent relationship between state-making, the construction of political authority, and the control of human reproduction. In chapter 3 we briefly traced over time the practices of everyday life, especially the means by which shifting understandings of public and private have been crucial in economic restructuring. As a set of comparisons complementary to these historical ones, chapter 4 turned to contemporary welfare states in western Europe and the United States, asking how the relationships between women, states, and economies are both similarly and differently structured in postsocialism and in welfare states. All of these systems are responsive and vulnerable to the international context that has seen a reorganization of global markets and encouraged cuts in social provisioning by states. Renewed political mobilization is one kind of response to such reorganization. In chapter 5 we turned to new patterns of political participation by men and women in the region. We examined the gendering of parliaments, civil societies, and mass media as arenas of political action, with particular attention to the proliferation of NGOs and the access that international humanitarian, nonprofit, religious, and market-oriented agencies now have to the region through them.

The end of communism created a significant challenge for social science. Preexisting models of societal change have often come to seem threadbare or ill-suited. Like other vast and somewhat comparable transformations—the transition from capitalism to socialism, the urbanization and industrialization of the nineteenth century or of the early communist era—these processes of transformation will continue to be at the center of scholarly controversy, creating the puzzles that provoke and inspire the production of knowledge. We have added a gendered perspective to recast general assumptions about postsocialism.

Here we return to two basic questions raised in the introduction. First, what are the broader implications of this gendered analysis for the way in which we understand the processes of change after socialism? What further questions does such a perspective suggest, and what directions for research? "Transition" is now widely recognized as an inadequate metaphor with which to summarize social change happening in East Central Europe. Theories of "transformation" reject teleology and recognize continuities with the past. What more is gained for understanding the processes of change by our strategy of focusing on gender and on the dynamic discrepancies between discourses and institutional practices? Second, how are feminist approaches to states, political processes, and political participation modified or clarified by including evidence from state socialist and postsocialist gender regimes? And, how are analytical frameworks changed when, instead of thinking about the "West" studying the "East," West and East are considered within a single gendered framework and used to shed light on each other? In taking up these issues, we draw again on the examples presented in previous chapters, but juxtapose them in different ways to bring out their implications for this broader set of questions.[1]

With respect to patterns of change, one can readily cite dramatic ruptures and subtle continuities in social life since 1989. But "rupture" and "continuity" are inadequate to the complexity of the situations at hand. Our work has instead foregrounded processes with varying rates and temporalities, and proposed a number of analytical concepts for exploring them. These concepts highlight the shifting interpretive frameworks through which people understand and experience stasis and change in everyday life. Because gender relations are mediated by age and location in the life cycle, evidence about gender relations and generational differences underscores the importance of attending to continuities of different tenacity and duration, to precedent-setting sequences, and to historical trajectories. The concepts we have marshalled for analyzing such changes include: *recontextualization, fractal distinction, revaluation, borrowed/erased tradition, coded morality*, and redefinition or *constitution of subjects*. We say a few words about each of these in discussing examples of processes with differing temporalities.

Some phenomena are new to the region. Since 1989, for instance, the public sphere has been democratized, and there has been a massive influx of pornography. Market economies are being successfully instituted, and there is an increase in officially recognized unemployment. Other developments suggest continuities but they have roots of differing time-depth. To understand the tenacity of the public and private distinction, for instance, and the changing cultural associations of men and women to each, we first traced the emergence of the bourgeois public and private in the nineteenth century across Europe, as well as its twists and transformations through the socialist era. In contrast, the relative self-confidence of many educated women in the region and their assumption that they are the equals of men in many respects are legacies of socialist educational and employment policies.

But "legacies"—another term for continuities—are mixed in effect, especially among different generations. Yet another legacy of communism is the fear of sexuality and the alienation from their bodies that are reported by Romanian women who reached pubescence during the Ceauşescu regime. Among Hungarian women, different aspects of communism have had other "legacies." In the case of entrepreneurial women, for example, their sense of entitlement to supportive "partners" in marriage—arguably a result of communist ideology about gender equality—has enabled their upward mobility in these new circumstances. But for the women cannery workers in the same town, their total reliance on communism's factory system left them bereft of kin networks and resources when their factory was privatized.

With respect to communist ideological forms, it might well be that the teachings least identified as communist, the ones that are taken-for-granted assumptions, are the ones most likely to be retained in the bricolage of beliefs with which people operate. For example, the sense of justice voiced by the cannery workers, their deep feeling that workers are a valuable stratum, that entrepreneurial activity is somehow suspect, and that people are entitled to the right to work, are widespread opinions strongly influenced by communist tenets, and sure to resonate for some time to come.

Many studies of postsocialism have emphasized the importance of trajectories from the past as well as the determining force of sequences of events. In the realm of gender relations this is perhaps most obvious if we consider decisions about industrial restructuring. The countries of the region vary in the unemployment rates of women and men, depending on which industries and which parts of industries were privatized and streamlined first. This results in large measure from the gendered occupational segregation discussed in chapter 3. Hence, what looks like a significant difference in unemployment rates between men and women could, of course, be a temporary effect of such restructuring, or could be the start of a broad trend resulting in the feminization of poverty. The sequence in which the two genders enter into the managerial ranks of new capitalist enterprises that are being established in the region will also have long-term consequences on the relative economic ranks of men and women. When powerful or lucrative positions are initially identified as better suited to the strengths, virtues, or special qualities of men, this imagery will be difficult to change later. The order in which the governments of the region have withdrawn from social provisioning—which policies are first to go in the different countries, which ones are retained, and by what criteria these are chosen—also sets the stage for further developments, redefining subjects, marking some populations for the long term as deserving and others as unworthy.

Differential rates of change within the realm of gender relations seem particularly interesting, raising the question of where and why rapid transformations are possible. Despite the dearth of explicitly feminist organizations, numerous hotlines for domestic violence against women and children were initiated all over East Central Europe. This is an impressive achievement even if the hotlines are sometimes short-lived and if the small networks that run them often experience burnout and frustration. Even more impressive is the success these organizations have had in changing public perceptions. Domestic violence, acknowledged for centuries as a normal if regretable part of life, is now revalued and seen as a social problem. The speed of this change is striking. The contexts that made it possible deserve further research. Another similarly rapid change is the imagery for sexualized femininity and aggressive masculinity apparent in magazines and job advertisements throughout the region. Employers seek women who are properly groomed with made-up faces, stylish clothes, and shaved legs. Varied responses notwithstanding, the generations under forty have taken on many of these images as their own.

In contrast to these relatively swift transformations, there is the persistence of older women's self-images as "brave victims," even if these are no longer valued in their own households. Their sense of self thus creates emotional difficulties for them, a feeling of being useless. Another persistent phenomenon is the household division of labor. Women, largely regardless of generation, have continued to be responsible for the greatest portion of housework and childcare despite communist ideals of gender equality and full employment for women, despite a backlash against that ideology in the 1960s and 1980s, and now despite the reorganization of employment and of public support for childcare in postsocialism, as well as changing self-images of men and women. Yet, polls across the region show that even with the advent of the "stay-at-home wife" as a new status symbol, most women want to continue working for wages, even if their families do not need the money. Opinion polls reveal another persistent finding: Across the region attitudes about the legality and advisability of abortion have stayed relatively constant despite heated public debate about the subject in most of the countries since 1989.

It is an important and interesting problem, in this respect, to analyze how people's understandings of time and of rates of social change are formed. Impressions of continuity and rupture are relative and are mediated by standards of measurement that are themselves subject to change. So the widespread view throughout the region that the "family" is a haven of constancy in a rapidly changing world depends on a comparison between changing families and institutions that are undergoing even more rapid reorganization. But it also depends on the creation of a sense of continuity through the kind of semiotic processes we described in tracing the public/private dichotomy. As long as the fractal distinction itself survives, it provides a resource for the ordering of fundamental social innovations in such a way that they seem familiar to social actors. The practices themselves have the recursive character that makes new subdivisions seem like versions of the same old thing. At the same time, because the discourse retains the same terms, basic shifts in the valences of public and private, and its realignments with similarly fractal distinctions such as man/woman and us/them, can be obscured effectively.

This brings up the broader question of disjunctures between discourses and practices as a significant component in the process of postsocialist transformations. What seem like the same activities are recontextualized; they gain new meanings and consequences as their contexts have changed. Thus, for instance, men and women in socialist countries that had thriving second economies have for decades been accustomed to taking multiple jobs in order to make enough money to satisfy their needs. By law, one of these had to be an official job in some recognized enterprise so that the individual would count as "employed" no matter how little time he or she actually spent on that job. The necessity of multiple jobs was denounced as one of the abominations of state socialism, proof that it was an inefficient and inhumane system. The necessity of multiple jobs, however, has survived the collapse of communism, as has, for some, the need to have at least one that provides official status. This status is now required not for legal purposes but as a source of social benefits. And the fact of multiple jobs is now generally understood not as a fault of any system but as a necessary labor strategy for properly "flexible" workers under new forms of capitalism. The phenomenon of shopping provides another example of the same sort of process. The large number of hours spent by women and elders on procuring household provisions in a shortage economy was a familiar complaint during the socialist years; often only the informal and sometimes illegal socialist markets located outside of cities could supply needed goods. Since 1989, however, many women have spent similarly long hours in household shopping. In a time of steep inflation and lowered incomes, travel to distant flea markets and careful comparisons of prices are necessary to find affordable products.

Striking examples of a similar process involve the revaluation of long-standing skills. Women's skills in a wide range of services, formerly part of a barter economy, can now be used for waged income. It is also the case that women's education in languages and accounting, for instance, have become more valuable in a postindustrial capitalist environment with multinational corporations and increasing tourism than the training for heavy industry and engineering that were the more masculine forms of higher education in the socialist era. But there is a certain irony here. As jobs in economics, finance, and accounting become lucrative, men are being retrained for such careers, and women's skills, gained in the communist system, might suffer another and negative revaluation. Finally, it seems worth pointing to another continuity based on revaluation, this time in political practice. The orientation to the centralized state, familiar from socialism, now takes the form of NGOs and local governments focused on applying to the center, on its own terms, for whatever money and assistance it has deemed worth giving. While in the communist era this was widely resented as the imposition of a distant power structure on local government, it is now reinterpreted. The administrators of towns, counties, and local organizations are eager to engage in the competition. Accommodating to the commands of the state bureaucracy is nothing new, but now it appears as "grantsmanship."

If what seem like old practices are transformed because they are being interpreted in new ways, the opposite is also a lively process. What appear to be new arrangements and solutions are given legitimacy and authority by linking them to old patterns. The novelty of some ideas and practices is hardly noticed, as they are cloaked in the guise of continuity. The permutations of the cultural distinction between public and private—in contrast to what public and private have meant in practice—is perhaps the most striking example of this, but there are numerous more specific ones. Many of those women who are becoming stay-at-home wives and mothers imagine themselves to be reclaiming older patterns of bourgeois femininity, or imagined Western forms as our evidence from Hungary suggests. But closer examination of what these women actually do, their various compromises and innovations, suggests that the link with the past is very much a form of "invention of tradition." Politicians, parties, and governments relying on discourses about reproduction to create their own legitimacy are engaging in similar strategies of making the new seem old, or at least "natural" and, as such, a source of authority. It is noteworthy that the ideology of communism, certainly in the early years, valorized "modernity" and the new, as have earlier revolutions. In the postsocialist era, by contrast, and especially in politics, it is the aura of age—and borrowing from varying hues of political tradition in Western Europe—that has gained a similar ability to authorize the present.

The borrowing of tradition and the erasure of tradition go hand in hand; they are simultaneous features of transformation itself. Current efforts at "feminist" organizing, whether these are based in universities or not, often seem caught in the middle of accusations that feminism is illegitimate, foreign to the region, versus other accusations or assertions that it is just a continuation of pre-war patterns of international activism by women. The understanding of the income bifurcation increasingly evident in the region is also a case in which people argue about what is old and what is new: Are these "new rich" just descendants of the old nomenklatura, having taken advantage of their former networks to gain a different kind of power? Or are they the talented few—for instance, women who headed banks when these were low priority enterprises— who have been able to sell old talents in new ways to make money in the new capitalism?

Turning now to the second set of questions, we review the ways in which integrating the evidence about gender relations from East Central Europe within feminist theory broadens our understanding about the relationship of men and women to states and political processes. The mirroring and mutual watching by "East" and "West" that were so typical of the Cold War era are further clarified by a gender analysis that puts the two sides together, thereby highlighting similarities rather than only differences. We have already described, in the introduction, the intriguing parallels in public discussion about "families" and their crises. Allegorical discussions of reproduction—coded morality tales—that authorized politics have been as common in the West as in the East. Naturalizations of gender difference also occurred on both sides during the 1970s and 1980s. As sociobiology gained influence in American social science, pitched against more constructionist approaches to gender, the official communist rhetoric of equality between the sexes coexisted with a social scientific and popular understanding of men and women as fundamentally different. This set the stage for developments after 1989, when the idealized bourgeois family was re-presented as natural, and early communist ideals to change it were used by anticommunists as evidence for communism's violation of natural law.

Integrating evidence from East Central Europe more closely with evidence about gender from other regions also adds nuance and complexity to feminist arguments about the nature of women's "dependence." The comparison contributes additional twists to the contradictions apparent in Anglo-American notions of "dependence" and the view of "independence" these imply. One strain of Western feminism celebrates the ideal of women's autonomy. As we have discussed, there are good historical reasons for the fact that sometimes, as in the case of reproductive decisions, most East Central Europe women are eager not for autonomy from husbands and male partners, but rather for their increased involvement. "Autonomy" and "independence" are usefully relativized and culturally contextualized in this kind of comparison.

There is currently nostalgia among the poor and working poor of East Central Europe for the state subsidies they have lost during the 1990s. Women workers in privatized factories, for instance, complain that their hard work no longer gets them the institutional services and benefits that they had come to see as their entitlements under socialism. One might view this as dependence on the state, and their brittle marriages as the kind of independence from individual men that was made possible by state support. But many such workers in East Central Europe sense clearly what is often forgotten in American and some Western European feminist arguments about independence from states and men: Selling one's labor without the support of kin and social benefits is not necessarily emancipation. It can also be a kind of dependence, this time on unpredictable and unaccountable market forces.

Studies of gender in East Central Europe also contribute to feminist analyses of political participation. Arenas of political activity—parliaments, voluntary associations, charity and humanitarian efforts, international NGOs—are themselves gendered, and their coding as "male" or "female" changes over time. Political action depends, in part, on publicly available categories through which people can construct "interests" or identities. But there is a great range of possibilities in how people actually take up, embrace, act on, and inhabit such identities. Through their policies and rhetoric, states try in various ways to classify people, to constitute subjects as "citizens," "workers," "mothers." Similarly, social movements perform the same sort of action, presupposing that they have a constituency and "calling" on subjects in movement activities and discourses.

But people's selves, their subjectivities, are not so closely tied to such political discourses and practices. This is suggested by many kinds of evidence we have presented. One example is people's outright opposition, subversion, or seeming complicity with laws about reproductive behavior through which states try to constitute their subjects. Another example appears in letters-to-the-editor columns of communist era newspapers in which women sometimes took on but at other times protested against images of themselves as "brave victims." Closer to current events, further evidence is provided by the reluctance of many women in East Central Europe at this historical juncture to declare themselves "feminists" despite the facts of gender discrimination and the increasing availability of the category as a political rubric. To put it another way: there is no automatic link between subjectivities created out of the patterns and practices of everyday life on the one hand and the identity categories evident in the discourses of political movements and state agencies on the other. Political discourse succeeds in mobilizing people only when they recognize themselves as its addressees. Such recognitions must be actively created, and when successfully done, their construction is later effectively obscured.

For the better part of the twentieth century, East Central Europe has been marked by dramatic political and economic changes coexisting with often less remarked long-term continuities. Otherwise stated, different kinds of change have had differing temporalities. And since 1989 "East" and "West" have become less starkly divergent. Global trends are similarly affecting Europeans, east and west. For example, the number of international, humanitarian, and socially activist NGOs has increased noticeably. In the economic realm, social provisioning by states has decreased while financial insecurity for workers has increased. However, for those in East Central Europe, these trends are postsocialist phenomena, occurring in the context of democracies and market economies in formation. Over the last decade, there have been rapid changes in opportunity structures as well as in the structuring of inequalities. Widening differences in wealth and standards of living are striking, now almost as great within the countries of the region as between them and their western neighbors. How people interpret these changes is a crucial aspect of transformation—and of its analysis. Our own understanding is informed as much by cultural as by political and economic frameworks. We have explored conceptual and empirical foundations for analyzing how gender shapes the everyday lives of men and women in what are often insecure and unpredictable new circumstances. Moreover, throughout this essay we have argued for the constitutive role of gender in the very processes of political and economic change. In sum, a gendered perspective is central to understanding the dynamics of postsocialism.

Notes

Chapter 1
After Socialism

1. We build on a growing, if separate, body of research on the situation of women in East Central Europe. This work is rich in essayistic reflections as well as empirical analyses and theoretical formulations. See, for instance, Corrin (1992, 1993); DeSoto and Anderson (1993); Einhorn (1993); Feischmidt, Magyari-Vincze, and Zentai (1997); Funk and Mueller (1993); Jaquette and Wolchik (1998b), Moghadam (1993); Posadskaya (1994); Rai, Pilkington, and Phizaklea (1992); Renne (1997); Rueschemeyer (1994), among others. Doubtless we have omitted many worthy works because the literatures in this and some of the other subfields we engage in this essay are too large for full coverage.

2. This definition relies on Joan Scott's (1988) influential essay. We have also been stimulated in thinking about the effects of gender on postsocialist politics by several traditions of feminist work on states and politics, including the early Marxist approaches, the critiques of liberal theory, various formulations of "patriarchy," Scandinavian and other European contributions about welfare states as gendered phenomena, and critical poststructuralist approaches to states as discursive constructions. We discuss these works in detail in the chapters that follow.

3. The East/West opposition is a form of orientalism, emanating from centers of power in Western Europe and taken up—for their own purposes and often with alacrity—at first by elites in the region, later in popular imaginings as well. It identifies the East as the negative end of a cultural contrast that pits civilization against barbarism, wealth against poverty, development against backwardness, among other oppositions. But knowing that regional categories are culturally and historically constructed does not mean we can dispense with them. We continue to use "East Central Europe" as a convenient label for an admittedly complex and changing situation. For an outline of the political economic relations in the last two centuries that made possible a category of East Central Europe and other contemporaneous regional categories, see Berend and Ránki (1974) and Janos (1982); for a longer view, see Szűcs (1988). Among the first and most notable of the coded discussions of the 1980s were those of Kundera (1984) and Timothy Garton Ash (1986); these as well as later works of Garton Ash (1999) and Judt (1996) were part of a lively international debate. For analysis of these durable and recursive imaginings about "East" and "West" see Gal (1991a). Wolff (1994) and Todorova (1997) provide detailed historical studies of the development of intra-European orientalist discourse. Burawoy and Verdery (1999:2–3) have underscored the particular significance of ethnographic research for analyzing the temporal and spatial dimensions of postsocialist transformations.

4. The tensions between East Central European and West European and American scholars were aired by the Hungarian journal *Replika* in 1992; the discussion continued in its first English language issue in 1996, where the article by Csepeli, Örkény, and Scheppele (1996) was published. The journal published their piece in Hungarian in 1998, when other scholars contributed further arguments. See Hadas (1998) in the same issue for a nuanced view that suggests there have been many models and forms for East Central European contributions. See Kornai (1980) and Hankiss (1988) for the concepts noted.

5. This book is a much expanded and rethought version of the original introduction to Gal and Kligman (2000). In that collaborative volume, fourteen original essays cover topics ranging from reproductive legislation to marriage patterns, women's business enterprises, nongovernmental organizations, as well as parliamentary politics and media representations of men and women. See the introduction to that book for details on choice of countries and for the project's intellectual evolution.

6. In the United States during the Cold War, the study of "East Central Europe," like the study of other regions considered of crucial military and strategic importance, became a separate, sometimes intellectually isolated, field of training, funding, and expertise. Since 1989, the interaction between government, private foundations, espionage, and the American research establishment has gained renewed attention from scholars excavating the nature of their own training. Area studies in the United States have become particularly problematic; they are in financial and intellectual "crisis," as the geopolitical relations that brought them into being are being tranformed. See Wallerstein (1998) and Simpson (1998) for historical and critical discussions.

7. As this paragraph makes particularly clear, we are less than consistent in our use of the terms—"communism," "socialism," and "state socialism"—to characterize the regimes of East Central Europe before 1989. There seems to be, nevertheless, a telling if unintended pattern to our choices. We thank Eva Fodor for her amusing observation, on reading the manuscript, that when we emphasize the oppressive qualities of the regimes, we tend to use "communism"; when we point to their more progressive features, we tend to use "socialism." Certainly, "communism" has long had perjorative connotations in the West. Rather than trying to change our usage, we underscore Fodor's suggestion that this might well be the way the terms are being discursively (re)constructed in the post-1989 era.

8. For example, Borneman (1992) discusses the reciprocal making of family policy in East and West Germany; many ethnographic accounts have noted, in passing, the importance of Western popular culture in East Central Europe; see most recently a special section, "Fogyasztói szocializmus" (Consumer socialism), of the Hungarian journal *Replika* in which the example of the kitchen debate is mentioned by Vörös (1997).

9. Much of the political science literature, as well as that in sociology, has been framed in terms of "transitions" to democracy that can be compared across regions, as in Greskovits (1998), Jaquette and Wolchik (1998b); Linz and Stepan (1996); Nelson (1994); and Przeworski (1991), or as transitions to market economics. For overviews of the latter, see Szelenyi and Kostello (1996) and

the entire Symposium on Market Transition in the *American Journal of Sociology* 101, no. 4 (1996). Dissatisfaction with the paradigm of "transition" was early voiced by many sociologists and anthropologists. Róna-Tas (1998) provides a useful assessment of the debates between "transition" theories and those that speak of "transformation"; see also Böröcz (1995) for a critique of the assumptions of "transition" and "transformation," and Stark and Bruszt (1998) and Burawoy and Verdery (1999) for more recent formulations. Pickles and Smith (1998), while using the term "transition," are among those who emphasize the significant diversity in transitions, the differences among countries in the strategies and pace by which changes happen. One difference between the two approaches is the rejection of teleology by those favoring the term "transformation"; another is the recognition that in East Central Europe, in contrast to Latin America and other regions, the processes were not only "transitions" to democracy but were simultaneously political, economic, and social "transformations."

Chapter 2
Reproduction as Politics

1. In pointing to the parallels among countries in the amount of attention paid to abortion, we do not want to minimize the substantial differences in the exact terms of their laws about abortion, the medical means by which abortions are performed, the costs, and other factors. See Gal and Kligman (2000) for discussions of abortion legislation across the region. David (1999) offers a useful, detailed guide to such policies.

2. For descriptions of the abortion debates in Germany, see DeSoto (1993); Maleck-Lewy (1995); Maleck-Lewy and Ferree (2000), Nelles (1991–92); and Nimsch (1991–92). On the Hungarian debate see Gal (1994), Huseby-Darvas (1996), and Sándor (ms). For Romania see Kligman (1992, 1998); on Serbia, Croatia, and Slovenia, see Bahovec (1991), Meznarić (n.d., 1997a, 1997b), Renne and Ule (1998); for Bulgaria see Daskalova (2000) and Petrova (1993); for Poland see Fuszara (1991) and Zielińska (2000), among many others. Many of these studies provide evidence from opinion polls showing that there were no examples of popular demand for restriction of access to abortion.

3. The feminist literature on public/private is voluminous, with Rosaldo's (1974) influential piece as one of the earliest contributions. In anthropology, a thorough critique of cross-cultural, universalist approaches appeared in Collier and Yanagisako (1987), with related arguments on the nature/culture dichotomy in MacCormack and Strathern (1990). See di Leonardo (1991) for a critical review. The political theorists in recent feminist writing have also made important contributions in thinking about this dichotomy, as have social historians. We discuss their work in detail in chapters 3 and 4.

4. This means that within a discursive approach such as the one we take here, functionalist theories are but one set among many other arguments that justify intervention (or restraint) in managing and controlling reproduction. Biological reproduction is not the same as social reproduction, although some social theories have inadvertently collapsed the two.

5. On monarchical systems see the classic work of Kantorowicz (1957) and

the critical discussions of Feeley-Harnik (1985) and Hunt (1991). Gallagher (1987) and Jordanova (1995) provide useful analyses of changing European ideas about population and reproduction into the nineteenth century. Foucault's work on governmentality has inspired a large literature; for the first wave of this see Donzelot (1979) and the articles in Burchell, Gordon, and Miller (1991); Hirshman (1977) juxtaposes the two forms of rule.

6. The example of Frederick the Great comes from Foucault's (1991) discussion of governmentality, which engages the same issue. Among the many questioning Foucault's dichotomy we have found Lindenfeld (1997) particularly useful.

7. Offen (1984) characterized nineteenth-century France's demographic problems described in the previous paragraph. She also suggested that welfare and population must be studied together with feminism and nationalism, and on the terrain of reproduction. Some of the feminist literature on the development of welfare states explores the particular implications of this aspect of state power for women: see Abramovitz (1988); Bock and Thane (1991); and Brown (1992). Hacking (1990); Herzfeld (1987); and Linke (1990) are among the many useful analyses of the development of scholarly disciplines in the context of state regulation; Lindenfeld (1997) discusses the German "sciences of state."

8. There have been many criticisms of the unified, personified view of the state; we have found Abrams (1988 [1977]) and Connell (1990) particularly helpful, as well as the feminist work on the welfare state. Kligman's study of Romania is an ethnography of the state from the perspective of reproduction, noting: "States are always given form through the actions of people" (1998:4). See also Brown (1992) and discussion in chapter 4. In contrast to rhetorics of the "retreat" of states in East Central Europe, we examine the changed forms of their continued presence.

9. An excellent overview of feminist historiography on family strategies and social reproduction in Europe is Brenner and Laslett (1984); Watkins (1991) is exemplary in exploring the relationship of family strategies about reproduction to increasing state and market integration in Western Europe over the last century and a half. See also Kertzer and Hogan (1989), Schneider and Schneider (1996), and Skinner (1997) for anthropological views on demography and family strategy.

10. We will return to the reproductive ideology of nationalism and communism in later sections; Michel and Koven (1990) provide a useful synthesis of developments in the maternalist feminisms of Western Europe. For a variety of feminist ideologies of reproduction see also Bock and Thane (1991); Bridenthal, Grossman, and Kaplan (1989) discuss eugenics, sex reformers, and other social movements in twentieth-century Germany.

11. Note that in points 1, 2, and 4 reproductive issues are directly involved in constructing politics. In the third point, by contrast, discussions of reproduction are indirectly involved; they mediate other concerns.

12. For a general overview of denunciations and their effects in the European context through the last few centuries, see Fitzpatrick and Gellately (1996). The mechanism of denunciations in the various communist states has a large litera-

ture: Romania is discussed in Kligman (1998); Poland in Gross (1988) and Toranska (1987); Germany in Gellately (1997); Hungary in Rév (1987) and Hodos (1987), among others.

13. For intriguing discussions of this aspect of fascism, see Berezin (1997) and Spackman (1996) as well as deGrazia (1992).

14. We note that although the discourses and practices of state agencies "hail" subjects—to use Althusser's terminology—this does not assure that people will actually "take up" or inhabit such positions; nor does it explain how and through what meaning-making processes people come to live in the subjectivities offered by institutions and movements. We return to this issue in chapters 5 and 6.

15. For details on the Hungarian abortion debate, see Gal (1994). Contemporaneous with the abortion debates in Germany was a controversy about the status and treatment of non-European and southern European immigrants, about German xenophobia and the definition of German citizenship. It would be interesting to see how these two debates drew on each other, discussing different but related aspects of "rights" and identity. In the United States the pitting of women's rights against fetal rights in the abortion debate is arguably a veiled comment about American ideals of citizenship. Here too there are hidden echoes of illegal immigration issues. Berlant (1993) has suggested that the ideal American citizen is the innocent, politically passive, and helpless fetus, rather than the sexually active, and therefore less than "innocent," woman. Mosse (1985) and more recently Povinelli (1997), among others, have discussed the ways in which citizenship is often linked to normative sexuality. Zielińska (2000) discusses the implications of the abortion debate for Polish politics.

16. The scholarship on nationalism used to distinguish sharply between ethnic and civic forms. It has also sometimes been claimed that either one or the other form characterized entire countries and even regions, frequently locating civic nationalism in the "West" and ethnonationalism to the "East." More recently, scholars have noted that far from being mutually exclusive, civic- and ethnonationalism coexist as different positions within a political field, both potentially available for elites to mobilize. Nationalisms are therefore more usefully distinguished as different stances within a single arena of argument. As we are suggesting here, reproductive arguments within single countries often center on whether women should be considered "citizens" (a term of civic nationalism) or "mothers of the nation." See Brubaker (1998) for a review of these approaches to nationalism. As many scholars have pointed out, the two categories of nation share many aspects of common origin. For instance, both were involved in early modern attempts to justify the sovereignty of "peoples" against monarchs.

17. A recent event will illustrate this phenomenon. In 1997, a Czech couple brought home a Romani child from a children's home; however, the child was of Slovak nationality. Although she had been born in the Czech Republic, her birth parents had not applied for permanent residence. The Czech couple attempting to adopt the child was soon denied childcare benefits. The social benefits law had changed, and because the child did not have Czech citizenship, this meant the family was ineligible. Moreover, because a foreigner had been

incorporated into the family, they lost the benefits for which they had been eligible on behalf of their own biological child. See "Adopting a Child? Don't Want a Foreigner." *Mlada Fronta Denes*, October 23, 1997.

18. The feminist literature on nation and gender covers most contemporary nation-states. The collection by Anthias and Yuval-Davis and their introduction to it (1989) were important early contributions. More recently, special issues of *Gender and History* (Hall et al. 1993), and of *Feminist Review* (Whitehead et al. 1993), have further explored these relationships. Not all the contributors distinguish clearly between nation and state. Verdery (1996) discusses gender and nationalism in Eastern Europe, as do many of the studies on women in East Central Europe cited in the first note of chapter 1. While most of these studies are about gender in general, Heng and Devan (1992) on state fatherhood has particular relevance for our discussion of reproduction. Chatterjee (1993) develops the important notion of postcolonial nationalism as based in the domestic and spiritual, as linked to women. See Băban (2000) for an example of contraceptive technologies in East Central Europe as signs of modernity.

19. There is a growing literature on rape as a weapon of war in the Balkans, although some of this writing is problematic because of its ahistorical approach. See Stiglmayer (1994).

20. Brubaker (1996). Violence in the Balkans has repeatedly started in areas where ethnic minorities perceived themselves to be under threat; Benderly (1997), Bracewell (1996), Mežnarić (1994), and Mostov (1995) discuss and analyze cases of rape and rumors about rape that mobilized nationalist sentiment in Kosovo and Serbia. The classic case of discouraging "unworthy" populations is Nazism; see Bock (1991).

21. See Mežnarić (n.d., 1997a, 1997b) for details of this process. Those who migrate out form ethnic diasporas and consider themselves members of the nation, emphasizing relation to an "imagined community" rather than inhabitance of a territory.

22. For instance, in contrast to those in Eastern and Western Europe, American battles about abortion have been posed as questions about the bounds of "privacy," women's self-determination, and images of the sort of female life worth living (e.g., Ginsburg [1989], Luker [1984], Petchesky [1990]). In Western Europe the terms of debate have formed around the responsibilities of the state to women (see Glendon 1987), and women's natural desires to mother; in China, as also in many postcolonial countries, around the meanings of modernity (Anagnost 1995).

23. Socialist states were chronically weak. See, for instance, the early discussions of this in Fehér, Heller, and Márkus (1984); also see Gross (1988), Przeworski (1991), Rév (1987), Sztaniszkis (1991), and Verdery (1996). For their inheritors, state forms continue to be deeply contested. Linz and Stepan (1996) make the point that "statehood" cannot be taken for granted, in fact must be constructed, in situations of "transition." They note, as well, that at least for those cases they investigated, markets do not legitimate democratic politics; rather, democratic politics set the stage for popular acceptance of markets and privatization that often produce unpalatable and highly visible differences in wealth. For a parallel discussion, see also Stark and Bruszt (1998). We note that

there is considerable controversy about the sequencing of marketization and democratization.

24. Postsocialist countries have no monopoly on morality tales created out of the reproductive behavior of women. In this, there is much continuity with the communist past, and such tactics are everywhere characteristic of reproductive politics.

25. The construction of authority through rhetorical devices such as "quotatives" and reported speech that invoke other realms (e.g., the ancestors or the past) and allow leaders to take on the voice of already recognized, authoritative social entities (to "ventriloquize" them, so to speak) is a theme in linguistic anthropology. See Lucy (1993), and Silverstein and Urban (1996) for detailed examples and exegesis.

26. The German example comes from the work of Dölling, Hann, and Scholze (2000); for more information on the Serbian and Albanian cases, see once again Mežnarić (1994) and Mostov (1995), among others.

27. We have earlier discussed nationalist and communist visions of women; the example of the colonial state is from Stoler (1991); Stone (1996) and Mosse (1985) provide examples of republican motherhood, stressing the differences between republican and liberal notions of citizenship, and discussing women's roles in making male citizenship. The contradictions of liberal states on the issue of reproductive rights have been discussed by Petchesky (1990), among others.

28. For a description of how a collection of names protesting abortion regulations in Hungary became a dangerous political act in 1973, see Kőrösi (1984). The organization of Polish women around abortion is described by Fuszara (1991); for Hungary see Szalai (1991)

29. Watson (1993) has argued persuasively that the "masculinization" of Polish politics is an active process involving the revaluation of male virtues. Further evidence about the masculinization of politics is provided by Kligman (1996) and by Băban, Daskalova, and Grunberg, all in Gal and Kligman (2000).

30. See Brown (1992) for a synthesis of the various feminist analyses of the state that all fit under the first characterization; Connell (1990) also follows this general strategy. The second sort of study is best exemplified by Koven and Michel's (1993) comparison of the effects of feminist movements on state policies across western Europe, but is characteristic as well of much writing on the possiblities of activism in the welfare state; see for instance Sassoon (1987) and Siim (1988).

31. For fuller discussion of such maneuvers, see, for instance, Kligman (1998).

32. Einhorn (1993) and Corrin (1993) have argued that the attempt to eject women from work is a way of dealing with unemployment.

33. The actions of other governments are also important. When the Reagan and Bush administrations in the United States denied international funding of abortion-related activities, they were appealing to domestic audiences, shoring up their own morality stances. Ironically, however, Ceauşescu's anti-abortion policies were not publicly criticized until after 1989, although the horrors had been increasingly known abroad. For the international context of women's rights and related issues, see Molyneux (1994). For discussion of the Irish case

in which abortion became an issue for the European Court, see Phelan (1992) and Peebles (1997); Sándor (ms) addresses the effects on the Hungarian court.

Chapter 3
Dilemmas of Public and Private

1. Some observers, especially feminists, have decried the supposed return to past forms; others welcome and advocate them. Journal articles, for instance, discuss the "redomestication of women" or going "back to the future" (see, for instance, Renner and Ule 1998).

2. See especially Pateman (1988a), whose feminist critique is a direct response to the writings of eighteenth-century political theory. In other cases, such as Landes (1989) and Fraser (1989, 1997), the response is also an engagement with Habermas (1989), whose influential work on the public sphere reoriented discussions of public/private, but without directly taking up questions of gender.

3. The Marxist view on public/private usually took the form of debates about the relation of production to reproduction, with Engels's work on the origins of the family as the earliest contribution. This tradition is discussed at length by feminists; see, for example, Young, Wolkowitz, and McCullagh (1981). The parallel arguments about public/private in structural-functionalist social theory are analyzed by Collier and Yanagisako (1987), who reject an earlier universalism and argue for cultural specificity of the distinctions, as we do here. The liberal and conservative discussions of related distinctions are reviewed, in the context of a history of the notion of "civil society," by Keane (1988a,b). We take these up in chapter 5. For a discussion of Habermas's views on public/private and further evidence of popular and scholarly European notions, see Calhoun (1992). The feminist literature on the public/private distinction is voluminous; feminist theorists have discussed this opposition in the context of states, politics, and patriarchy. See for instance, Eisenstein (1984), Hartsock (1985), Pateman (1988a), and Phillips (1990). The recent collection edited by Landes (1998) brings together some of the most important works of the last two decades.

4. See especially parts 2 and 4 of Habermas (1989).

5. We draw here on Benhabib's (1998 [1992]) discussion, as well as comments throughout Landes (1998). Others have typologized philosophical approaches to public/private on other grounds—for instance, on the question of where, in which sphere (public or private), the individual political actor is constituted.

6. In ethnographic and textual studies it is crucial to pay close attention to the meanings of terms used by actors to name the spheres we are here calling by the English terms "public" and "private." There are rarely exact semantic correspondences of such terms across languages, despite frequent cognates throughout Europe. Importantly, however, the semiotic processes that establish opposed domains of this kind do not depend on similar lexical items to name the domains, but rather on the widespread pragmatic possibility of using in interac-

tion a variety of indexicals—deictics and shifters—in ways that signal more proximate versus more distanced relationships, or front-stage and backstage events. See Peirce's writings (as assembled in 1940) on indexicals and the tripartite theory of signs. For shifters see Jakobson (1990 [1957]), and see Silverstein (1976) on the social significance of shifters. Goffman's (1979) notion of footing and Bakhtin's (1981) voicing are somewhat different approaches to the same phenomena.

7. For further explication of how such fractal semiotic processes work, see Gal (1991a), Gal and Irvine (1995), Irvine and Gal (2000), on language ideologies. See Abbott (1990) for a general discussion of the self-similarity of a wide range of social structures, cultural processes and the imagery of fractals. Earlier writers such as Evans-Pritchard and Gregory Bateson noted similar processes of opposition and differentiation in segmentary kinship and gender systems. A familiar example of public and private that can be understood as a fractal distinction is the division of space in bourgeois residences. The privacy of the entire living area (when contrasted to the street) is itself divided into more public parlors/living rooms and more private bedrooms. Examples of divisions of space as well as more fluid self-similar embeddings of public/private can be found in much ethnographic work. Goffman's (1959) analysis of frontstage and backstage can serve as a model of how, even without legal or conventional spatial divisions, public events are often subdivided into more private moments and more public parts. A private exchange can be embedded in a public one (and vice versa) by changing the forms of talk and gesture in interactional routines. The general conceptual point is that the public/private distinction resembles other cultural divisions (East/West, male/female, modern/traditional) in having the semiotic feature of being self-similar, and indexically applicable to different contexts, identities, and relationships.

8. For instance, in the United States, it was in part second wave feminist activism that created a "public" inside the private by arguing that households (private) are as conflict-ridden as other institutions, and by saying that they ought to be run on democratic (public) principles.

9. The investigation of "separate spheres" in Europe has produced a sizable literature. See, for example, Brenner and Laslett (1984). Frader and Rose (1996) attend especially to this issue among the working classes. Davidoff (1995: chap. 8) discusses in detail the approaches taken by feminist historians of Europe to this dichotomy. Many of the works cited in note 3 also provide analyses of the historical development of the division of labor in the household and workplace. We found that as an ethnographically detailed historical study, the work of Davidoff and Hall (1987) was especially useful on gender division in the making of the English middle class.

10. Frader and Rose (1996) review the arguments among social and cultural historians about the gendered effects of industrialization and class formation. Similarly, Honeyman and Goodman (1991) synthesize the monographic literature to provide an outline of the development of a gendered division of labor in manufacturing. The gender imagery of the middle classes came to signify, in part, the moral superiority that would legitimate middle-class political power. Significantly, middle-class morality and respectability soon became the emblem

of national identity in many European nations; see for instance Mosse (1985) and Frykman and Lofgren (1987). The studies collected in deGrazia (1996) provide evidence of these shifts; Folbre (1991) traces the devaluation of household work in the nineteenth century.

11. For the relationship of Eastern and Western European economic change, see Berend and Ránki (1974) and Janos (1982). Much social historical work, for instance by Hungarian historians such as Hanák (1975, 1998), Gerő (1993), and Gyáni (1997, 1999), has documented the rise of bourgeois patterns across the urban areas of the region.

12. It would be interesting to investigate the arrangements of the aristocracy as well. The patterns outlined in this and the previous paragraph are based on descriptions of gender arrangements among agricultural workers in Hungary by Lampland (1995) and of patrilineal systems in Romania (Kligman 1988) and Yugoslavia (Denitch 1974). The historical background of recent changes in Bulgaria also provides supportive evidence; see Todorova (1993), Petrova (1993), and Meurs (1998).

13. Discussions of the utopian moment in Soviet gender ideology include Buckley (1989), Stites (1991), and Clements (1997). Lapidus (1978) also speaks to these and related issues.

14. This description of the interwar period draws on a range of sources. The ideology of reformers is discussed by Grossman (1983) as well as in several studies in Bridenthal, Grossman, and Kaplan (1989); for the strategies and representations of communist parties in this period see Weitz (1996) and Buckley (1989).

15. The first two sections of Wolchik and Meyer (1985) provide valuable information about gender relations and the organizing of women's movements in the interwar period in several countries of East Central Europe, stressing the differences in economic development and demographic patterns across the region.

16. Many feminist theorists have found the term "patriarchy" adequate for describing the whole range of systems of male dominance we are analyzing here, distinguishing between "private patriarchy" and "public patriarchy"; see for instance Siims (1988), Sassoon (1987), and Walby (1990). Jones and Jónasdóttir (1988) is also relevant here. Broadly, patriarchies operate by excluding women from the ownership of the key resources necessary for successful participation in the public, but these resources, and the means of exclusion, will vary across different types of patriarchies. We agree with the importance of such exclusion, but want in addition to draw attention to how various institutions such as agencies of the state, labor markets, and education are organized around cultural conceptions of gender difference. We use the term "gender regime" because it evokes a continuing concern not only for the practices of gender relations, but also for the assumptions through which gender arrangements are understood and through which they control social actors. There are many permutations in the way that gender difference is conceptualized and used to secure the subordination of women. We use "regime" somewhat differently than does Connell (1987), and with an awareness of the irony of the term in the region about which we write.

17. For a discussion of the homogenizing ideal of socialism, see Lefort (1986), as well as Kligman (1992), who provides the example of Stakhanovite mothers. The attempt to erase gender difference is a good empirical example of the feminist insight that gender has varying salience in social life, and is not always equally significant. Fodor (1997a) discusses the policy strategies of homogenizing versus differentiating women.

18. It is interesting to note the contrast with second wave feminism in the United States and Western Europe, which also voiced fundamental critiques of the public/private distinction and recommended women's entry into waged work. But American feminism of that period took a different tack. Rather than advocating that housework and reproduction be "eliminated" by making them public, many strands of second wave feminism argued that men should do more work in the private, a sphere that was itself redefined as political and in need of democratization.

19. We will return to the comparison with Western developments and welfare states in chapter 4. McIntyre (1985) as well as authors of other articles collected in Wolchik and Meyer (1985) describe the policies concerning households in this period. Fodor (1997a) demonstrates persuasively how policy makers viewed women's political potential during the communist period.

20. There is a voluminous literature on the definition, development, and importance of the "second economy," or informal economy, in many of the countries of the region. The most accessible review of this empirical and theoretical work in English is the collection edited by Nee and Stark (1989).

21. Recent work on Hungary suggests, moreover, that there was much deliberate manipulation of the public and private distinction in trying to reform the communist economic system. Planners working within what they perceived as the rigid constraints of Soviet orthodoxy were creative in subtly redefining and subdividing legal terms that delineated public and private (Selény 1994). The results of these regulations are described by Stark (1996), who provides an account of the mixed forms within Hungarian firms during the communist period. People in their domestic practices, facing the same structural rigidities, were also creative with these distinctions, and in similarly fractal ways. For instance, Kenedi (1981) describes with wry wit the building of a private house in Budapest, using such mixed (public and private) resources.

22. Among the many ethnographic descriptions across the region of the kind of atomization and complicity we are alluding to here, see Kligman (1998) on Romania; Gal (1997a), Kenedi (1981), and Rév (1987), among others, on Hungary; Toranska (1987) and Wedel (1986) on Poland; Kukutz and Havemann (1990) and Gellately (1997) among others on Germany; Humphrey (1994) on Soviet examples. The interpenetration—rather than separation—of two distinct ethical systems, of public and private, and of kin and government have been noted by observers. We are highlighting, in addition, the way the fractal embedding of public/private dichotomies allowed people to switch unself-consciously between levels of contrast in ethics/people/activities, reframing and thus relativizing their moral judgments as they recast their relation to acts or persons as public or private. A brief report by Wedel from Poland is illustrative of how theft could be reframed: "An employee took a desk from a state-owned

factory, intending to resell it. He left the desk in a truck near his apartment building until it could be delivered to the intended purchasers. But to his dismay, it disappeared. He complained bitterly that 'people are dishonest and immoral'" (1986:15).

23. This property of abstraction is crucial in understanding ideological formations. One approach to describing it more precisely is through the semiotic distinction between "indexical" expressions and "referentiality." Because the referential meaning of shifters is always in part linked to the moment of interaction—the speech event—their denotation varies by context. It is possible, however, to use such indexical expressions (public/private, we/they) as though they did not have this property, but were instead simply labels for objects or activities that then appear to be fixed features of the world. This possibility is an ordinary aspect of communication, but with evident ideological possibilities and consequences. See Silverstein (1976) and Bauman and Briggs (1990) for further discussion. See also Bourdieu's (1991:131–34) notion of "theory effect," although he does not attend to how communicative principles allow this effect to occur.

24. The gender politics of "antipolitics" is discussed by Goven (1993).

25. The many citations in note 1 of the introduction all allude to these conditions, as have virtually all ethnographic accounts of the region in the last twenty years. See especially Einhorn (1993) for a useful overview of studies about the double and triple burden. In Romania one must understand the triple burden to include forced childbirth. In some countries grandfathers were as important to the maintenance of the household as grandmothers.

26. For vivid and persuasive studies of media images during the communist period see Dölling (1993) and Rosenberg (1985). In our discussion in this and the next paragraphs we have relied on the recent work of Marody and Giza-Poleszczuk, Băban, Mršević, Kovács and Váradi, Daskalova and Dölling et al., all in Gal and Kligman (2000). See also the work of Blagojević (1996) on related issues.

27. Note that for highly educated women in the West, this was followed by another phase, in which a sense of incompetence was not entirely overcome, but was compounded by the impossible double bind with its expectations of overachievement in all domains, domestic as well as professional. There was thus an ironic mirroring between the socialist "superwoman" and the image of "superwoman" developed in the West at roughly the same time.

28. The descriptions in this paragraph draw on research by Băban, Kovács and Váradi, Marody and Giza-Poleszczuk, and Mršević, all in Gal and Kligman (2000).

29. See Kornai (1994) for an influential analysis of these dramatic economic changes—what he calls transformational recession—especially the virtually unprecedented drop in production after 1989. Blanchard (1997) provides a concise summary of economists' debates on production, disorganization, and apparent recuperation since 1994. Economic assessments of the region, while wary of the unreliable statistics, nevertheless concur that those with lower wages have suffered greater losses than the well paid. Furthermore, in many countries the incidence of low-paid workers (defined as those earning less than two-thirds of

the median wage) has increased to as much as one-fifth of all workers. In some cases, a small portion of the population, often the highly educated or those located in rapid growth sectors, have experienced increasing incomes. Thus, the "compressed" earnings distribution characteristic of central planning has been quickly changed into distributions similar to the OECD countries. These figures do not include the effects of growing "informal" economies in all countries, in some cases estimated to account for as much as 30% of GDP (see Milanović 1998, Rutkowski 1996). For a discussion of the institutional aspects of the economic crisis, see Elster, Offe, and Preuss (1998). Einhorn (1993) summarizes women's economic situation in the region since 1989.

30. This choice of topics is evident in an extensive review of the past decade's work on postsocialist economic change in the disciplines of economics and economic sociology (Róna-Tas 1998).

31. Burawoy and Lukács (1992) describe the development of labor markets within state socialism, in Hungary. Ironically, after 1989, it was often those men working in heavy indusry—what had earlier been a highly valued sector—who were among the first to be laid off and who have often had the most difficult time finding alternate work.

32. We have drawn on Reskin and Roos (1990) in outlining this approach to analyzing gender segregation in the labor force. In East Central Europe, as elsewhere, gender distinctions—much like the public/private opposition we have focused on—were recursively applied even within occupations to produce a fine-grained gender segregation of work. The details of this segregation have been changing since 1989—in tandem with the changing understanding of public and private—but the general principle persists.

33. In this discussion we have relied on Fodor's (1997b) analysis of employment and unemployment in Hungary, Poland, and Slovakia, using the notion of gender segregation. Paukert (1995), Fong and Paull (1993), and Kligman (1996) also provide information on the gendering of labor markets. Kotowska (1995) and Heinen (1995) discuss the reasons for women's unemployment in postsocialist Poland. Such reasons include outright discrimination based on an employer's expectation that women should play "traditional" roles. Woodward (1995) treats the paradox of socialist unemployment, and how planners dealt with what was not supposed to occur in Yugoslavia. Note the important point that the categories by which statistics on employment were gathered before 1989 were based on ideological assumptions of full employment. They are not at all comparable to the categories routinely used by the ILO. Therefore, it is impossible to compare unemployment statistics before and after 1989. Valid comparisons are possible only since the period during which the statistical bureaus of Eastern Europe have switched to ILO categories.

34. See Szalai (1991, 2000) on women's strategies. Fodor (1997b) discusses this process in several countries of the region, and outlines the notion of "revalued" resources.

35. The cultural assumption that men are more suited to retraining and management than women is parallel to the idea we noted earlier that men are more suited to the new forms of democratic politics. For this kind of redefinition in Poland, see Kotowska (1995) and Heinen (1995). Some analysts have also

pointed out that women with the double burden of wage work and housework often do not have the time to engage in retraining programs. For a description of gendered changes in the Hungarian banking industry, see Bihari (1993); for the same trend in East Germany, and gender segregation more generally see Nickel and Schenk (1994), Huening and Nickel (1998). On the mobility of Hungarian women into social work, see Horváth (1993–96).

36. Paukert (1995) emphasizes the location of women's jobs in the public sector in Poland, Hungary, and the Czech and Slovak Republics. See also Fong and Paull (1993). Ferge (1997, 1998) discusses long-term developments of this kind in Hungary.

37. Prostitution supposedly did not exist under socialism, because it was officially "unnecessary," but empirical evidence suggests otherwise; see Buckley (1993:88–89). For further discussion of prostitution in the socialist period, and its relation to other kinds of work by women, see Volgyes and Volgyes (1977); Ferenc (1997) also includes the post-1989 situation. Like some other expanding occupations, sex work is sometimes run by multinational networks. The relatively low wages of East Central Europe limit expenses as these entrepreneurs market the region to sex tourists from Germany and Northern Europe, touting it as a geographically convenient substitute for East Asia, and a means of avoiding the danger of AIDS there (Kligman 1996).

38. Note that in addition to the incentives for employers to engage in these arrangements and thereby avoid the expense of employee benefits, there are also incentives for workers who, in many countries, can thereby sometimes partially avoid high payroll taxes. For evidence of the current, mixed, multiple-job strategy of women in Hungary see the work of Szalai (2000) and her colleagues; for rural Romania, see Sampson (1995:174–75); Poland's strong second economy in the socialist period suggests the likelihood of a parallel development; Standing (1996) mentions similarly informal and multiple employment arrangements in the Czech Republic. It is interesting that virtually all the women who participated in the comparative research project from which this book emerged were holding multiple jobs at the time of the research (see Gal and Kligman 2000). "Recombinant property" is Stark's (1996) term for the "mixed" nature of property in large firms since 1989. Despite fundamental differences, there are also some parallels between the secure and insecure jobs in East Central Europe, and what has been called the segmented labor market of the United States, where, however, in contrast to East Central Europe, job insecurity is linked to low wages.

Chapter 4
Forms of State, Forms of "Family"

We thank Carole Pateman for her comments on this chapter and for her collegial goodwill.

1. Deacon (1992b) and Deacon and Szalai (1990) are important exceptions to the general lack of direct comparison, Esping-Anderson (1996) is a more recent example. Many of the reports from the World Bank and other agencies that we cite later now rely on comparisons with Western countries. As Deacon

(1992a) implies in a preface, when East/West comparative issues were first raised, they were too often addressed either by economists blind to the negative consequences of unbridled marketization or by socialists blind to the striking failures of the Soviet and East European experience.

2. See Molyneux (1994) for a discussion of the international climate that the new states of East Central Europe face. See Standing (1996:230) for the claim of historically unprecedented international influence.

3. Much of the empirical evidence about changes in social provisioning across East Central Europe—relied on by all who discuss the region—comes from the work of welfare economists commissioned or funded by the World Bank, who themselves point out the indeterminacies and lacunae in their data. We have found the following works especially useful: Barr (1994), Milanović (1998), and Rutkowski (1996). For more detailed analysis we have turned to country reports for the region: on Bulgaria (Hassan and Peters 1995); Hungary (Allison and Grootaert 1996); Poland (Rutkowski 1998); and the Czech Republic (Svejnar 1995).

4. The juxtaposition of efficiency as against equality has long dominated social policy debates. For a discussion of the "crisis," its global reach, and neoliberal inspiration, see the studies in Esping-Andersen (1996). On the basis of comparative data from the highly industrialized states, Blank (1994) takes an anticrisis stance, and suggests that a larger safety net does not necessarily entail less economic flexibility.

5. Choices must be made that have significantly different consequences for various segments of the population as well as for government spending. What to do about the long-standing programs such as pensions, maternal leaves, family allowances, free services, as well as the newer ones such as poverty assistance, unemployment insurance, and health insurance are all subjects of policy debate in the region. Sources of funding under discussion include: national budgets, employer funds, employee contributions, nonprofit and volunteer organizations, private insurance plans, pay-as-you-go schemes, or various combinations. In this chapter we have relied on the following assessments of the current situation of social policy in East Central Europe: Deacon (1992b), Deacon and Szalai (1990), Ferge (1998), Ferge and Kohlberg (1992), Kapstein and Mandelbaum (1997), Kornai, Haggard, and Kaufman (2000), Offe (1993), Pestoff (1995), and the World Bank reports and country reports mentioned earlier.

6. The most influential categorization of welfare states has been that of Esping-Anderson (1990, building on Titmuss 1963). For a feminist critique of Esping-Anderson's work, see Orloff (1993), and the chapters by Hobson (1994) and others in Sainsbury (1994). For the general approach to the gendering of the welfare state that has inspired our own account, we have drawn on Borchorst (1999), Orloff (1996), Pedersen (1993), Pateman (1988b), and Sainsbury (1996), all providing critical discussions of feminist responses. See Hernes (1987) for the notion of state feminism, which has since been applied to China and Egypt among other states.

7. Walby (1990) discusses public patriarchy, Brown's (1992) essay is a condemnation of women's relation to states.

8. See Siim (1988). Eduards (1991) makes the same argument, using examples from Swedish policy debates in which women's political activism has been acknowledged and has had practical effect. Gordon (1990) reviews much of this debate, and Leira (1992) makes the same points with reference to the specific case of motherhood. The variation among welfare states is emphasized in all these works. Leira notes that the Scandinavian cases, which are usually lumped together, actually differ significantly in their policies toward motherhood, and feminist discussions of Scandinavian welfare states differ greatly in that some are optimistic, some pessimistic assessments. Since these works were written, various global and domestic factors have led to the rethinking of welfare policies in all the Scandinavian countries. Note that the choice between public or private support for welfare has only recently been reintroduced—after earlier historical experience with it—into Western European policy debate, with considerable resistance from citizens.

9. Specialists within the region who criticized socialist welfare systems and had proposed a variety of mixed solutions have since lost credibility or have converted to market approaches. Foreign experts have certainly contributed to the ascendance and prestige of market solutions in the region, yet they have also sometimes warned of an overreliance on market mechanisms. As one Hungarian commentator remarked: "domestic analysts would be promptly accused of retrograde anti-market behavior if they formed the same statements" (Ferge 1995:156). Greskovits (1998: chaps. 3, 4), in analyzing policy debates in several countries, shows how opinions narrowed in the 1980s and 1990s, so that even without direct outside influence, neoliberal positions triumphed. There continue to be exceptions, however. Deacon and Szalai (1990) present a greater range of advice and opinion than later publications, sometimes by the same authors. As many have remarked, in several countries the arguments for market mechanisms during the 1980s were powerful because they were coded messages that alluded not only to economics but to the desire for a democratic politics that could not be openly discussed at that time.

10. On U.S. statistics and discourses about welfare, especially its historical dimension, see Skocpol (1992) and the articles collected in Gordon (1990), though recent changes in U.S. welfare legislation are, of course, not registered there. For Swedish statistics, see Carlson (1990) and Esping-Andersen (1996).

11. For discussion of opinions about the reasons for mortality and morbidity rates, see Eberstadt (1993), Standing (1996), and Watson (1995).

12. See Goven (1993) and Lapidus (1978) for discussions of women being blamed for societal ills. Perhaps the most famous examples of the political valorization of the family and the private sphere were the writings of Konrád, Havel, and others on anti-politics, as we noted in chapter 3. But there are many other instances, including the works of social scientists in the East and West who have also analyzed East European families in this way. For a thoughtful summary and presentation of these views see Einhorn (1993). The changing vital statistics and family patterns of East Central European countries are summarized in Mitchell (1992).

13. In Hungary the 1980s saw the development of a vociferous antifeminism, although there was no feminist movement; in other countries such as Ro-

mania, the danger of capitalism was foregrounded. See Gedeon (1995), Offe (1993), and Szalai (1993–96) for some examples of what aspects of social policy were receiving most discussion in the region during the mid-1990s.

14. Esping-Andersen (1990) provides a detailed examination of the differences in policies, effects, and historical development of these different types of states. See also Barbalet (1988) for a different and illuminating discussion of the development of welfare rights as opposed to political rights. The major significant distinction here is between universalist state provisions and those which are means tested and therefore easily stigmatized.

15. On the nearly opposite policy decisions of Hungarian and Romanian policy makers, see McIntyre (1985); see Deacon (1992b) for the new category.

16. The breadwinner dimension was proposed by Lewis and Astrom (1992), and later refined (Lewis 1997). See the reactions of other scholars in the special issue of *Social Politics* (4:3, 1997). Similar criticisms were formulated by Hobson (1994) and other authors in Sainsbury (1994).

17. On pensions and changes in pension systems in the region, see Fox (1994), Nelson (2000), and Andrews (1996).

18. See Sajó (1996) for a critical discussion of the Hungarian case. Polish attempts to limit family allowances are discussed in Rutkowski (1998) and Barr (1994).

19. For examples of such plans see Svejnar (1995). For similar examples from other countries, see Roxin and Hóos (1995), Sipos (1994), Vinton (1993), and Okolicsányi (1993).

20. For a parallel discussion of the problem of "carework" in Western welfare states, see Knijn and Ungerson (1997). The ethnographic evidence for East Central European views is reported in Gal and Kligman (2000).

21. The conditions of women's work in East and West have differed in other ways as well. Even in those welfare states, such as Sweden, where as many as 80 percent of women work, women's work is very often part-time. By contrast, in East Central Europe where the labor force participation of women is also high (varying by country from 50 percent to near 80 percent), full-time jobs remain the norm for everyone, though women increasingly engage in part-time work, often in addition to their full-time jobs.

22. Ferge (1997) discusses the thorny issue of coercion. Szalai (2000) makes the case for coercion, but see also Daskalova (2000), Einhorn (1993), Petrova (1993), and other authors in the Funk and Mueller collection for this widespread view. Lewis and Astrom (1992) provide the analysis of the Swedish case we rely on here. It appears that the Swedish decision to recruit women into the labor force was motivated in part by the desire to keep immigrant populations out.

23. Currently, welfare economists routinely distinguish among income transfers such as "social assistance," which is poverty relief given on the basis of an income test with no contribution by recipient; "social insurance," which is meant to cover particular contingencies on the basis of past contributions and is limited to insurable losses such as age and unemployment; "universal benefits," which require no contribution or income test but are linked to some specified event such as the birth of a child; "family benefits" which are aimed at mothers

and children, usually with no income tests (Barr 1994). A further question we have not detailed here is the extent to which the state shares responsibility with voluntary, nonprofit, or nongovernmental organizations (see Götting 1995; Szémán 1995). Hobson (1994) and Barbalet (1988) provide useful discussions of what roles and role relations are grounds for claims by women in various Western states, and the important effects of these differences for women. Pedersen (1993) describes the unintended and differential effects of universal versus targeted aid to children and mothers in England and France.

24. For early criticism within the region, see for example Szalai (1991). Berdahl (1999) provides an ethnographic account of stratification according to one's "connections" in East Germany; see Kligman (1998), among many other studies, for Romania. The numeous discussions of abortion policy in the region provide evidence of the capricious distribution of health and reproductive care.

25. For more details see Goven (2000).

26. See Haney (1997 and forthcoming) on the redefinition of Hungarian mothers. Although the exact terms of the Hungarian welfare regulations have since changed, the conceptual points remain telling; Kligman (1998) discusses the ways in which reproduction in Romania is stratified through strictures on adoption. Among the many studies of the stratifying effects of reproduction in the German situation, see Dölling, Hann, and Scholz (2000), and Zielińska (2000) on Poland.

27. Rutkowski (1998) provides details on Polish income distributions.

28. We note again the instructive contrast between the situation of East Central European women and those in Sweden. Swedish women's jobs are largely part-time and adequately paid, the terms of employment secured by law. Jobs are accompanied by social welfare benefits, and child-care is widely available. See Szalai (2000) for more detail on Hungarian women's strategies. Despite the encouragement of nationalist and religious leaders in East Central Europe urging women to be full-time mothers, polls taken since 1989 consistently show that the majority of women in the countries across the region say they would want to keep their jobs even if their money were not essential to the household; see data reported in the chapters of Gal and Kligman (2000).

29. In Poland, it is men who are more commonly involved in the informal economy (Fuszara 2000). For further details about such informal arrangements and the various means of financing benefits—general government budget, insurance paid by employer and employee—across the region, see Standing (1996).

30. See also Szelenyi et al. (1988) for a discussion of family legacies in the making of a new entrepreneurial class.

31. Gal, fieldnotes summer 1998.

32. In addition to Fraser and Gordon (1994) see also Siim (1988) on the history of the idea of dependence. Orloff (1993) provides a framework analyzing welfare states in terms of rights of independent citizens.

33. See Kligman (1998) for a detailed version of this argument.

34. See for instance Ferge (1995), Rutkowski (1998), and Milanović (1999), who report the results of opinion polls. We thank Eva Fodor for drawing our attention to survey data on this question.

Chapter 5
Arenas of Political Action

1. Several works have stimulated our thinking about these matters, especially Scott, Kaplan, and Keates (1997) and essays in Butler and Scott (1992). The literature on women's political participation in East Central Europe is large. We have relied on recent works edited by Funk and Mueller (1993), Rueschemeyer (1994), Jaquette and Wolchik (1998b), Gal and Kligman (2000), and Scott, Kaplan, and Keates (1997), as well as papers by Regulska (1995), Graham and Regulska (1997), Waylen (1994), Matynia (1995), *UCLA Women's Law Journal* (1994), and the orienting studies by Einhorn (1993), Szalai (1998), and Fuszara (1991), among others. Fodor (1997a) provides a rich theoretical and historical comparison of women's political participation in Hungary and Austria, as examples of socialist and capitalist societies.

2. There are a great many discussions of civil society in East Central Europe, both theoretical and empirical. See Arato (1981) for one of the earliest examples; Keane's (1988b) collection is a much-consulted source; see also Tismăneanu (1992) and the articles collected in Hann (1990) and Hann and Dunn (1996), and Kligman (1990), who is one of those expressing skepticism.

3. We cite only a few among the many useful general sources for discussion of the history of the concept of civil society: Cohen and Arato (1992) and Colas (1997) provide the long view, the former tracing the German tradition, the latter going as far back as the classical Greeks. Keane's survey (1988a) is valuable as a resource; Taylor (1991) makes the important distinction between economistic and self-organizing views, linking the first to the Scottish Enlightenment, the second to the French tradition. Kumar (1993), Tester (1992), and Seligman (1992) all review the history and provide critical commentary.

4. For instance, see Kumar (1993) and Calhoun (1995) for discussions of the use of the concept in Western Europe and China, respectively. Greskovits (1998) and Jaquette and Wolchik (1998b) compare Latin America and Eastern Europe in terms recognizably related to civil society; Putnam (1995) is among those who have invoked the idea to claim a deterioration in American democracy.

5. The effects of recontextualization as a semiotic process on the creation of power and unity or disunity among groups are discussed in Bauman and Briggs (1990); feminists have pointed to this process, for instance in debates about abortion (see Gal [1994]) and in theorizing about international coalitions (see Tsing [1997]).

6. For examples and further discussion of this argument about redefinitions see Gal (1997a), Szalai (1998), and Vajda (1993). Grunberg (2000) notes the fiscal skimming by states.

7. See Fuszara (2000) for the importance of parliaments, despite feminist focus on less formal political activities and more local political participation of women. Many explanations have been proposed for women's low rates of participation in national politics worldwide. They range from the observation that women, carrying a double or triple burden, simply have no time for formal

politics, which is routinely scheduled to fit the lives of men who are not responsible for household and reproductive activities; to discursive factors that define women as unsuited for the rough and tumble of politics; to the finding that women are voted into office significantly more when electoral rules eschew majoritarian principles and instead adopt proportional representation with candidates chosen by parties. See Phillips (1991) for a general discussion of women's political participation in Western states.

8. Kligman (1996) has noted the irony of women's current prominence in NGOs; Watson (1997) has argued for the related politicization of "difference" in civil societies. For the detailed description and analysis of Romanian women's NGOs we have relied on Grunberg (2000).

9. The previous three paragraphs draw on the work of Grunberg (2000), as well as on Sampson's (1996) trenchant discussion of East European NGOs viewed from the inside and Wedel's (1994) description of the policy perspective. Carothers (1996) is a detailed assessment of how Western assistance has worked in Romania. Hann's introduction in Hann and Dunn (1996) also provides useful commentary.

10. This description of the Belgrade hotline relies on the work of Mršević (2000); allusions to other cities of the region derive from field notes of Gal and Kligman. For a detailed close-up of one country's experience with NGOs, their regulation, benefits, and problems since 1992, see Bullain and Simon (1999) on Hungary.

11. A suggestive case of diaspora women's organizing that is overshadowing local mobilization is provided by Hrycak (1999).

12. The early expectations for a flowering of feminism are evident in newspapers and magazine reports of the period. More recently, Ferge (1997) has called for civil societies to protect women. Offen (1984), Skocpol (1992), Koven and Michel (1993), Bock and Thane (1991), and Hobson and Lindholm (1996) all discuss the history of American and European maternalist movements, and movements for women's social citizenship, arguing about their effects on politics. The first half of Jaquette and Wolchik (1998b) is devoted to the contributions of Latin American women to transition politics in that region. Einhorn (1993) remains a handy reference for data on wage discrepancies and measures of discrimination against women in East Central Europe. See also World Bank reports on related issues .

13. For evidence of feminist activism in East Germany around the "Wende," see Merkel et al. (1990); for the demobilization of East German feminism, see Ferree (1994). According to opinion polls described by Fuszara (2000), in Poland *feminism* is most often thought to be a code word for man-hating, frustrated women, lesbianism, and trivial extremism. Grunberg (2000) provides similar evidence for Romania; Goven (1993) and Szalai (1998) make the same point about Hungary; Daskalova (2000) about Bulgaria; Bútorová and Bútorov (1996) provide similar evidence from opinion polls in Slovakia.

14. On the American side, Funk (1993) and Snitow (1995, 1997) both have discussed these problematic yet ultimately productive encounters. The exchange between East and West German feminists predated these meetings.

15. The East Central Europeans who have written frankly and critically in

English about their views on these matters include Šiklová (1996), Marody (1993), Havelková (1997), Drakulić (1993), Adamik (1993). Virtually every account of women in postsocialist East Central Europe has commented on this phenomenon. Neményi (1994) interestingly claims the term "feminist" for herself, and at the same time explains the dilemmas, discussed below, of using the phrase "the personal is political" in Hungary. Salecl (1994) discusses the difficulties of feminism in the Yugoslav context, which differs significantly from the others. Miroiu (1995), Nicolaescu (1996), and Blagojević, Duhaček, and Lukić (1995) are examples of attempts to create nation-specific feminisms in the region.

16. This was often framed as a difference between socialist paternalism and public or private patriarchy (Walby 1990). For the debate between East and West German feminists, see Rosenberg (1991, 1995) and Ferree (1992, 1995). We rely here and in the following paragraphs on these, as well as on the East European commentaries listed in note 15.

17. Feminists from the Third World have been vocal in protesting the homogenization of "Third World women" in Western feminist discourse; see, for instance, Mohanty (1991). But ironically, "Western" feminism does the same homogenizing to itself at moments of self-representation.

18. For the historical arguments about the forms of women's movements, see the citations in note 12; for a fuller discussion of contemporary debates about women's relation to states, see chapter 4. Olsen (1997) discusses what the "West" can learn from the "East." Faludi (1991), Ginsburg (1989), and Burkett (1998) provide examples of the splits and conficts among American women on various issues within feminism.

19. For discussions of feminism as a circulating discourse, see Tsing (1997) and Gal (1997b). Several recent collections treat feminism as a global phenomenon, or raise the possibility of this. See the articles in Basu (1995), Moghadam (1994), and Scott, Kaplan, and Keates (1997), among others. The similarities and differences among Third World women's movements have been discussed in Jayawardena (1986) and Mohanty, Russo, and Torres (1991). The studies in Katzenstein and Mueller (1990) compare women's movements in the United States and Western Europe; Cott (1987) and Ferree and Hess (1985) remain important sources for the history of American feminism. Rupp and Taylor (1999) discuss the making of international feminism at the turn of the century.

20. Information about political activities of this kind requires local research. Fábián (1995) gives a picture of developments in Hungary; Matynia (1995) covers Polish, Czech, Slovak, and Hungarian cases. Grunberg (2000) provides an overview of activity in Romania; Daskalova (2000) in Bulgaria, and the articles and collections cited in note 1 are all informative on this question. Regulska and Graham (1996) have emphasized the importance of considering all of women's politics, not only that labeled "feminism." Ferenc (1997) discusses Hungarian approaches to prostitution; Havelková (1997) gives prostitution as an example of nongendered thinking in the Czech Republic.

21. Watson (1997) and Gal (1997a) have noted the need to reject definitions of civil society as "empty space" with respect to gender. Interestingly, the recognition of difference in the postsocialist states has focused primarily on the

rights of ethnic groups, rather than on those of women. International attention to women's rights as human rights was heightened by the cases of rape in the Balkan wars.

22. The argument about the discursive construction of political identities versus subjectivities draws on recent feminist work that is semiotic and/or poststructuralist. For instance, the articles in Butler and Scott (1992), Gal (1991b), and Salzinger (in press) provide ethnographic approaches to these conceptual differences. Matynia (1995) gives some striking examples of interviews in which women leaders reveal their changing "consciousness" of gender issues since 1989 in the way we are describing here.

23. Lukić (2000) as well as Fuszara (2000) describe notable examples of this phenomenon from Serbia and Poland, respectively.

24. Throughout the book we have cited the way newspapers and magazines frame and define gender issues; see especially Dölling, Hann, and Scholz (2000), Marody and Giza-Poleszcsuk (2000), as well as Dölling (1993), Lukić (2000), and Băban (2000), among many other insightful analyses. See Berdahl (1999) for an example of postsocialist patterns of consumption and their relation to political identity.

25. The collaborative, cross-national research project out of which this book emerged is one example. We ourselves do not know whether the other members of the project publicly label themselves feminists, nor was this relevant to the research itself. It was all the more surprising to us that several participants included discussions of feminism in their initial reports, even though the state of feminism in their countries was not an integral feature of their research, nor of the project. We believe that this is revealing of what East Central European researchers assume is expected by Western feminists such as ourselves, and is another example of the effects of international contacts. On the other hand, our participation in the project forced us to rethink some of our assumptions, for instance about differences between feminisms in "East" and "West," which we discuss in the text.

26. For the recent literature on the history of women's movements in East Central Europe, see articles by Daskalova, Fuszara, Lang, Malecky-Lewy, and Pető collected in Scott, Kaplan, and Keates (1997), as well as Kovács (1994) and Pető (1998), among others. Many more studies are currently underway.

Chapter 6
Gender and Change

1. In earlier chapters, these examples are described in fuller detail, with citations to the authors and studies on which we rely. Our contribution in this section is to integrate these studies—drawing out further implications—in order to reconsider the patterns and processes of change that emerge when they are brought together.

Bibliography

Abbott, Andrew. 1990. "Self-Similar Social Structures." Department of Sociology, University of Chicago. Manuscript.

Abramovitz, Mimi. 1988. *Regulating the Lives of Womem: Social Welfare Policy from Colonial Times to the Present*. Boston: South End Press.

Abrams, Philip. 1988 [1977]. "Notes on the Difficulty of Studying the State." *Journal of Historical Sociology* 1, no. 1: 58–89.

Acsády, Judit. 1997. "'A Huszadik Század Asszonya' A Századforduló Magyar Feminizmusának Nőképe" ("Woman of the Twentieth Century:" Images of Women in Hungarian Feminism at the Turn of the Century). In *Szerep és Alkotás: Női Szerepek a Társadalomban és az Alkotóművészetben* (Role and creation: Images of Women in Society and the Arts), ed. Beata Nagy and Margit S. Sárdi, 243–53. Debrecen: Csokonai Kiadó.

Adamik, Mária. 1993. "Feminism and Hungary." In *Gender Politics and Post-Communism: Reflections from Eastern Europe and the Former Soviet Union*, ed. Nanette Funk and Magda Mueller, 207–12. New York: Routledge.

Allison, Christine, and Christiaan Grootaert. 1996. *Hungary: Poverty and Social Transfers*. A World Bank Country Study. Washington, D.C.: The World Bank.

Anagnost, Ann. 1995. "A Surfeit of Bodies: Population and the Rationality of the State in Post-Mao China." In *Conceiving the New World Order: The Global Politics of Reproduction*, ed. Faye Ginsburg and Rayna Rapp, 22–41. Berkeley: University of California Press.

Andrews, Emily S. 1996. *The Financing of Pension Systems in Central and Eastern Europe: An Overview of Major Trends and Their Determinants, 1990–1993*. Technical Paper no. 339. Washington, D.C.: World Bank.

Anthias, Floya, and Nira Yuval-Davis. 1989. "Introduction." In *Woman—Nation—State*, ed. Floya Anthias and Nira Yuval-Davis, 1–16. New York: St. Martin's Press.

Arato, Andrew. 1981. "Civil Society Against the State: Poland 1980–1981." *Telos* 47: 23–47.

Băban, Adriana. 2000. "Women's Sexuality and Reproductive Behavior in Post-Ceaușescu Romania: A Psychological Approach." In *Reproducing Gender: Politics, Publics, and Everyday Life after Socialism*, ed. Susan Gal and Gail Kligman. Princeton: Princeton University Press.

Bahovec, E., ed. 1991. *Abortus Pravica elo izbire? Pravni, medicinski, sociološki, moralni in politični. vidiki*. (Abortion). Ljubljana: Skupina ženske za politiko.

Bakhtin, Mikhail 1981. "Discourse in the Novel." In *The Dialogic Imagination: Four Essays*, trans. Caryl Emerson and Michael Holquist, ed. Michael Holquist, 259–422. Austin: University of Texas Press.

Barbalet, J. M. 1988. *Citizenship: Rights, Struggle and Class Inequality*. Minneapolis: University of Minnesota Press.

Barr, Nicholas, ed. 1994. *Labor Markets and Social Policy in Central and Eastern Europe: The Transition and Beyond.* Oxford: Oxford University Press and The World Bank.

Basu, Amrita, ed. 1995. *The Challenge of Local Feminisms: Women's Movements in Global Perspective.* Boulder, Colo.: Westview Press.

Bauman, Richard, and Charles Briggs. 1990. "Poetics and Performance as Critical Perspectives on Social Life." *Annual Review of Anthropology* 19: 59–88.

Benderly, Jill. 1997. "Balkans: Rape, Feminism, and Nationalism in the War in Yugoslav Successor States." In *Feminist Nationalism,* ed. Lois West, 59–74. Routledge: New York.

Benhabib, Seyla. 1998 [1992]. "Models of Public Space: Hannah Arendt, the Liberal Tradition, and Jürgen Habermas." In *Feminism, the Public, and the Private,* ed. Joan B. Landes, 65–99. New York: Oxford University Press.

Berdahl, Daphne. 1999. *Where the World Ended: Re-unification and Identity in the German Borderland.* University of California Press: Berkeley.

Berend, Iván, and György Ránki. 1974. *Economic Development in East Central Europe in the 19th and 20th Centuries.* New York: Columbia University Press.

Berezin, Mabel. 1999. "Political Belonging: Emotion, Nation and Identity in Fascist Italy." In *State/Culture: State Formation after the Cultural Turn,* ed. George Steinmetz, 355–77. Ithaca: Cornell University Press.

Berlant, Lauren. 1993. "The Theory of Infantile Citizenship." *Public Culture* 5:395–410.

Bihari, Zsuzsanna. 1993. "Nők a Pénzintézeti Szféra Vezetésében" (Women in the Management of Financial Business). *Tér és Társadalom* 1–2: 69–88.

Blagojević, Marina. 1996. "'Transition,' Everyday Life and Parenthood: The Case of Serbia." Paper presented at the Conference on Gender, Women and the Transition, Il Ciocco, Italy.

Blagojević, Marina, Daša Duhaček, and Jasmina Lukić, eds. 1995. *What Can We Do for Ourselves?* Belgrade: Center for Women's Studies Research and Communication.

Blanchard, Olivier. 1997. *The Economics of Post-Communist Transition.* Oxford: Clarendon Press.

Blank, Rebecca. 1994. "Does a Larger Social Safety Net Mean Less Economic Flexibility?" In *Working under Different Rules,* ed. Richard B. Freeman, 157–88. New York: Russell Sage Foundation.

Bock, Gisela, 1991. "Antinatalism, Maternity, and Paternity in National Socialist Racism." In *Maternity and Gender Policies: Women and the Rise of the European Welfare States, 1880–1950s,* ed. Gisela, Bock and Pat Thane, 233–55. New York: Routledge.

Bock, Gisela, and Pat Thane, eds. 1991. *Maternity and Gender Policies: Women and the Rise of the European Welfare States 1880–1950s.* New York: Routledge.

Borchorst, Anette. 1999. "Feminist Thinking about the Welfare State." In *Revisioning Gender,* ed. Myra Marx Ferree, Judith Lorber, and Beth B. Hess, 99–127. London: Sage Publications.

Borneman, John. 1992. *Belonging in the Two Berlins: Kin, State, Nation.* New York: Cambridge University Press.

Böröcz, József. 1995. "Social Change by Fusion." Department of Sociology, Rutgers University. Manuscript.

Bourdieu, Pierre. 1991. *Language and Symbolic Power*. Cambridge: Harvard University Press.

Bracewell, Wendy. 1996. "Women, Motherhood and Contemporary Serbian Nationalism." *Women's Studies International Forum* 19, no. 1/2: 25–33.

Brenner, Johanna, and Barbara Laslett. 1989. "Gender and Social Reproduction: Historical Perspectives." *Annual Review of Sociology* 15: 381–404.

Bridenthal, Renate, Atina Grossmann, and Marion Kaplan, eds. 1984. *When Biology Becomes Destiny: Women in Weimar and Nazi Germany*. New York: Monthly Review Press.

Brown, Wendy. 1992. "Finding the Man in the State." *Feminist Studies* 18, no. 1: 7–34.

Brubaker, Rogers. 1996. *Nationalism Reframed: Nationhood and the National Question in the New Europe*. New York: Cambridge University Press.

———. 1998. "Myths and Misconceptions in the Study of Nationalism." In *Ernest Gellner and the Theory of Nationalism*, ed. John Hall, 272–306. New York: Cambridge University Press.

Buckley, Mary. 1989. *Women and Ideology in the Soviet Union*. Ann Arbor: University of Michigan Press.

———. 1993. *Redefining Russian Society and Polity*. Boulder, Colo.: Westview Press.

Bullain, Nilda, and Ildikó Simon, eds. 1999. *Utazás a Nonprofit Törvény Körül*. (A Trip around the Nonprofit Law). Budapest: CTF Alapitvány.

Burawoy, Michael, and János Lukács. 1992. *The Radiant Past: Ideology and Reality in Hungary's Road to Capitalism*. Chicago: University of Chicago Press.

Burawoy, Michael, and Katherine Verdery, eds. 1999. *Uncertain Transitions: Ethnographies of Change in the Postsocialist World*. Lanham, Md.: Rowman and Littlefield.

Burchell, Graham, Colin Gordon, and Peter Miller, eds. 1991. *The Foucault Effect: Studies in Governmentality*. Chicago: University of Chicago Press.

Burkett, Elinor. 1998. *The Right Women: A Journey through the Heart of Conservative America*. New York: Scribner.

Butler, Judith, and Joan W. Scott, eds. 1992. *Feminists Theorize the Political*. New York: Routledge.

Bútorová, Zora, and Martin Bútora, eds. 1996. *She and He in Slovakia: Gender Issues in Public Opinion*. Bratislava: Focus.

Calhoun, Craig, ed. 1992. *Habermas and the Public Sphere*. Cambridge: MIT Press.

———. 1993. "Civil Society and the Public Sphere." *Public Culture* 5, no.2: 267–80.

Carlson, Allan. 1990. *The Swedish Experiment in Family Politics: The Myrdals and the Interwar Population Crisis*. New Brunswick, N.J.: Transaction Publishers.

Carothers, Thomas. 1996. *Assessing Democracy Assistance: The Case of Romania*. Washington, D.C.: Carnegie Endowment Book.

Chatterjee, Parth. 1993. *The Nation and Its Fragments: Colonial and Postcolonial Histories.* Princeton: Princeton University Press.

Clements, Barbara Evans. 1997. *Bolshevik Women.* New York: Cambridge University Press.

Cohen, Jean L., and Andrew Arato. 1992. *Civil Society and Political Theory: Conjoined Histories.* Cambridge: MIT Press.

Colas, Dominique. 1997. *Civil Society and Fanaticism.* Stanford, Calif.: Stanford University Press.

Collier, Jane F., and Sylvia Yanagisako. 1987. *Gender and Kinship: Essays toward a Unified Analysis.* Stanford, Calif.: Stanford University Press.

Connell, R. W. 1987. *Gender and Power: Society, the Person, and Sexual Politics.* Stanford, Calif.: Stanford University Press.

———. 1990. "The State, Gender, and Sexual Politics: Theory and Appraisal." *Theory and Society* 19, no. 5: 507–44.

Corrin, Chris, ed. 1992. *Superwoman and the Double Burden: Women's Experience of Change in Central and Eastern Europe and the Former Soviet Union.* Toronto: Second Story Press.

———. 1993. *Magyar Women: Hungarian Women's Lives, 1960s–1990s.* New York: St. Martin's Press.

Cott, Nancy. 1987. *The Grounding of Modern Feminism.* New Haven: Yale University Press.

Csepeli, György, Antal Őrkény, and Kim Lane Scheppele. 1996. "Acquired Immune Deficiency Syndrome in Social Science in Eastern Europe." *Social Research* 63, no. 2: 487–509.

Daskalova, Krassimira. 2000. "Women's Problems, Women's Discourses in Bulgaria." In *Reproducing Gender: Politics, Publics, and Everyday Life after Socialism,* ed. Susan Gal and Gail Kligman. Princeton: Princeton University Press.

David, Henry. 1999. *From Abortion to Contraception: A Research Guide to Public Policies and Reproductive Behavior in Central and Eastern Europe from 1917 to the Present.* Westport, Conn.: Greenwood Press.

Davidoff, Leonore. 1995. *Worlds Between: Historical Perspectives on Gender and Class.* Cambridge: Polity Press.

Davidoff, Leonore, and Catherine Hall. 1987. *Family Fortunes: Men and Women of the English Middle Class, 1780–1850.* Chicago: University of Chicago Press.

Deacon, Bob, 1992a. "East European Welfare: Past, Present, and Future in Comparative Context." In *The New Eastern Europe: Social Policy Past, Present, and Future,* ed. Bob Deacon, 1–30. New York: Sage Publications.

———. ed. 1992b. *The New Eastern Europe: Social Policy Past, Present, and Future.* New York: Sage Publications.

Deacon, Bob, and Júlia Szalai, eds. 1990. *Social Policy in the New Eastern Europe: What Future for Socialist Welfare?* Avebury: Aldershot.

deGrazia, Victoria. 1992. *How Fascism Ruled Women: Italy, 1922–1945.* Berkeley: University of California Press.

———, ed. 1996. *The Sex of Things: Gender and Consumption in Historical Perspective.* Berkeley: University of California Press.

DeSoto, Hermine G., 1995. "'In the Name of the Folk:' Women and Nation in the New Germany." *UCLA Women's Law Journal* 5, no. 1: 83–101.

DeSoto, Hermine G., and David G. Anderson, eds. 1993. *The Curtain Rises: Rethinking Culture, Ideology, and the State in Eastern Europe.* Atlantic Highlands, N.J.: Humanities Press.

Denitch, Bette S. 1974. "Sex and Power in the Balkans." In *Woman, Culture, and Society,* ed. Michelle Rosaldo and Louise Lamphere, 243–62. Stanford, Calif.: Stanford University Press.

di Leonardo, Micaela. 1991. "Introduction." In *Gender at the Crossroads of Knowledge: Feminist Anthropology in the Postmodern Era,* ed., Micaela di Leonardo, 1–50. Berkeley: University of California Press.

Dölling, Irene. 1993. "'But the Pictures Stay the Same . . .': The Image of Women in the Journal *Für Dich* before and after the 'Turning Point.'" In *Gender Politics and Post-Communism: Reflections from Eastern Europe and the Former Soviet Union,* ed. Nanette Funk and Magda Mueller, 168–79. New York: Routledge.

Dölling, Irene, Daphne Hann, and Sylka Scholz. 2000. "'Birth Strike' in the New Federal States: Is Sterilization an Act of Resistance?" In *Reproducing Gender: Politics, Publics, and Everyday Life after Socialism,* ed. Susan Gal and Gail Kligman. Princeton: Princeton University Press.

Donzelot, J. 1979. *The Policing of Families.* New York: Pantheon Books.

Drakulić, Slavenka. 1993. "Women and the New Democracy in the Former Yugoslavia." In *Gender Politics and Post-Communism: Reflections from Eastern Europe and the Former Soviet Union,* ed. Nanette Funk and Magda Mueller, 123–30. New York: Routledge.

Eberstadt, Nicholas. 1993. "Mortality and the Fate of Communist States." *Communist Economies and Economic Transformation* 5, no. 4: 499–517.

Eduards, Maud, L. 1991. "Toward a Third Way: Women's Politics and Welfare Policies in Sweden." *Social Research* 58, no. 3: 677–705.

Einhorn, Barbara. 1993. *Cinderella Goes to Market: Citizenship, Gender, and Women's Movements in East Central Europe.* London: Verso.

Eisenstein, Zillah R. 1984. *Feminism and Sexual Equality: Crisis in Liberal America.* New York: Monthly Review Press.

Elster, Jon, Claus Offe, and Ulrich K. Preuss. 1998. *Institutional Design and Post-communist Societies: Rebuilding the Ship at Sea.* New York: Cambridge.

Esping-Andersen, Gøsta. 1990. *The Three Worlds of Welfare Capitalism.* Princeton: Princeton University Press.

———, ed. 1996. *Welfare States in Transition: National Adaptations in Global Economies.* London: Sage Publications.

Fábián, Katalin. 1995. "Nőmozgalmak" (Women's Movements). *INFO-Társadalomtudomány* 32:57–64.

Faludi, Susan. 1991. *Backlash: The Undeclared War against American Women.* New York: Crown.

Feeley-Harnik, Gillian. 1985. "Issues in Divine Kingship." *Annual Review of Anthropology* 14: 273–313.

Fehér, Ferenc, Ágnes Heller and György Márkus. 1983. *Dictatorship over Needs: An Analysis of Soviet Societies.* Oxford: Basil Blackwell.

Feischmidt, Margit, Enikő Magyari-Vincze, and Violetta Zentai, eds. 1997. *Women and Men in East European Transition.* Cluj-Napoca: Editura Fundaţie pentru Studii Europene.

Ferenc, Lenke. 1997. "Bűnözés és Prostitució" (Crime and Prostitution). In *Szerepváltozások* (Role Changes), ed. Katalin Lévai and György István Tóth, 139–50. Budapest: Tárki-Munkaügyiminisztérium.

Ferge, Zsuzsa. 1995. "Challenges and Constraints in Social Policy." In *Question Marks: The Hungarian Government, 1994–1995*, ed. Csaba Gombár, Elemér Hankiss, László Lengyel, and Györgyi Varnia, 144–71. Budapest: Korridor.

Ferge, Zsuzsa. 1997. "Women and Social Transformation in Central-Eastern Europe: The 'Old Left' and the 'New Right.'" *Czech Sociological Review* 5, no. 2: 159–78.

———. 1998. *Fejezetek a Magyar Szegénypolitika Történetéből* (Chapters from the History of Hungarian Policy toward the Poor). Budapest: Kávé Kiadó.

Ferge, Zsuzsa, and Jon Eivind Kolberg, eds. 1992. *Social Policy in a Changing Europe.* Frankfurt: Campus Verlag.

Ferree, Myra Marx,. 1992. "The Wall Remaining: Two Women's Movements in One German State." Department of Sociology, University of Connecticut. Manuscript.

———. 1994. "'The Time of Chaos Was the Best': Feminist Mobilization and Demobilization in East Germany." *Gender and Society* 8, no. 4: 597–623.

———. 1995. "Patriarchies and Feminisms: Two Women's Movements in Post-Unification Germany." *Social Politics* (Spring): 10–24.

Ferree, Myra Marx, and Beth B. Hess. 1985. *Controversy and Coalition: The New Feminist Movement.* Boston: Twayne Publishers.

Fitzpatrick, Sheila, and Robert Gellately, eds. 1997. *Accusatory Practices: Denunciation in Modern European History, 1789–1989.* Chicago: University of Chicago Press.

Fodor, Éva. 1997a. "Power, Patriarchy, and Paternalism: An Examination of the Gendered Nature of State Socialist Authority." Ph.D. thesis, Department of Sociology, University of California, Los Angeles.

———. 1997b. "Gender in Transition: Unemployment in Hungary, Poland, and Slovakia." *East European Politics and Societies* 11, no. 3: 470–500.

Folbre, Nancy. 1991. "The Unproductive Housewife: Her Evolution in 19th Century Economic Thought." *Signs* 16, no. 3: 463–84.

Fong, Monica, and Gillian Paull. 1993. "Women's Economic Status in the Restructuring of Eastern Europe." In *Democratic Reform and the Position of Women in Transitional Economies*, ed., Valentine Moghadam, 217–47. Oxford: Clarendon Press.

Foucault, Michel 1991. "Governmentality." In *The Foucault Effect: Studies in Governmentality*, ed. Graham Burchell, Colin Gordon, and Peter Miller, 87–104. Chicago: University of Chicago Press.

Fox, Louise. 1994. *Old Age Security in Transitional Economies.* Policy Research Working Paper No. 1257. Washington, D.C.: World Bank.

Frader, Laura L., and Sonya O. Rose. 1996. "Introduction." In *Gender and Class in Modern Europe*, ed. Laura L. Frader and Sonya O. Rose, 1–33. Ithaca: Cornell University Press.

Fraser, Nancy, 1989. "What's Critical about Critical Theory? The Case of Habermas and Gender." In *Unruly Practices: Power, Discourse, and Gender in Contemporary Social Theory*, 113–44. Minneapolis: University of Minnesota Press.

———. 1997. "Rethinking the Public Sphere: A Contribution to the Critique of Actually Existing Democracy." In *Justice Interruptus: Critical Reflections on the "Postsocialist" Condition*, 69–98. New York: Routledge.

Fraser, Nancy, and Linda Gordon. 1994. "'Dependency' Demystified: Inscriptions of Power in a Keyword of the Welfare State." *Social Politics* 1, no. 1: 4–31.

Frykman, Jonas, and Orvar Löfgren. 1987. *Culture Builders: A Historical Anthropology of Middle-Class Life*. New Brunswick, N.J.: Rutgers University Press.

Funk, Nanette. 1993. "Feminism East and West." In *Gender Politics and Post-Communism: Reflections from Eastern Europe and the Former Soviet Union*, ed. Nanette Funk and Magda Mueller, 318–30. New York: Routledge.

Funk, Nanette, and Magda Mueller, eds. 1993. *Gender Politics and Post-Communism: Reflections from Eastern Europe and the Former Soviet Union*. New York: Routledge.

Fuszara, Małgorzata. 1991. "Legal Regulation of Abortion in Poland." *Signs* 17, no. 1: 117–28.

———. 2000. "New Gender Relations in Poland in the 1990s." In *Reproducing Gender: Politics, Publics, and Everyday Life after Socialism*, ed. Susan Gal and Gail Kligman. Princeton: Princeton University Press.

Gal, Susan. 1991a. "Bartók's Funeral: Representations of Europe in Hungarian Political Rhetoric." *American Ethnologist* 18: 440–58.

———. 1991b. "Between Speech and Silence: The Problematics of Research on Language and Gender." In *Gender at the Crossroads of Knowledge: Feminist Anthropology in the Postmodern Era*, ed. Micaela di Leonardo, 175–203. Berkeley: University of California Press.

———. 1994. "Gender in the Post-Socialist Transition: The Abortion Debate in Hungary." *East European Politics and Societies* 8, no. 2: 256–87.

———. 1997a. "Feminism and Civil Society." In *Transitions, Environments, Translations: Feminisms in International Politics*, ed. Joan Scott, Cora Kaplan, and Debra Keates, 30–45. New York: Routledge.

———. 1997b. "Movements of Feminism: The Circulation of Discourses about Women in East Central Europe." Paper presented at the 96th Annual Meeting of the American Anthropological Association, Washington, D.C., November.

Gal, Susan, and Judith T. Irvine. 1995. "The Boundaries of Languages and Disciplines: How Ideologies Construct Difference." *Social Research* 62, no. 4: 967–1001.

Gal, Susan, and Gail Kligman, eds. 2000. *Reproducing Gender: Politics, Publics, and Everyday Life after Socialism*. Princeton: Princeton University Press.

Gallagher, Catherine. 1987. "The Body versus the Social Body in the Works of Thomas Malthus and Henry Mayhew." In *The Making of the Modern Body*, ed.

Catherine Gallagher and Thomas Laqueur, 83–106. Berkeley: University of California Press.

Garton Ash, Timothy. 1986. "Does Central Europe Exist?" *New York Review* 33, No. 15 (9 October).

———. 1999. "The Puzzle of Central Europe." *New York Review* 46, no. 5.

Gedeon, Péter. 1995. "Hungary: Social Policy in Transition." *East European Politics and Societies* 9, no. 3: 433–58.

Gellately, Robert. 1997. "Denunciations in Twentieth-Century Germany: Aspects of Self-Policing in the Third Reich and the German Democratic Republic." In *Accusatory Practices: Denunciation in Modern European History, 1789–1989*, ed. Sheila Fitzpatrick and Robert Gellately, 185–222. Chicago: University of Chicago Press.

Gerő, András. 1993. *Magyar Polgárosodás* (Hungarian Embourgeoisement). Budapest: Atlantisz.

Ginsburg, Faye. 1989. *Contested Lives: The Abortion Debate in an American Community.* Berkeley: University of California Press.

Ginsburg, Faye, and Rayna Rapp. 1991. "The Politics of Reproduction." *Annual Review of Anthropology* 20: 311–43.

———, eds. 1995. *Conceiving the New World Order: The Global Politics of Reproduction.* Berkeley: University of California Press.

Glendon, Mary. 1987. *Abortion and Divorce in Western Law.* Cambridge: Harvard University Press.

Goffman, Erving. 1959. *The Presentation of Self in Everyday Life.* New York: Anchor Books.

———. 1979. "Footing." *Semiotica* 25, nos. 1/2: 2–29.

Gordon, Linda, ed. 1990. *Women, the State, and Welfare.* Madison: University of Wisconsin Press.

Götting, Ulrike. 1995 "Welfare State Development in Post-Communist Bulgaria, Czech Republic, Hungary, and Slovakia: A Review of Problems and Responses (1989–1993)." In *Reforming Social Services in Central and Eastern Europe: An Eleven Nation Overview*, ed. Victor A. Pestoff, 349–93. Cracow: Cracow Academy of Economics, Friedrich Ebert Stiftung.

Goven, Joanna. 1993. "Gender Politics in Hungary: Autonomy and Antifeminism " In *Gender Politics and Post-Communism: Reflections from Eastern Europe and the Former Soviet Union*, ed. Nanette Funk and Magda Mueller, 224–40. New York: Routledge.

———. 2000. "New Parliament, Old Discourse? The Parental Leave Debate in Hungary." In *Reproducing Gender: Politics, Publics, and Everyday Life after Socialism*, ed. Susan Gal and Gail Kligman. Princeton: Princeton University Press.

Graham, Ann, and Joanna Regulska. 1997. "Expanding Political Space for Women in Poland: An Analysis of Three Communities." *Communist and Post-Communist Studies* 30:65–82.

Greskovits, Béla. 1998. *The Political Economy of Protest and Patience: East European and Latin American Transformations Compared.* New York: Central European University Press.

Gross, Jan. 1988. *Revolution from Abroad: The Soviet Conquest of Poland's Western Ukraine and Western Belorussia*. Princeton: Princeton University Press.

Grossman, Atina. 1983. "The New Woman and the Rationalization of Sexuality in Weimar Germany." In *Powers of Desire: The Politics of Sexuality*, ed. Ann Snitow, Christine Stansell and Sharon Thompson, 153–76. New York: Monthly Review Press.

Grunberg, Laura. 2000. "Women's NGOs in Romania." In *Reproducing Gender: Politics, Publics, and Everyday Life after Socialism*, ed. Susan Gal and Gail Kligman. Princeton: Princeton University Press.

Gyáni, Gábor. 1997. "A Cselédkép Változásai a Századforduló Diskurzusában" (Changing Images of the Servant in Turn-of-the-Century Discourse). In *Szerep és Alkotás: Női Szerepek a Társadalomban és az Alkotóművészetben* (Role and Creation: Women's Roles in Society and the Arts), ed. Beata Nagy and Margit S. Sárdi, 227–33. Debrecen: Csokonai Kiadó.

———. 1999. *Az Utca és a Szalon: Társadalmi Térhasználat Budapesten, 1870–1940* (The Street and the Salon: The Social Use of Space in Budapest, 1870–1940). Budapest: Új Mandátum.

Habermas, Jürgen. 1989. *The Structural Transformation of the Public Sphere: An Inquiry into a Category of Bourgeois Society*. Translated by Thomas Burger and Frederick Lawrence. Cambridge: MIT Press.

Hacking, Ian. 1990. *The Taming of Chance*. New York: Cambridge University Press.

Hadas, Miklós. 1998. "Bartók, a Természettudós" (Bartók, the Natural Scientist]. *Replika* 33–34 (Special Issue on the Colonization of Scholarship): 21–33.

Hall, Catherine, Jane Lewis, Keith McClelland, and Jane Rendall, eds. 1993. "Gender, Nationalisms and National Identities." *Gender and History* 5, no. 2 (Special issue).

Hanák, Péter. 1975. *Magyarország a Monarchiában: Tanulmányok* [Hungary in the Monarchy]. Budapest: Magvető.

———. 1998. *The Garden and the Workshop: Essays on the Cultural History of Vienna and Budapest*. Princeton: Princeton University Press.

Haney, Lynne. 1997. " 'But We Are Still Mothers:' Gender, and the Construction of Need in Post-Socialist Hungary." *Social Politics* 4, no. 2: 208–44.

———. Forthcoming. *Inventing the Needy: The Gender Transformation from Socialist Welfare to Welfare Capitalism in Hungary*. Berkeley: University of California Press.

Hankiss, Elemér. 1988. "The 'Second Society:' Is There an Alternative Social Model Emerging in Contemporary Hungary?" *Social Research* 55, no. 1–2: 13–45.

———. 1990. *East European Alternatives*. Oxford: Clarendon Press.

Hann, Chris, ed. 1990. *Market Economy and Civil Society in Hungary*. London: Frank Cass.

———. 1996. "Introduction: Political Society and Civil Anthropology." In *Civil Society: Challenging Western Models*, ed. Chris Hann and Elizabeth Dunn, 1–26. London: Routledge.

Hann, Chris, and Elizabeth Dunn, eds. 1996. *Civil Society: Challenging Western Models*. London: Routledge.

Hartsock, Nancy. 1985. *Money, Sex, and Power: Toward a Feminist Historical Materialism*. Boston: Northeastern University Press.

Hassan, Fareed, and R. Kyle Peters. 1995. *Social Safety Net and the Poor during the Transition: The Case of Bulgaria*. Washington, D.C.: World Bank.

Havelková, Hana. 1997. "Transitory and Persistent Differences: Feminism East and West." In *Transitions, Environments, Translations: Feminisms in International Politics*, ed. Joan Scott, Cora Kaplan, and Debra Keates, 56–64. New York: Routledge.

Heinen, Jacqueline. 1995. "Unemployment and Women's Attitudes in Poland." *Social Politics* 2, no. 1: 91–110.

Heng, Geraldine, and Janadas Devan. 1992. "State Fatherhood: The Politics of Nationalism, Sexuality, and Race in Singapore." In *Nationalisms and Sexualities*, ed. Andrew Parker, Mary Russo, Doris Sommers, and Patricia Yaeger, 343–64. New York: Routledge.

Hernes, Helga M. 1987. *Welfare State and Woman Power: Essays in State Feminism*. Oslo: Norwegian University Press.

Herzfeld, Michael. 1987. *Anthropology through the Looking Glass: Critical Ethnography in the Margins of Europe*. New York: Cambridge University Press.

Hirschman, Albert O. 1977. *The Passions and the Interests: Political Arguments for Capitalism before Its Triumph*. Princeton: Princeton University Press.

Hobson, Barbara. 1994. "Solo Mothers, Policy Regimes, and the Logics of Gender." In *Gendering Welfare States*, ed. Diane Sainsbury, 170–87. London: Sage Publications.

Hobson, Barbara, and Marika Lindholm. 1996. "Collective Identities, Women's Power Resources, and the Making of Welfare States." Paper presented at the Tenth International Conference of Europeanists, Chicago, Ill.

Hodos, George H. 1987. *Show Trials: Stalinist Purges in Eastern Europe, 1948–1954*. New York: Praeger.

Honeyman, Katrina, and Jordan Goodman. 1991. "Women's Work, Gender Conflict, and Labor Markets in Europe, 1500–1900." *Economic History Review* 44, no. 4: 608–28.

Horváth, Ágota. 1993–1996. "Roads to Social Work in Hungary." *East Central Europe* 20–23, parts 3–4: 147–70.

Hrycak, Alexandra. 1999. "Transnational Social Movement Organizations and the Formation of the Post-Soviet Women's Movement: Grass Roots Mobilization from Above." Department of Sociology, Reed College. Manuscript.

Huening, Hasko, and Hildegard-Maria Nickel, eds. 1998. *Finanzmetropole Berlin: Strategien betrieblicher Transformation* (Berlin as Finance Metropolis: Strategies of Industrial Transformation). Opladen: Leske and Budrich.

Humphrey, Caroline. 1994. "Remembering an 'Enemy:' The Bogd Khann in 20th Century Mongolia." In *Memory, History and Opposition under State Socialism*, ed. Rubie S. Watson, 21–44. Santa Fe: School of American Research Press.

Hunt, Lynn, ed. 1991. *Eroticism and the Body Politic*. Baltimore: Johns Hopkins University Press.

Huseby-Darvas, Eva. 1996. "'Feminism, the Murderer of Mothers:' The Rise and Fall of Neo-nationalist Reconstruction of Gender in Hungary." In *Women Out of Place: The Gender of Agency and the Race of Nationality*, ed. Brackette Williams, 161–85. New York: Routledge.

Informator organizac i inicjatyw kobiecych w Polsce. 1997. "Information on This Dynamic Phenomenon—The Women's Movement in Poland." Directory of Women's Organizations and Initiatives in Poland. Warsaw: Centrum Promocji Kobiet.

Irvine, Judith T., and Susan Gal. 2000. "Language Ideology and Linguistic Differentiation." In *Regimes of Language*, ed. Paul Kroskrity. Santa Fe: School of American Research Press.

Jakobson, Roman. 1990 [1957]. "Shifters and Verbal Categories." In *On Language: Roman Jakobson*, ed. Linda R. Waugh and Monique Monville-Burston, 386–92. Cambridge: Harvard University Press.

Janos, Andrew C. 1982. *The Politics of Backwardness in Hungary, 1825–1945*. Princeton: Princeton University Press.

Jaquette, Jane S. and Sharon L. Wolchik. 1998a. "Women and Democratization in Latin America and Central and Eastern Europe: A Comparative Introduction." In *Women and Democracy: Latin America and Central and Eastern Europe*, 1–28, ed. Jane S. Jaquette and Sharon Wolchik. Baltimore: Johns Hopkins University Press.

———, eds. 1998b. *Women and Democracy: Latin America and Central and Eastern Europe*. Baltimore: Johns Hopkins University Press.

Jayawardena, Kumari. 1986. *Feminism and Nationalism in the Third World*. London: Zed Books.

Jones, Kathleen B. and Anna G. Jónasdóttir, eds. 1988. *The Political Interests of Gender: Developing Theory and Research with a Feminist Face*. Newbury Park, Calif.: Sage Publications.

Jordanova, Ludmilla. 1995. "Interrogating the Concept of Reproduction in the 18th Century." In *Conceiving the New World Order: The Global Politics of Reproduction*, ed. Faye Ginsburg and Rayna Rapp, 369–86. Berkeley: University of California Press.

Judt, Tony. 1996. *A Grand Illusion? An Essay on Europe*. New York: Hill and Wang.

Kantorowicz, Ernst H. 1957. *The King's Two Bodies: A Study in Medieval Political Theology*. Princeton: Princeton University Press.

Kapstein, Ethan B., and Michael Mandelbaum, eds. 1997. *Sustaining Transition: The Social Safety Net in Postcommunist Europe*. New York: Council on Foreign Relations.

Katzenstein, Mary F., and Carol M. Mueller, eds. 1990. *The Women's Movements of the United States and Western Europe: Consciousness, Political Opportunity and Public Policy*. Philadelphia: Temple University Press.

Keane, John. 1988a. "Introduction." In *Civil Society and the State: New European Perspectives*, ed. John Keane, 1–32. London: Verso.

Keane, John, ed. 1988b. *Civil Society and the State: New European Perspectives.* London: Verso.

Kenedi, János. 1981. *Do It Yourself: Hungary's Hidden Economy.* London: Pluto Press.

Kertzer, David, and Dennis P. Hogan. 1989. *Family, Political Economy, and Demographic Change: The Transformation of Life in Casalecchia, Italy, 1861–1921.* Madison: University of Wisconsin Press.

Kligman, Gail. 1988. *The Wedding of the Dead: Ritual, Poetics, and Popular Culture in Transylvania.* Berkeley: University of California Press.

———. 1990. "Reclaiming the Public: A Reflection on Creating Civil Society in Romania." *East European Politics and Societies* 4, no. 3: 393–438.

———. 1992. "The Politics of Reproduction in Ceauşescu's Romania." *East European Politics and Societies* 6, no. 3: 364–418.

———. 1994. "The Social Legacy of Communism: Women, Children, and the Feminization of Poverty." In *The Social Legacy of Communism*, ed. James R. Millar and Sharon L. Wolchik, 252–70. Washington, D.C., and New York: Woodrow Wilson Center and Cambridge University Press.

———. 1996. "Women and the Negotiation of Identity in Post-Communist Eastern Europe." In *Identities in Transition: Russia and Eastern Europe after Communism*, ed. Victoria Bonnell, 68–91. Berkeley: International and Area Studies.

———. 1998. *The Politics of Duplicity: Controlling Reproduction in Ceauşescu's Romania.* Berkeley: University of California Press.

Knijn, Trudie, and Clare Ungerson, eds. 1997. "Special Issue: Care Work and Gender in Welfare Regimes." *Social Politics* 4, no. 3: 323–421.

Kőrösi, Suzanne. 1984. "Hungary: The Nonexistence of 'Women's Emancipation.'" In *Sisterhood is Global: The International Women's Movement Anthology*, ed. Robin Morgan, 289–93. Garden City, N.Y.: Anchor Press.

Kornai, János. 1980. *Economics of Shortage.* Amsterdam: North-Holland Publishing Company.

———. 1994. "Transformation Recession: The Main Causes." *Journal of Comparative Economics* 19, no. 1: 39–63.

Kornai, János, Stephen Haggard, and Robert Kaufman, eds. 2000. *Reforming the State: Fiscal and Welfare Reform in Post-Socialist Countries.* Cambridge: Cambridge University Press.

Kotowska, Irena E. 1995. "Discrimination against Women in the Labor Market in Poland During the Transition to a Market Economy." *Social Politics* 2, no. 1: 76–90.

Kovács, Katalin, and Monika Váradi. 2000. "Women's Life Trajectories and Class Formation in Hungary." In *Reproducing Gender: Politics, Publics, and Everyday Life after Socialism*, ed. Susan Gal and Gail Kligman. Princeton: Princeton University Press.

Kovács, Mária. 1994. "A Magyar Feminizmus Korszakfordulója" (A Turning Point of Hungarian Feminism). *Cafe Babel* 14, no. 1–2: 179–84.

Koven, Seth, and Sonya Michel, eds. 1993. *Mothers of a New World: Maternalist Politics and the Origins of Welfare States.* New York: Routledge.

Kukutz, Irena, and Katja Havemann. 1990. *Protected Source: Conversations with Monika H., Alias Karin Lenz.* Berlin: Basisdruck Verlag.

Kumar, Krishan. 1993. "Civil Society: An Inquiry into the Usefulness of a Historical Term." *British Journal of Sociology* 44, no. 3: 375–95.

Kundera, Milan. 1984. "The Tragedy of Central Europe." *New York Review of Books*, 26 April, 33–38.

Lampland, Martha. 1995. *The Object of Labor: Commodification in Socialist Hungary.* Chicago: University of Chicago Press.

Landes, Joan. 1989. *Women and the Public Sphere in the Age of the French Revolution.* Ithaca: Cornell University Press.

———, ed. 1998. *Feminism, the Public and the Private.* New York: Oxford University Press.

Lapidus, Gail. 1978. *Women in Soviet Society: Equality, Development and Social Change.* Berkeley: University of California Press.

Lefort, Claude. 1986. *The Political Forms of Modern Society: Bureaucracy, Democracy, Totalitarianism.* Cambridge: Polity Press.

Leira, Arnlaug. 1992. *Welfare States and Working Mothers: The Scandinavian Experience.* Cambridge: Cambridge University Press.

Lewis, Jane. 1997. "Gender and Welfare Regimes: Further Thoughts." *Social Politics* 4, no. 2: 160–77.

Lewis, Jane, and Gertrude Astrom. 1992. "Equality, Difference, and State Welfare: Labor Market and Family Policies in Sweden." *Feminist Studies* 18, no. 1: 59–87.

Lindenfeld, David F. 1997. *The Practical Imagination: The German Sciences of State in the 19th Century.* Chicago: University of Chicago Press.

Linke, Uli. 1990. "Folklore, Anthropology and the Government of Social Life." *Comparative Studies in Society and History* 32, no. 1: 117–48.

Linz, Juan J., and Alfred Stepan. 1996. *Problems of Democratic Transition and Consolidation: Southern Europe, South America, and Post-Communist Europe.* Baltimore: Johns Hopkins University Press.

Lucy, John, ed. 1993. *Reflexive Language: Reported Speech and Metapragmatics.* New York: Cambridge University Press.

Luker, Kristin. 1984. *Abortion and the Politics of Motherhood.* Berkeley: University of California Press.

Lukić, Jasmina. 2000. "Media Representations of Men and Women in Times of War and Crisis: The Case of Serbia." In *Reproducing Gender: Politics, Publics, and Everyday Life after Socialism*, ed. Susan Gal and Gail Kligman. Princeton: Princeton University Press.

MacCormack, Carol P., and Marilyn Strathern. 1980. *Nature, Culture, and Gender.* New York: Cambridge University Press.

Maleck-Lewy, Eva. 1995. "Between Self-Determination and State Supervision: Women and the Abortion Law in Post-Unification Germany." *Social Politics* 2, no. 1: 62–76.

Maleck-Lewy, Eva, and Myra Marx Ferree. 2000. "Talking about Women and Wombs: The Discourse of Abortion and Reproductive Rights in the GDR during and after the 'Wende.'" In *Reproducing Gender: Politics, Publics, and*

Everyday Life after Socialism, ed. Susan Gal and Gail Kligman. Princeton: Princeton University Press.

Marody, Mira. 1993. "Why I Am Not a Feminist: Some Remarks on the Problem of Gender Identity in the United States and Poland." *Social Research* 60, no. 4: 853–64.

Marody, Mira, and Anna Giza-Poleszczuk. 2000. "Changing Images of Identity in Poland: From the Self-Sacrificing to the Self-Investing Woman?" In *Reproducing Gender: Politics, Publics, and Everyday Life after Socialism,* ed. Susan Gal and Gail Kligman. Princeton: Princeton University Press.

Matynia, Elzbieta. 1995. "Finding a Voice: Women in Postcommunist Central Europe." In *The Challenge of Local Feminisms: Women's Movements in Global Perspective,* ed. Amrita Basu, 374–404. Boulder, Colo.: Westview Press.

McIntyre, Robert J. 1985. "Demographic Policy and Sexual Equality: Value Conflict and Policy Appraisal in Hungary and Romania." In *Women, State and Party in Eastern Europe,* ed. Sharon L. Wolchik and Alfred G. Meyer, 270–85. Durham, N.C.: Duke University Press.

Merkel, Ina, et al. 1990. *Ohne Frauen ist kein Staat zu machen* (No New State without Women). Hamburg: Argument-Verlag.

Meurs, Mieke. 1998. "Imagined and Imagining Equality in East Central Europe: Gender and Ethnic Differences in the Economic Transformation of Bulgaria." In *Theorising Transition: The Political Economy of Post-Communist Transformations,* ed. John Pickles and Adrian Smith, 330–46. London: Routledge.

Mežnarić, Silva. N.d. "The Discourse of Endangered Nation: Demography, Gender, and Reproductive Policies in Croatia." Manuscript.

———. 1994. "Gender as an Ethnomarker: Rape, War and Identity Politics in the Former Yugoslavia." In *Identity Politics and Women: Cultural Reassertions and Feminisms in International Perspective,* ed. Valentine M. Moghadam, 76–97. Boulder, Colo.: Westview Press.

———. 1997a. "Populacionizam i demokracija: Hrvatska nakon osamostaljenja" (Populationism and Democracy: Croatia after Independence). *Erasmus* 19: 58–63.

———. 1997b. "Populacija, nacija, broj: demografija i politika etnosa modernoj Europi" (Population, Nation, Number: Demography and the Politics of Ethnos in Modern Europe). *Revija za sociologiju* 28, nos. 1–2: 19–33.

Michel, S., and S. Koven. 1990. "Womanly Duties: Maternalist Politics and the Origins of the Welfare State in France, Germany, Great Britain and the United States, 1880–1920." *American Historical Review* 95, no. 4: 1076–108.

Milanović, Branko. 1998. *Income, Inequality, and Poverty during the Transition from Planned to Market Economy.* Washington, D.C.: World Bank.

Milanović, Branko, et al. 1995. *Understanding Poverty in Poland: A World Bank Country Study.* Washington, D.C.: World Bank.

Miroiu, M. 1995. *Gândul umbrei: Abordări feministe în filozofia contemporană* (In the Shadow of Reason: Feminist Approaches to Contemporary Philosophy). Bucharest: Editura Alternativa.

Mitchell, Brian R. 1992. *International Historical Statistics, Europe, 1750–1988.* 3rd ed. New York: Stockton Press.

Moghadam, Valentine M., ed. 1993. *Democratic Reform and the Position of Women in Transitional Economies.* Oxford: Clarendon Press.

———. 1994. "Introduction: Women and Identity Politics in Theoretical and Comparative Perspective." In *Identity Politics and Women: Cultural Reassertions and Feminisms in International Perspective,* ed. Valentine M. Moghadam, 3–26. Boulder, Colo.: Westview Press.

Mohanty, Chandra T. 1991. "Under Western Eyes: Feminist Scholarship and Colonial Discourse." In *Third World Women and the Politics of Feminism,* ed. Chandra Mohanty, Ann Russo, and Lourdes Torres, 51–80. Bloomington: Indiana University Press.

Mohanty, Chandra T., Ann Russo, and Lourdes Torres, eds. 1991. *Third World Women and the Politics of Feminism.* Bloomington: Indiana University Press.

Molyneux, Maxine. 1994. "Women's Rights and the International Context: Some Reflections on Post-Communist States." *Millennium: Journal of International Studies* 23, no. 2: 287–313.

Mosse, George L. 1985. *Nationalism and Sexuality: Middle-Class Morality and Sexual Norms in Modern Europe.* Madison: University of Wisconsin Press.

Mostov, Julie. 1995. "'Our Women'/'Their Women': Symbolic Boundaries, Territorial Markers, and Violence in the Balkans." *Peace and Change* 20, no. 4: 515–29.

Mršević, Zorica. 2000. "Belgrade's SOS Hotline for Women and Children Victims of Violence: A Report." In *Reproducing Gender: Politics, Publics, and Everyday Life after Socialism,* ed. Susan Gal and Gail Kligman. Princeton: Princeton University Press.

Nee, Victor and David Stark, with Mark Selden, eds. 1989. *Remaking the Economic Institutions of Socialism: China and Eastern Europe.* Stanford, Calif.: Stanford University Press.

Nelles, Ursula. 1991–1992. "Abortion, the Special Case: A Constitutional Perspective." *German Politics and Society* 24–25 (Special issue on Gender and Politics): 111–21.

Nelson, Joan, ed. 1994. *Intricate Links: Democratization and Market Reforms in Latin America and Eastern Europe.* New Brunswick, N.J.: Transaction Publishers.

———. 2000. "The Politics of Pension and Health Care Reforms in Hungary and Poland." In *Reforming the State: Fiscal and Welfare Reform in Post-Socialist Countries,* ed. János Kornai, Stephen Haggard, and Robert Kaufman. Cambridge: Cambridge University Press.

Neményi, Mária. 1994. "A Kötelező Heteroszexualitástól a Kötelező Feminizmusig" (From Compulsory Heterosexuality to Compulsory Feminism). *Cafe Babel* 14, nos. 1–2: 163–70.

Nickel, Hildegard-Maria, and Sabine Schenk. 1994. "Prozesse geschlechtsspezifischer Differenzierung im Erwerbssystem" (Processes of Gender-specific Differentiation in Employment). In *Erwerbsarbeit im Umbruch* [Reorganization of Employment], ed. Hildegard-Maria Nickel, Jürgen Kuelh, and Sabine Schenk, 259–82. Berlin: Akademie-Verlag.

Nicolaescu, M., ed. 1996. *Cine suntem noi? Despre identitatea femeilor din românía modernă* (Who are we? About women's identity in modern Romania). Bucharest: Editura Anima.

Nimsch, M. 1991–1992. "Abortion as Politics." *German Politics and Society* 24–25 (Special issue on Gender and Politics): 128–34.

Offe, Claus. 1993. "The Politics of Social Policy in East European Transitions: Antecedents, Agents, and Agenda of Reform." *Social Research* 60, no. 4: 649–684.

Offen, Karen. 1984. "Depopulation, Nationalism and Feminism in Fin-de-Siècle France." *American Historical Review* 89, no. 3: 648–76.

Okolicsányi, Károly. 1993. "Hungary's Misused and Costly Social Security System." *RFE/RL Research Report* 2. no. 17:12–16.

Olsen, Frances. 1997. "Feminism in Central and Eastern Europe: Risks and Possibilities of American Engagement." *Yale Law Journal* 106, no. 7: 2215–57.

Orloff, Ann S. 1993. "Gender and the Social Rights of Citizenship: The Comparative Analysis of Gender Relations and Welfare States." *American Sociological Review* 58, no. 3: 303–28.

———. 1996. "Gender in the Welfare State." *Annual Review of Sociology* 22: 51–78.

Pateman, Carole. 1988a. *The Sexual Contract*. Stanford, Calif.: Stanford University Press.

———. 1988b. "The Patriarchal Welfare State." In *Democracy and the Welfare State*, ed. Amy Gutmann, 231–60. Princeton: Princeton University Press.

Paukert, Liba. 1995. *Economic Transition and Women's Employment in Four Central European Countries, 1989–1994*. International Labour Organization, Labour Market Papers, no. 7.

Pedersen, Susan. 1993. *Family, Dependence, and the Origins of the Welfare State: Britain and France, 1914–1945*. Cambridge: Cambridge University Press.

Peebles, Gustav. 1997. "'A Very Eden of the Innate Rights of Man'? A Marxist Look at the European Union Treaties and Case Law." *Law and Social Inquiry* 22, no. 3: 581–618.

Peirce, Charles S. 1940. "Logic as Semiotic: The Theory of Signs." In *The Philosophy of Peirce: Selected Writings*, ed. Justus Buchler. London: Routledge, Kegan Paul.

Pestoff, Victor, A. ed., 1995. *Reforming Social Services in Central and Eastern Europe: An Eleven Nation Overview*. Cracow: Cracow Academy of Economics, Friedrich Ebert Stiftung.

Petchesky, Rosalind. 1990. *Abortion and Woman's Choice: The State, Sexuality, and Reproductive Freedom*. 2nd ed. Boston: Northeastern University Press.

Pető, Andrea. 1998. *A Politizáló Magyar Nők Történetéből, 1945–1951* (On the History of Politically Active Hungarian Women, 1945–1951). Budapest: Seneca.

Petrova, Dimitrina. 1993. "The Winding Road to Emancipation in Bulgaria." In *Gender Politics and Post-Communism: Reflections from Eastern Europe and the Former Soviet Union*, ed. Nanette Funk and Magda Mueller, 22–29. New York: Routledge.

Phelan, Diarmuid Rossa. 1992. "Right to Life of the Unborn v. Promotion of Trade in Services: The European Court of Justice and the Normative Shaping of the European Union." *Modern Law Review* 55, no. 5: 670–89.

Phillips, Anne. 1991. *Engendering Democracy*. University Park: Pennsylvania State University Press.

Pickles, John, and Adrian Smith, eds. 1998. *Theorising Transition: The Political Economy of Post Communist Transformations*. London: Routledge.

Posadskaya Anastasia, ed. 1994. *Women in Russia: A New Era of Russian Feminism*. London: Verso.

Povinelli, Elizabeth. 1997. "Sex Acts and Sovereignty: Race and Sexuality in the Construction of the Australian Nation." *Diacritics* 24, no. 2–3: 122–50.

Przeworski, Adam. 1991. *Democracy and the Market: Political and Economic Reforms in Eastern Europe and Latin America*. New York: Cambridge University Press.

Putnam, Robert D. 1995. "'Bowling Alone': America's Declining Social Capital." *Journal of Democracy* 6, no. 1: 65–78.

Rai, Shirin, Hilary Pilkington, and Annie Phizacklea, eds. 1992. *Women in the Face of Change: The Soviet Union, Eastern Europe, and China*. New York: Routledge.

Regulska, Joanna. 1995. *Women's Participation in Political and Public Life*. Background document EG/EGM 95, no. 10. Strasbourg: The Council of Europe.

Regulska, Joanna, and Ann Graham. 1996. "When Political Meets Women: Creating Local Political Space." Paper presented at the Tenth Annual Conference of Europeanists, Chicago, Ill.

Rener, Tanja, and Mirjana Ule. 1998. "Back to the Future: Nationalism and Gender in Post-Socialist Societies." In *Women, Ethnicity and Nationalism: The Politics of Divided Societies*, ed. Rick Wilford and Robert L. Miller, 120–31. New York: Routledge.

Renne, Tanya. 1997. *Ana's Land: Sisterhood in Eastern Europe*. Boulder, Colo.: Westview Press.

Reskin, Barbara, and Patricia A. Roos. 1990. *Job Queues, Gender Queues: Explaining Women's Inroads into Male Occupations*. Philadelphia: Temple University Press.

Rév, István. 1987. "The Advantages of Being Atomized." *Dissent* 34, no. 3: 335–50.

Róna-Tas, Ákos. 1998. "Path-Dependence and Capital Theory: Sociology of the Post-Communist Economic Transformation." *East European Politics and Societies* 12, no. 1: 107–31.

Rosaldo, Michelle. 1974. "Woman, Culture, and Society: A Theoretical Overview." In *Woman, Culture and Society*, ed. Michelle Rosaldo and Louise Lamphere, 17–42. Stanford, Calif.: Stanford University Press.

Rosenberg, Dorothy. 1985. "The Emancipation of Women in Fact and Fiction." In *Women, State and Party in Eastern Europe*, ed. Sharon L. Wolchik and Alfred Meyer, 344–61. Durham: Duke University Press.

———. 1991. "Shock Therapy: GDR Women in Transition from a Socialist Welfare State to a Social Market Economy." *Signs* 17, no. 1: 129–51.

———. 1995. "Step-Sisters: On the Difficulties of German-German Feminist Cooperation." In *Communication in Eastern Europe: The Role of History, Culture and Media in Contemporary Conflict*, ed. Fred L. Casmir, 81–109. Mahwah, N.J.: Lawrence Erlbaum.

Roxin, Violet, and János Hóos. 1995. "Social Services in Eleven Central and East European Countries—Comparative Aspects." In *Reforming Social Services in Central and Eastern Europe: An Eleven Nation Overview*. ed. Victor A. Pestoff, 281–301. Cracow: Cracow Academy of Economics, Friedrich Ebert Stiftung.

Rueschemeyer, Marilyn, ed. 1994. *Women in the Politics of Postcommunist Eastern Europe*. Armonk, N.Y.: M. E. Sharpe.

Rupp, Leila J., and Verta Taylor. 1999. "Forging Feminist Identity in an International Movement." *Signs* 24, no. 2: 363–86.

Rutkowski, Jan J. 1996. *Changes in the Wage Structure during Economic Transition in Central and Eastern Europe*. World Bank Technical Paper no. 340. Washington, D.C.: World Bank.

———. 1998. *Welfare and the Labor Market in Poland: Social Policy during Economic Transition*. World Bank Technical Paper no. 417. Washington, D.C.: World Bank.

Sainsbury, Diane, ed. 1994. *Gendering Welfare States*. New York: Sage Publications.

———. 1996. *Gender, Equality and Welfare States*. Cambridge: Cambridge University Press.

Sajó, András. 1996. "How the Rule of Law Killed Hungarian Welfare Reform." *East European Constitutional Review* 5, no. 1:31–41.

Salecl, Renata. 1994. *The Spoils of Freedom: Psychoanalysis and Feminism after the Fall of Socialism*. New York: Routledge.

Salzinger, Leslie L. In press. *Gender under Production: Constituting Subjects in Mexico's Global Factories*. Berkeley: University of California Press.

Sampson, Steven. 1995. "All is Possible, Nothing is Certain: The Horizons of Transition in a Romanian Village." In *East European Communities: The Struggle for Balance in Turbulent Times*, ed. David A. Kideckel, 159–78. Boulder, Colo.: Westview Press.

———. 1996. "The Social Life of Projects: Importing Civil Society to Albania." In *Civil Society: Challenging Western Models*, ed. Chris Hann and Elizabeth Dunn, 121–42. London: Routledge.

Sándor, Judit, ed. 1992. *Abortusz és . . .* (Abortion and . . .). Budapest: Literatura Medica.

———. 1999. "Abortion Laws in 'Crisis': Commentary on the Recent Decision of the Hungarian Constitutional Court." Manuscript.

Sassoon, Anne Showstack, ed. 1987. *Women and the State: The Shifting Boundaries between Public and Private*. London: Hutchinson.

Schneider, Jane C., and Peter T. Schneider. 1996. *Festival of the Poor: Fertility Decline and the Ideology of Class in Sicily, 1860–1980*. Tucson: University of Arizona Press.

Scott, Joan W. 1988. *Gender and the Politics of History*. New York: Columbia University Press.

Scott, Joan W., Cora Kaplan, and Debra Keates, eds. 1997. *Transitions, Environments, Translations: Feminisms in International Politics*. New York: Routledge.

Selény, Anna. 1994. "Constructing the discourse of Transformation: Hungary, 1979–1982." *East European Politics and Societies* 8, no. 3: 439–66.

Seligman, Adam B. 1992. *The Idea of Civil Society*. New York: Free Press.

Siim, Birte. 1988. "Towards a Feminist Rethinking of the Welfare State." In *The Political Interests of Gender: Developing Theory and Research with a Feminist Face*, cd. Kathleen B. Jones and Anna G. Jónasdóttir, 160–86. London: Sage Publications.

Šiklová, Jiřina. 1996. "Feminism and the Roots of Apathy to Politics among Women in the Post-Communist Countries: The Case of the Czech Republic." Paper presented at the Collegium Budapest, Budapest, Hungary.

Silverstein, Michael. 1976. "Shifters, Linguistic Categories, and Cultural Description." In *Meaning in Anthropology*, ed. Keith H. Basso and Henry A. Selby, 11–55. Albuquerque: University of New Mexico Press.

Silverstein, Michael, and Greg Urban, eds. 1996. *Natural Histories of Discourse*. Chicago: University of Chicago Press.

Simpson, Christopher, ed. 1998. *Universities and Empire: Money and Politics in the Social Sciences during the Cold War*. New York: New Press.

Sipos, Sándor, 1994. "Income Transfers: Family Support and Poverty Relief." In *Labor Markets and Social Policy in Central and Eastern Europe: The Transition and Beyond*, ed. Nicholas Barr, 227–59. Oxford: Oxford University Press and The World Bank.

Skinner, G. William. 1997. "Family Systems and Demographic Processes." In *Anthropological Demography: Toward a New Synthesis*, ed. David J. Kertzer and Tom Fricke, 53–95. Chicago: University of Chicago Press.

Skocpol, Theda. 1992. *Protecting Soldiers and Mothers: The Political Origins of Social Policy in the United States*. Cambridge: Harvard University Press, Belknap Press.

Smith, Adrian, and John Pickles. 1998. "Introduction." In *Theorising Transition: The Political Economy of Post-Communist Transformations*, ed. John Pickles and Adrian Smith, 1–53. London: Routledge.

Snitow, Ann. 1995. "Feminist Futures in the Former East Bloc." In *What Can We Do for Ourselves?* ed. Marina Blagojević, Daša Duhaček, and Jasmina Lukić, 141–54. Belgrade: Center for Women's Studies.

———. 1997. "Response." In *Transitions, Environments, Translations: Feminisms in International Politics*, ed. Joan W. Scott, Cora Kaplan, and Debra Keates, 176–84. New York: Routledge.

Spackman, Barbara. 1996. *Fascist Virilities: Rhetoric, Ideology, and Social Fantasy in Italy*. Minneapolis: University of Minnesota Press.

Standing, Guy. 1996. "Social Protection in Central and Eastern Europe: A Tale of Slipping Anchors and Torn Safety Nets." In *Welfare States in Transition: National Adaptations in Global Economies*, ed. Gøsta Esping-Andersen, 225–55. London: Sage Publications.

Stark, David. 1996. "Recombinant Property in East European Capitalism." *American Journal of Sociology* 101, no. 4: 993–1027.

Stark, David, and László Bruszt. 1998. *Postsocialist Pathways: Transforming Politics and Property in East Central Europe*. New York: Cambridge University Press.

Stiglmayer, Alexandra, ed. 1994. *Mass Rape: The War against Women in Bosnia-Herzegovina*. Lincoln: University of Nebraska Press.

Stites, Richard. 1991. *The Women's Liberation Movement in Russia:*

Feminism, Nihilism, and Bolshevism, 1860–1930. Princeton: Princeton University Press.

Stoler, Ann. 1991. "Carnal Knowledge and Imperial Power: Gender, Race and Morality in Colonial Asia." In *Gender at the Crossroads of Knowledge: Feminist Anthropology in the Postmodern Era*, ed. Micaela di Leonardo, 51–101. Berkeley: University of California Press.

Stone, Judith F. 1996. "Republican Ideology, Gender and Class: France, 1860s-1914." In *Gender and Class in Modern Europe*, ed. Laura L. Frader and Sonya O. Rose, 238–59. Ithaca: Cornell University Press.

Svejnar, Jan, ed. 1995. *The Czech Republic and Economic Transition in Eastern Europe*. San Diego: Academic Press.

Szalai, Júlia. 1991. "Some Aspects of the Changing Situation of Women in Hungary." *Signs* 17, no. 1: 151–70.

———, ed. 1993–1996. "Old and New Poverty in Post-1989 Central Europe." *East Central Europe-L'Europe du Centre-Est* 20–23 (Special issue): 3–4.

———. 1998. "Women and Democratization: Some Notes on Recent Changes in Hungary." In *Women and Democracy: Latin America and Central and Eastern Europe*, ed. Jane S. Jaquette and Sharon L. Wolchik, 185–202. Baltimore: Johns Hopkins University Press.

———. 2000. "From Informal Labor to Paid Occupations: Marketization from Below in Hungarian Women's Work." In *Reproducing Gender: Politics, Publics, and Everyday Life after Socialism*, ed. Susan Gal and Gail Kligman. Princeton: Princeton University Press.

Szelényi, Iván, with Robert Manchin, Pál Juhász, Bálint Magyar, and Bill Martin. 1998. *Socialist Entrepreneurs: Embourgeoisement in Rural Hungary*. Madison: University of Wisconsin.

Szelenyi, Ivan, and Kostello, Eric. 1996. "The Market Transition Debate: Toward a Synthesis?" *American Journal of Sociology* 101, no. 4: 1082–96.

Szémán, Zsuzsa. 1995. "The Role of NGOs in Social Welfare Services in Hungary." In *Reforming Social Services in Central and Eastern Europe: An Eleven Nation Overview* ed. Victor A. Pestoff, 323–47. Cracow: Cracow Academy of Economics Friedrich Ebert Stiftung.

Sztaniszkis, Jadwiga. 1991. *The Dynamics of the Breakthrough in Eastern Europe: The Polish Experience*. Trans. Chester A. Kisiel. Berkeley: University of California Press.

Szűcs, Jenő. 1988. "Three Historical Regions of Europe." In *Civil Society and the State: New European Perspectives*, ed. John Keane, 291–332. London: Verso.

Taylor, Charles. 1991. "Modes of Civil Society." *Public Culture* 3, no. 1: 95–118.

Tester, Keith. 1992. *Civil Society*. New York: Routledge.

Tismăneanu, Vladimir. 1992. *Reinventing Politics: Eastern Europe from Stalin to Havel*. New York: Free Press.

Titmuss, Richard M. 1963. *Essays on 'The Welfare State.'* London: Allen and Unwin.

Todorova, Maria. 1993. "The Bulgarian Case: Women's Issues or Feminist Issues?" In *Gender Politics and Post-Communism: Reflections from Eastern Eu-*

rope and the Former Soviet Union, ed. Nanette Funk and Magda Mueller, 30–38. New York: Routledge.

———. 1997. *Imagining the Balkans*. New York: Oxford University Press.

Toranska, Teresa. 1987. *"Them": Stalin's Polish Puppets*. New York: Harper and Row.

Tsing, Anna Lowenhaupt. 1997. "Transitions as Translations." In *Transitions, Environments, Translations: Feminisms in International Politics*, ed. Joan W. Scott, Cora Kaplan, and Debra Keates, 253–72. New York: Routledge.

UCLA Women's Law Journal. 1994. "Women in Central and Eastern Europe: Nationalism, Feminism, and Possibilities for the Future." 5, no. 1 (special issue).

Vajda, Ágnes. 1993. "Foundations and Associations: Citizen Initiatives and the Denationalization of the Non-Profit Sector." In *Participation and Changes in Property Relations in Post-Communist Societies*, ed. Mihály Laki et al. Budapest: Active Society Foundation.

Verdery, Katherine. 1996. *What Was Socialism, and What Comes Next?* Princeton: Princeton University Press.

Vinton, Louisa. 1993. "Poland's Social Safety Net: An Overview." *RFE/RL Research Report* 2, no. 17: 3–11.

Volgyes, Ivan and Nancy Volgyes. 1977. *The Liberated Female: Life, Work, and Sex in Socialist Hungary*. Boulder, Colo.: Westview Press.

Vörös, Miklós. 1997. "Életmód, Ideológia, Háztartás" (Lifestyle, Ideology, Household). *Replika* 26 (June): 31–46.

Walby, Sylvia. 1990. *Theorizing Patriarchy*. Oxford: Basil Blackwell.

Wallerstein, Immanuel. 1998. "The Unintended Consequences of Cold War Area Studies." In *The Cold War and the University: Toward an Intellectual History of the Postwar Years*, ed. Noam Chomsky et al., 195–230. New York: New Press.

Watkins, Susan Cotts. 1991. *From Provinces into Nations: Demographic Integration in Western Europe, 1870–1960*. Princeton: Princeton University Press.

Watson, Peggy. 1993. "The Rise of Masculinism in Eastern Europe." *New Left Review* 198: 71–82.

———. 1995. "Explaining Rising Mortality among Men in Eastern Europe." *Social Science and Medicine* 41, no. 7: 923–34.

———. 1997. "Civil Society and the Politics of Difference in Eastern Europe." In *Transitions, Environments, Translations: Feminisms in International Politics*, ed. Joan W. Scott, Cora Kaplan, and Debra Keates, 21–29. New York: Routledge.

Waylen, Georgina. 1994. "Women and Democratization: Conceptualizing Gender Relations in Transition Politics." *World Politics* 46: 327–54.

Wedel, Janine. 1986. *The Private Poland*. New York: Facts on File.

———. 1994. "U.S. Aid to Central and Eastern Europe 1990–1994: An Analysis of Aid Models and Responses." In *East-Central European Economies in Transition: Study Paper Submitted to Joint Economic Committee, Congress of the United States*, 299–335. Washington, D.C.: U.S. Government Printing Office.

Weitz, Eric. 1996. "The Heroic Man and the Ever-Changing Woman: Gender and Politics in European Communism, 1917–1950." In *Gender and Class in Modern Europe*, ed. Laura L. Frader and Sonya O. Rose, 311–52. Ithaca: Cornell University Press.

Whitehead, Annie, Clara Connolly, Erica Carter, and Helen Crowley, eds. 1993. "Nationalisms and National Identities." *Feminist Review* 44 (Special issue): 1–111.

Wolchik, Sharon L. 1994. "Women's Issues in Czechoslovakia in the Communist and Post-Communist Period." In *Women and Politics Worldwide*, ed. Barbara Nelson and Najma Chowdhury. New Haven: Yale University Press.

———. 2000. "Reproductive Policies in the Czech and Slovak Republics." In *Reproducing Gender: Politics, Publics, and Everyday Life after Socialism*, ed. Susan Gal and Gail Kligman. Princeton: Princeton University Press.

Wolchik, Sharon L., and Alfred G. Meyer, eds. 1985. *Women, State and Party in Eastern Europe*. Durham, N.C.: Duke University Press.

Wolff, Larry. 1994. *Inventing Eastern Europe: The Map of Civilization on the Mind of the Enlightenment*. Stanford, Calif.: Stanford University Press.

Woodward, Susan L. 1995. *Socialist Unemployment: The Political Economy of Yugoslavia, 1945–1990*. Princeton: Princeton University Press.

Yack, Bernard. 1996. "The Myth of the Civic Nation." *Critical Review* 10, no. 2: 193–211.

Young, Kate, Carol Wolkowitz, and Roslyn McCullagh. 1981. *Of Marriage and the Market: Women's Subordination in International Perspective*. London: CSE Books.

Yuval-Davis, Nira. 1997. *Gender and Nation*. London: Sage Publications.

Zielińska, Eleonora. 2000. "Between Ideology, Politics and Common Sense: The Discourse of Reproductive Rights in Poland." In *Reproducing Gender: Politics, Publics, and Everyday Life after Socialism*, ed. Susan Gal and Gail Kligman. Princeton: Princeton University Press.